LIFTING THE WEIGHT

LIFTING THE WEIGHT

Understanding Depression in Men,
Its Causes and Solutions

Martin Kantor, M.D.

Westport, Connecticut
London

Library of Congress Cataloging-in-Publication Data

Kantor, Martin.
  Lifting the weight : understanding depression in men, its
causes and solutions / Martin Kantor.
    p. ; cm.
  Includes bibliographical references and index.
  ISBN 978-0-275-99372-6 (alk. paper)
  1. Depression in men. I. Title.
    [DNLM: 1. Depressive Disorder—etiology. 2. Depressive
  Disorder—therapy. 3. Men—psychology. WM 171 K16L 2007]
  RC537.K352   2007
  616.85′270081—dc22   2007020660

British Library Cataloguing in Publication Data is available.

Library of Congress Catalog Card Number: 2007020660
ISBN: 978-0-275-99372-6

First published in 2007

Praeger Publishers, 88 Post Road West, Westport, CT 06881
An imprint of Greenwood Publishing Group, Inc.
www.praeger.com

Printed in the United States of America

The paper used in this book complies with the
Permanent Paper Standard issued by the National
Information Standards Organization (Z39.48-1984).

10 9 8 7 6 5 4 3 2 1

To M.E.C.

Contents

Preface

The topic of depression in men is so extensive that one book on the disorder can only hope to have limited goals and deal with selected highlights. My goal for this book is therefore a specific and modest one: to focus on the human dimension of depression as it appears in men, to give the reader an underlying sense of what it feels like to be a man who is depressed, and to give the depressed man an intimation of how to get over a current depression and avoid experiencing one in the future. I certainly hope that my book will give the depressed man some ideas on how to lift his depression so that he can crawl out from under his burden and find relief from his suffering. My method is to focus on the personal details that some texts omit in their emphasis on research and formal theory. I therefore emphasize the microscopic doings of the depressed man's inner and outer life, going beyond such generalities found throughout the literature as depression is both an interpersonal and an auto-aggressive disorder to describe exactly what happens when men develop the red hot blues—precisely how they beat themselves up, often over little or nothing, and find (and keep) others to help them do just that. My belief is that if I retrace the details of the baby steps a man takes to get into his depression, I can help him take a giant step forward out of it—off the path of danger and onto higher, safer ground.

I have not avoided unveiling some of the darker sides of depression in men, aspects of the disorder that the more politically sensitive clinicians generally do not even mention. The navel of the underbelly of depression is often painful for all concerned to contemplate. Depressed men who complain that people abandon them have often in fact driven these people away. Some are too self-preoccupied to be accepted by and acceptable to others, and some are mean and angry and even delight in torturing other people the same way they seem to delight in torturing themselves. For such depressed men unfavorable character traits are more than just byproducts of their depression. They are some of its prime movers. I cannot just ignore these, even if it seems that by including them I appear to be criticizing men who are not bad but ill. It is true that depressed men are stigmatized to the point that they need favorable public relations. But what is even truer is that depressed men have an illness that needs not only better publicity but also a more favorable therapeutic outcome.

My theoretical stance is an eclectic one, for I do not believe that one school of thought contains all the clinical wisdom and provides all the answers. Mine is a holistic approach to understanding and treating depression that does not prematurely discount anything that could help its sufferers. I strive to intervene psychodynamically, cognitively, behaviorally, and interpersonally in a supportive interpersonal context. In my experience all depressed men—no matter how much they deny it—are needy individuals—babies in a sense who, longing to have their hands held, predictably respond negatively to purely psychodynamic and cognitive approaches if these are presented in the same remote, disdainful, controlling, critical interpersonal way that created their depression in the first place.

I advocate avoiding therapeutic approaches that I believe can and do make depression worse, and can turn a serious illness into a fatal one. I especially avoid those methods that if only in spirit resemble primal scream techniques, where keeping it all in is bad, and getting it all out is good. Such approaches may not adequately respect a man's depression and how it is there for a purpose. For example, Terrance Real's suggestion to "crack [the depressed man] open"[1] implies a philosophy that is generally antithetical to mine, which has as its goal putting the depressed man together so that he heals as naturally as possible. That he cannot do if I render him asunder as his therapist, constantly opening up old wounds, then pouring salt into them.

What follows is based more on my clinical experience than on pure research. This is in part because the pure research I have encountered is often too inconsistent to guide me reliably. For example, I have not been able to determine how to reconcile two opposing ideas frequently found in the literature: women are more sensitive than men and women are less sensitive than men.

This book is divided into three parts. In Part I, Description, I discuss the general manifestations of depression as they occur in both sexes and attempt to contrast the clinical features of a man's and a woman's depression.

In Part II, Causation, I detail some of the important causes of depression in both men and women, with a focus on the factors that foment depression in men.

In Part III, Treatment, I describe some general remedies that apply to both men and women, and outline some specific remedies geared to treating depression in men. I also offer the man struggling with depression some ways to feel better using self-help approaches involving:

- Self-contemplating, for example, "Why do I get so depressed, and what can I do about it?" in preparation for self-understanding based on working out psychodynamics within a self-affirmative context—accepting the need to self-criticize, but balancing that with the need to self-soothe.

- Coming to grips with past traumata that are difficult to shake.

- Reducing guilt, leading to a less punitive self-evaluation involving being kinder to oneself and giving oneself a vote of confidence—"chilling out" by accepting that "I am no more or less flawed than most everyone else."

- Becoming less interpersonally hypersensitive, especially distinguishing negative fantasy from positive reality in order to ascertain others' true attitudes and actual motives.

- Learning to become less irrationally angry and, after reducing anger to a minimum, smoothing over what anger remains and, when indicated, expressing it not in the form of tantrums but in a healthy, socially acceptable, relationship-saving way.

- Correcting cognitive errors about oneself, one's existence, and one's plight.

In many cases, as I point out, relief from depression may not require a radical revision of a man's inner and outer life. Often when it comes to depression, and especially depression in men, a small amount of change can create a large amount of improvement.

I also advance some ideas on how family and friends in the depressed man's orbit can help him feel less depressed while helping themselves cope with the often difficult and draining fallout from his disorder. So often friends, family, and partners who are the targets or "victims" of depressed men—people in the path of depression fallout—try to tolerate the man's depression by telling themselves, "He is sick" and "He cannot help himself." But that neither helps the depressed man's targets cope better nor heals the man himself, and the overpermissiveness may even make things worse for all concerned. Generally speaking, people who try to heal the depressed man intuitively, no matter how well-meaning and altruistic their intent, often find that the results they get from doing what comes naturally are unexpectedly and stunningly bad. Therefore, one of my goals is to offer these targets or victims a framework for responding to depressed men in a productive fashion through understanding their depression scientifically. With this in mind I try to answer such questions as, "How exactly should you talk to a depressed man? Should you be sympathetic and hand-hold or set limits instead? Do you give a depressed man advice or do you let him find his own way out of his quagmire, and if so, what kind of advice do you give him, and what kind of advice do you withhold?" My goal is to help a depressed man's loved ones develop a considered, effective, precise, and theoretically based healing interaction with the depressed men in their lives—sparing the depressed man some of the pain, while also sparing themselves some of the burden.

Martin Kantor, M.D.

PART I

DESCRIPTION

Chapter 1

An Overview

Depression in men differs from depression in women in its unique presentation, its idiosyncratic psychology, and its special treatment requirements. Both men and women who get depressed experience a similar intense, painful, diffuse, poignant suffering. Both hurt from that hollow rainy day feeling that is a composite of anxiety, fear, sadness, hopelessness, anger, guilt, and desperation. Both may need psychotherapy to help keep them from becoming emotional cripples who cannot enjoy life, have close relationships, and be productive on the job, and from developing emotionally based physical symptoms or an actual physical disorder such as cardiovascular disease or stroke.

Yet it is almost a truism that depression is less common in men, or at least in straight men, than in women. As much of the scientific and lay literature notes, the incidence of depression is about two times higher in women than it is in men. Indeed, Solomon suggests that the disparity may be even greater, for many therapists underrecognize and "undertreat women's depression because [they mistake] withdrawal . . . for [normal or natural] feminine passivity."[1]

But while some observers claim that numbers like this represent real and significant differences, others view the differences as illusory, or even as imaginary. They note that the disparity between men and women tends to diminish when age is factored in. Thus Cochran and Rabinowitz say that "age emerges as a salient confounding variable in the measurement of prevalence rates of depression."[2] Cochran and Rabinowitz note, "Before adolescence, little boys are generally diagnosed at least as frequently with depression as little girls [and only] at adolescence [does the] female preponderance of depressive disorders first begin . . . to emerge."[3]

Many observers also note that the disparity between men and women tends to diminish when the individual's status in life is factored in. For example, the differences in the rate of depression in men and women diminish in college populations. This is possibly because more highly educated men are more open about how they feel than men who are less educated, or, as Solomon puts it, "men who are at college are probably more open to acknowledging their illness than are less educated ... men."[4]

Too, many observers note that the difference in frequency of occurrence across the sexes is most relevant to a first episode, for after that the gap closes, and that the discrepancy between men and women, as Cochran and Rabinowitz suggest, is closed "with regard to bipolar affective disorder."[5]

Countertransference-based diagnostic errors also affect the numbers, for therapists are more likely to apply the term depression as a pejorative to women than to men, and male therapists, as Solomon notes, are likely to see women as depressed just for not "show[ing] the vitality that their husbands expect or demand."[6]

Because men are less psychologically minded than women, in men an extant depression often goes unremarked and undiagnosed because men fail to describe their symptoms precisely and accurately and instead repress their true, depressive selves out of the belief that by doing so they are being masculine by remaining emotionally strong. There is a notable male tendency to deny such a "shameful affliction" as depression. We are not surprised when a female says, "I'm depressed," but we are when a man says that. Women accept depression even though it is incompatible with their self-image, but men posit an acceptable self-image that is incompatible with feeling depressed. In this regard, men are often just echoing what society expects of them—to suffer in silence, and to fight, not yield to, their depression. Women seem more comfortable just being themselves, and less preoccupied with being a woman (and more concerned with just being a person) than men. Men, often overly concerned with being men, tend to be narrowly focused on projecting an image of masculinity. They might do almost anything to project the image that fits their macho ideal self—with depression no fit whatsoever. (Exceptions do, however, exist, as Kraemer[7] and Solomon[8] in their excellent books on depression prove, for both men are clearly in touch with their feelings, able to communicate emotions, know a great deal about themselves, and do not seem to be excessively concerned with this aspect of their images.)

Finally, men and women have different patterns of help-seeking behavior. Women, seeking treatment more than men, tend to be overrepresented in the sample populations found in research.

But to me it is our diagnostic criteria, and so the description and definition of depression, that are the most likely culprits to account for the statistical disparity. Depression is a man-made diagnosis, and too often it is one that is defined by the symptoms of the disease as they occur in women. Thus, as Cochran and Rabinowitz note, our "traditional diagnostic criteria [are] biased toward feminine means of expressing emotional distress."[9] As Real says, referring to the different presentations of depression in men and women, the incidence of depression is the same in men and women if when making the diagnosis "we factor into the equation 'personality disorders' [especially antisocial personality disorder] and chemical dependency"[10] as well as the atypical forms of depression.

Because the classical signs and symptoms of depression show some notable basic differences between men and women, clinicians who look only for the symptoms characteristic of depression in women risk missing the diagnosis in men. It is very common for depression in men to present atypically with the symptoms taking the form of "depressive equivalents" that constitute an indirect expression of the disorder. For example, depressed men do not cry as much as depressed women (*DSM-IV* criterion "appears tearful"[11]). Instead men often become irritable or develop somatic symptoms such as back pain or constipation—for they believe these to be more manly displays than expressions of raw, uncensored depressive emotion. Often, too, men deny their depression and shift into hypomania. If depression is a "woman's disease," hypomania is a "man's disease." It turns the sincere, hard-working, bright man with weighty matters on his mind and true love in his heart into a superficial, flighty, flippant, unreliable, selfish, self-centered individual doing everything he can to not look soft, passive, vulnerable, and defeated. Where once there was shyness and withdrawal, now there is attention-seeking behavior. Where once there was crying, now there is clowning. Where once there was sexual inhibition, now there is sexual preoccupation. Where once there was hypersensitivity, now there is insensitivity. Where once there was hostility/cruelty to oneself, now there is hostility/cruelty to others—characterized by truncated altruism and a lack of empathy—of the kind displayed by a man who said to his wife, "Boy, are you a mess. I sometimes wonder how I, or anybody else, can stand to live with you."

Women and men also tend to get depressed for different psychodynamic, cognitive-behavioral, and interpersonal reasons. The clinician who considers that loss is an integral part of the clinical picture of depression (and doesn't make the diagnosis unless a discernible loss has occurred) will risk overlooking depression in men. For men often get depressed without experiencing a significant, classical loss. For as we shall see, men can often tolerate losses better than they can tolerate feeling controlled; losing out to the competition in personal and professional power struggles; and losing—or what is so often being deprived of—their status and their manhood. In fact, the latter determinant is so central to the psychology of depression in men that I often say that while clinicians diagnosing women should look for evidence of *relationship* anxiety, clinicians diagnosing men should look for evidence of *castration* anxiety.

I have been impressed to find that so many of the depressed men I have treated tended to get depressed over mundane everyday troubles, making men's depression a much-ado-about-nothing illness with a tendency to spare the capacity to handle major, while affecting the capacity to handle minor, stress. As Queen Victoria, a monarch prone to severe melancholy, might have said about men when she was speaking of herself, "Great events make [them] quiet and calm; it is only trifles that irritate [their] nerves."[12] While often depression in men is a major disorder precipitated by minor events, these minor precipitants are sadly often overlooked by all concerned—clinicians, family, and friends alike. They say, "You are getting depressed over nothing" when they should be saying, "If you are getting depressed over something then it is something, not nothing, that is making you depressed." (Along related lines, too many of us make the assumption that if something is not of crushing importance to us personally, then it ought not to be of any importance whatsoever to anyone else.)

Of course, women get depressed over "nothing" too. But the mundane things that bother women the most tend to differ significantly from the mundane things that bother men the most. To oversimplify for purposes of clarity, women get depressed when they don't have a nice home to go to, while men get depressed when they have a nice home but cannot leave whenever they please—when the spirit of wanderlust (a particularly male thing) moves them. Some women tend to be understanding of a partner's infidelities and don't get depressed when they discover that their husbands have a mistress. In contrast, many men are unlikely to as readily accept a wife's infidelities; some become depressed and even violent if they so much as suspect that their wives are showing any interest at all in other men.

As we shall see, I advocate treating depression somewhat differently in women and in men. For both women and men I use an eclectic approach that embraces psychodynamic, cognitive-behavioral, interpersonal, supportive-affirmative, and pharmacological interventions. However, I tend to speak about different dynamics, correct different cognitive errors, and focus on different sources of personal and interpersonal stress in the two sexes. (These are also the things that friends and family of depressed men, and men trying to talk themselves up and out of a depression, should be thinking and talking about.) With both men and women I talk about excessive anger, irrational guilt, and an ego ideal that is either too lowly to reflect the individual's true strengths, or too lofty to do anything but leave the individual in the position of always seeing himself or herself as an underachiever. But with women I find myself speaking mostly about getting depressed over relationships gone sour, whereas with men I find myself speaking mostly about getting depressed over feeling rejected; feeling trapped, cornered, controlled, criticized, and put down; and feeling emasculated. To illustrate the latter with an anecdote from my own life, whenever I proudly mention that one of my books is doing okay, for example, "I just won an award" or "My book has been bought to be translated into a foreign language," a professor, whom I otherwise admire and respect, regularly responds by invalidating my accomplishment. Predictably she will ask, "How much money did they pay you?" and, just as predictably, go on to note that the really important thing is not that it is being translated into another language but whether it is going to be made into a movie. Then my self-esteem falls because I let it depend on whether or not someone validates my achievements. Next I go back for more, hoping this time for less. That way I put myself in the position of being invalidated, or to use a current term, "plutoed," not just once, but over and over again.

I often find myself communicating with men about how down they feel when those who should know better blame them for everything that happens in their relationships with women, and in particular in their relationships with their wives. I have had a number of men in therapy complain bitterly to me that they were being scapegoated by therapists who saw them as one hundred percent responsible for abusing their wives in situations where at least fifty percent of the problem involved their wives abusing them. In a general way, this exemplifies how men get especially depressed when they feel cut down to size by unsupportive people, and especially by people, both men and women, who remind them of their mother who never gave them positive feedback when they were boys but instead responded negatively when they tried to grow up and become a man. For example, a patient, a child prodigy who was an excellent pianist and composer, remembers being at home playing a thirty-minute piano sonata he composed at age nine—one that was full of passion and tenderness. But when the last chord sounded, his mother did not respond with "That was beautiful," but with "Did you finally get that all out of your system?" As a child I had a playmate of whom I was very fond. Her mother, whom I subsequently realized must have had a germ phobia, wouldn't let me touch her for fear that I would dirty and contaminate her. My resentment built, and one day I decided to break free and express myself by doing something spiteful to show them all what I really felt about their prissy ways and regimenting, controlling behaviors. So I took a handful of dirt and threw it into my playmate's carriage. Not surprisingly, there was an outcry heard round the neighborhood, and they never let me either forget it or atone. Forty years later I went to a party given by my old playmate, now a grown woman. When I entered her house after not having seen her for years, the first words out of her mouth were not "Hello" or "So good to see you again" but a less than life-affirming, "Look, everybody, here is that boy I told you all about—that brat who threw dirt in my stroller."

The psychotherapeutic process itself also differs in men and in women. Since I have generally found women to be more insightful than men, with men I often have to spend a lot of time attempting to convince them that they are in fact depressed, for example, that their stomach pains are not due to gas but to internalized rage, or that their head pains are not due to migraines but to tension. With men I have also found that I have to be especially alert to resistances to ongoing therapy. More men than women view therapy as a shameful undertaking. They feel that just being in treatment makes them a pathetic excuse for a human being. They also see having to be in therapy as one more episode in a lifetime of capitulating to authority and view their therapists as a force trying to take away their freedom and cut them down to size. All things considered, the depressed woman who clings to the therapist and to her therapy has as her counterpart the depressed man who will do anything to quit it—including having a flight into health, where he denies his disorder just so that he can appear to have been cured and have an excuse to leave treatment immediately.

Pharmacotherapeutic treatment for women and men also can proceed along somewhat different lines. Men with primarily atypical symptoms (more common in men than in women) tend not to respond to pharmacotherapy alone but additionally need psychotherapy directed to the depression hiding beneath the complaints. Too, the pharmacotherapy of Bipolar II Disorder and of Cyclothymia (a mild form of Bipolar II Disorder), both of which are also in my (perhaps unique) experience more common in men than in women, is different from the pharmacotherapy of classic Unipolar depression, the former sometimes requiring mood stabilizers in addition to antidepressants.

Finally, to the conventional wisdom that depression in men is underdiagnosed compared to depression in women, I add the cautionary statement that depression in both sexes is sometimes not *under-* but *over-* diagnosed. Of particular concern to me is that paranoid men are often incorrectly called depressed and antidepressants alone (without covering agents such as antipsychotic drugs) are prescribed, activating their paranoia and possibly causing them to become violent. In recent times there have been many news stories about men diagnosed as depressed who became violent when on antidepressants. Although there is no certain evidence of cause-and-effect, it makes sense to me that if antidepressants (as has been shown) can increase suicidality, which is violence toward the self, they can also potentially increase homicidality (as is not often appreciated), which is violence to others.

Chapter 2

Making the Diagnosis

DIAGNOSING DEPRESSION

Depression is an elusive, complex, multifaceted disorder with many subtypes, each of which has its own, often indistinct, boundaries. Diagnosis will vary depending on how strictly clinicians follow *DSM-IV* diagnostic criteria. It is, unfortunately, somewhat common for clinicians to fail to adhere strictly to *DSM-IV* criteria, even though by doing so they risk both under- and overdiagnosing depression.

Clinicians often *underdiagnose* depression when they allow their personal beliefs to fuel their clinical expectations. The clinician who believes that affective disorder is uncommon in men might assign the more manly diagnoses of psychopath, addiction, and impulse disorder to men who are in fact bipolar. Recently a man bought several houses in one day. Though I diagnosed him as basically suffering from an affective disorder, others dismissed him as a cad and a charlatan, while a few even complimented him for being a savvy "he-man" and said, "No fool he when it comes to investing in real estate."

Clinicians who diagnose depression strictly on the basis of self-tests also risk overlooking depression in men. Here is a commonly used self-test meant to discern the diagnosis of depression:

"During the past month, have you often been bothered by feeling down, depressed, or hopeless?

During the past month, have you often been bothered by little interest or pleasure in doing things?"[1]

A depressed woman, submissive and passive, as well as desirous of pleasing a tester from whom she sought succor and help, might answer "yes" to both questions and be diagnosed as depressed. Her counterpart, a man who was equally depressed, might see both questions as critical blaming attacks on him and as threatening to his macho self-image. Also, he would likely know what the tester wanted and might believe that only a "wuss" would yield and give it to him. He might also feel that the tester was attempting to humiliate and devalue him. So he might answer "no" to both questions just to maintain his positive self-view, project what he believed to be a correct, manly image, and goof on the person administering the test. Many women accept the medical context in which the questions are asked, give the tester sincere answers, and are correctly diagnosed as depressed. Many men take the questioning personally, as a reflection on their self-worth by someone who doesn't count anyway, rebel in order to make certain no "egghead" is going to put them in a bad light by calling them names, and deliberately cover up their depression so well that the disorder goes undiagnosed for a period of some months or even years.

Clinicians also often underdiagnose depression because they are willing to make the diagnosis only in the presence of that clear-cut depressive affect that may be hidden in men. But it is often appropriate to make the diagnosis even when depressive affect is merely inferred—as long as other defining symptoms such as withdrawal or irritability are present.

In contrast clinicians *overdiagnose* depression when they overlook its special nature and refer to any psychological phenomenon characterized by some degree of sadness, boredom, diminution of interest, modest slowing, anger, withdrawal, and reduced functionality as depression. As a result they may wrongly call men with Borderline Personality Disorder, Schizoid Personality Disorder, or Paranoid Personality Disorder depressed. Clinicians often overdiagnose depression in women after confounding feminine passivity with depressive withdrawal. Clinicians often overdiagnose depression in men when they classify the paranoid plaint, "He persecutes me" as the depressive plaint, "I feel unworthy and disliked." In both men and women clinicians too often confound the normal depressed mood from which many of us suffer from time to time with an actual clinical depression.

Finally, the diagnosis of depression is socioculturally bound. Therefore men from different cultures tend to display different symptoms, and clinicians from different cultures tend to interpret alerting signs and symptoms differently, resulting in problems with consensus about what constitutes normalcy and what constitutes depressive deviation from the norm. In my experience, clinicians from the more expressive cultures often minimize the significance of even major pathological affect displays, and so regularly miss the diagnosis of depression. In contrast, clinicians from the more reserved cultures often maximize the significance of minor affective displays, and with some frequency overdiagnose depression.

CLASSIFYING DEPRESSION

Depression can be profitably viewed as a specific symptom, as a disorder characterized by a constellation of symptoms, or as a syndrome where the identified constellation of symptoms is a destination reached by many roads. The constellation depression has a number of subclassifications, each of which in turn has somewhat indistinct boundaries.

Dysthymia (Dysthymic Disorder)

Dysthymia is a mild form of depression. It tends to be more long-lived and chronic than episodic. Dysthymia is often readily comprehensible in interactive human terms, for example, as the product of marital stress. According to some observers, Dysthymia exists on a continuum with Major Depression, making it at times difficult to distinguish between the two. I believe that one possible distinction is that Dysthymia and Major Depression have a different feel both to the man suffering from the depression and to those observing him. Men with Dysthymia tend to feel and look less sick than troubled, while men with a Major Depression tend to go beyond feeling emotionally ill to feeling almost physically sick. To me, however, that does not mean that Dysthymia is necessarily, and by definition, an emotional, and Major Depression is necessarily, and by definition, a biological, disorder.

Brief, Mild, and Atypical Depression

As Cochran and Rabinowitz note, there are "various subclinical syndromes composed of fewer diagnostic criteria compared with a major depressive episode...."[2] Some men experience minidepressions (*brief, mild depression*) where they throw their depressed feeling off in a few minutes, hours, or days—perhaps because they have learned from prior therapy how to abort a more prolonged episode by "psychotherapeutizing" themselves. Other men experience *atypical* depression. I describe the symptoms of atypical depression (often called "depressive equivalents" to indicate how they are in effect disguised depressive symptoms) in Chapter 6.

Major Depression (Major Depressive Disorder)/Depression with Psychotic Features/Melancholia

The term *Major Depression* (which overlaps conceptually and clinically with "black depression," otherwise known as "Melancholia") applies to the more severe forms of the disorder. These may be characterized by such serious "psychotic" symptoms as somatic delusions and even hallucinations, especially somatic hallucinations. Major Depression tends at times to be acute and is often recurrent. Because it can be difficult to comprehend in human interactive terms, that is, because it does not routinely appear to be a determinable response to specific interpersonal events or obvious environmental stresses, it is often called "endogenous" (innate). It is often believed to be organic in nature in part because it has a biological cast, that is, it looks and feels almost like a physical illness such as a flu prodrome.

When Major Depression occurs alone, that is, without alternating with mania or hypomania, we call the result *Unipolar Depression*. Cochran and Rabinowitz suggest that there are three types of Unipolar Depression, which they classify according to cause, family history, and associated disorders. These are:

1. Reactive depression ... secondary to bereavement or medical illness, or ... associated with a natural catastrophe.
2. Familial pure depressive disease [with] family histories of depression only and an absence of antisocial personality and alcoholism in relatives.
3. Depressive spectrum disease ... associated with ... emotional instability [and] anxiety disorders, alcoholism, substance abuse, and personality disorders in relatives.[3]

In what is called *Bipolar Disorder*, depressive episodes tend to recur and be interspersed with hypomania or mania. Bipolar Disorder may be divided into Type I and Type II. In *Bipolar Type I Disorder* major depressive episodes alternate with mania, while in *Bipolar Type II Disorder* major depressive episodes alternate with hypomania. While some men alternate between hypomania and depression, a few hypomanic men do not clearly manifest the depressive state at all but instead appear to be on a chronic unremitting high.

Some men suffer from a disorder called *Cyclothymic Disorder*. This is characterized by mood swings between mild depression and hypomania, that is, it is conveniently conceptualized as a mild form of Bipolar II Disorder. A feature of some forms of Cyclothymia is rapid cycling between down and up mood, with, however, each of the phases of the cycle of lesser amplitude than the mood swings of either Bipolar I Disorder or Bipolar II Disorder.

Chapter 3

Symptoms

In this chapter I focus on the symptoms of depression in men and emphasize how these tend to differ from the symptoms of depression in women.

AN OVERVIEW

Men who experience depression often experience an agonizing, distressing, at times almost unbearable, blue mood. They may want to cry but be unable to shed tears openly. Their self-esteem is low—they think little of themselves and feel defective and worthless. Sometimes there is a slowing of ideation and motility associated with feelings of fatigue and a diminished interest in enjoyable activity so that they become unable to experience pleasure from any source—other perhaps than from the "sweet suffering" of the depression itself. They speak of a pervasive gloominess and sense of finality and become preoccupied with feelings of personal and world decay. They become pessimistic individuals hyperaware of the somber and baneful side of life, and they think only of how hopeless their future is. They dwell on past and present mistakes they made and lose hope of doing better in the future. They anticipate the imminence of catastrophes, particularly losses, and as a result become highly anxious and excessively cautious. They have thoughts of dying and death that may be accompanied by suicidal ruminations. Sometimes they make a suicidal attempt, unsuccessful or successful, because they hate themselves for being inadequate, fear that life is most definitely over, or believe that all is most certainly lost.

AFFECT (MOOD)

The terms affect and mood are often used interchangeably. However, depressive *affect* is the semantic equivalent of "the general climate," as distinct from depressive *mood* which is the semantic equivalent of "today's weather." Depressive affect, often referred to as the blues, consists primarily of feelings of deep sadness along with feelings of depletion. The man feels physically worn out and anergic (without energy), and possibly empty, detached, blank, and alienated from himself and life. Real describes depressive affect as a "perverse sense of blackness, sadness, a grim coldness at the center of things [and a] state of dead disconnection. . . ."[1] Often feelings of panic also exist as do feelings of rage. In men who are depressed this combined depression, panic, and rage is often felt and expressed as agitation, where the man feels and expresses a sense of exploding anguish, as if he is almost literally about to "blow apart" from within.

However, not all depressed men (or women) develop the full picture of classical depressive affect in all or even in one of their depressive episodes. Some men feel mostly blank and detached, while others feel mostly irritable and angry. How the man feels depends on the severity and depth of the individual depressive episode; on the particular nature of the precipitant (if any) of a given episode (for example, the response to the loss of a person can look and feel different from the response to the loss of a job); and on past therapy received and present treatment in progress.

Depressed men often experience their blue feeling in the pit of their stomach or beneath their sternum. The feeling hurts and gnaws. While it comes from within it often feels as if it is coming from without—as if a vise being placed on the chest was being gradually but inexorably squeezed closed. It is a miserable, lost, and futureless feeling—as if the bottom has dropped out and one's body and soul are being blackened, awash in an endless, draggy, perpetually sad, downcast, joyless, and exhausting onslaught that drains and depletes, making life into an unfortunate play whose sad ending is predictable, virtually assured, and, alas, ultimately even desirable.

APPEARANCE

Changes in appearance are of some diagnostic and prognostic value and may assist in the monitoring of the course and prognosis of the disorder. However, we certainly must not judge the depth and extent of a man's depression by his appearance alone. Even depressed men who are severely ill will refuse to let their emotions significantly affect their appearance if they are trying to ward off, evade, and control disintegration on the outside in a desperate attempt to control it on the inside.

Certainly the man's suicidal potential bears little if any direct relationship to his appearance, and sometimes the better the man looks the worse he feels and the more likely he is to act. Some masochistically inclined depressed men with an excess of empathy try to keep up their appearance just to avoid burdening others with their despair, while others do so just so that they can succeed in a planned suicide attempt without anyone noticing and interfering. In contrast, some sadistically inclined men look bad just so that they can be clear about what is going on with them, perhaps to torture others with their suffering, to have company in their misery, and to sadistically bring others down to their level.

Specific changes in appearance can reflect a man's underlying personality structure/personality disorder. For example, *masochistic* depressed men often look just slightly out of style, a bit messy, or somewhat shabby, with a stooped posture, shuffling gait, and hangdog expression that is part of a cultivated "kick-me-because-I-am-down" look. These men often appear to be older than they actually are because they stoop when they walk, and look crestfallen, and they may even deliberately spoil their appearance by wearing a tie with a big spot on it, or pants with cuffs that are turned up and frayed. *Obsessive-compulsive* depressed men tend to look plain as they live out stoic Puritan fantasies in their appearance. As the joke goes, when one such depressed man was asked where he got his coat, he replied, "I didn't get it; I had it." Many such men are guilty about experiencing pleasure and want to look, to themselves as well as to others, as if they are not particularly enjoying themselves, or as if they are broke. *Passive-aggressive* depressed men may display a rigid facial musculature set in a gelatin of rage. The intent is twofold: to look as if they are about to attack, and to provoke others to provoke them back so that they can next justify, guilt free, the torrent of anger they plan to release. The more *psychopathic*, more manipulative depressed men deliberately contort their faces into expressions of anguish and pain as part of an almost conscious plan to elicit a sympathetic response they can use for their own ends.

BEHAVIOR

In the following section I describe characteristic depression behaviors, some of which are associated with severe consequences such as a loss of an important relationship or job, financial problems, or suicide.

However, many depressed men, splitting "how I feel" from "how I act," behave normal or close to normal to fight, not yield to, their depression. Ultimately, however, that fight takes its toll: in depletion of energy; depressive fatigue; and anhedonia (an inability to feel and to respond to much of anything), all because they have dissipated too much energy in a constant struggle to repress and disavow whole aspects of their feeling and thinking self.

Relationship Difficulties

Many depressed men have relationship difficulties and these are a source of their own misery and of the misery they create for others. Many men enter therapy at the behest of a desperate, and sometimes fed up, wife, partner, or friend, who is responding negatively to the depressed man's excessive distancing, excessive clinging, irritability and anger, rigid controlling stubbornness and uncooperativeness, undue hypersensitivity, excessive competitiveness, or a devaluing of others with the intent to overvalue himself by comparison.

In the realm of the depressed man's characteristic irritability, I was once in psychoanalysis with a doctor who insisted that I come for sessions in mid-morning, making it impossible for me to hold down my full-time position a long subway ride from his office. When I protested, he snapped at me, "We aren't getting along very well, are we?" and suggested that I leave analysis on the spot—no protestations, no second chances, and no refund for the unused part of the hour. Later I learned that he successfully committed suicide by jumping off his roof—in the presence of someone he had called to come over and help him get hospitalized before he tried to kill himself.

Men who present with a defensive hypomanic relatedness meant to undo feeling lonely and abandoned have many transitory superficial relationships characteristically shot through with excessive hostility, for example, antagonizing many of their middle-aged friends by calling them names such as "fatso" and "baldy." Some hypomanic men deal with feeling abandoned and lonely by stalking, an activity often associated with what Cochran and Rabinowitz refer to as "paranoia and increased interpersonal sensitivity."[2] Some depressed men deal with castration anxiety by developing restitutive paraphilias. They might *flash* to reassure themselves that they are still intact down there and retain the ability to elicit some reaction, even an unfavorable one, or develop *pedophilia* to feel that they are in full control of, and retain all the power in, a relationship.

Withdrawal

Some depressed men withdraw both personally and professionally. Their withdrawal as Cochran and Rabinowitz suggest may take the form of an "increased withdrawal from relationships [which] may be denied by [the] patient"[3] or of "decreased interest in activities."[4] Or it may take the form of atypical symptoms such as impaired sexuality characterized according to Cochran and Rabinowitz by a "shift in the interest level of sexual encounters"[5] as well as difficulty achieving orgasm (easily mistaken for a side effect of antidepressants). A shift into hypomania with an increase in sexual desire along with a frantic seeking of sexual gratification may eventually appear.

In the depressed man withdrawal might signify:

- A living out the feeling that "I am not worth relating to."
- A defensive way to avoid being rejected based on a pervasive fear of rejection that is often the product of an extreme sensitivity to potential slights.
- A fear of being traumatized in a relationship just as one was before (often in childhood).
- An angry, spiteful withholding of love.
- A self-hatred lived out by relinquishing the pleasures and rewards of close loving relationships.
- A self-love with narcissistic gratification "all I need."
- A searching for another mother or father, only to give up after discovering that no one can ever fully take the original's place.
- A preference for and the enjoyment of being isolated.

However, there is an important differential diagnosis of what looks at first to be depressive withdrawal. Some so-called depressive withdrawal is actually schizoid remoteness, avoidant distancing due to relationship anxiety, or schizotypal quirkiness used to pull back from a feared, despised, or uncomprehending "establishment."

Blocking

Blocking often occurs and takes one of several forms:

- Motivational lack
- Obsessional, unproductive brooding
- An inability to be as successful professionally as one might otherwise have become
- Depressive anhedonia/burnout
- Paralysis of self-expression leading to creative block
- Relationship difficulties due to a fear of often imagined interpersonal calamities.

The depressed man's familiar inability to cry can be a form of blocking. It is often due to the fear that expressing feelings is weak and feminine. There may be an associated desire to convince oneself that one is manly just because one is acting stoically.

Erratic Impulsive Action

Depressed men can be unpredictable and erratic. They may swing from being sensible, rational, and reliable individuals with little or no semblance of behavioral abnormality to manifesting poor judgment in the form of self-destructive behavior or a hypomanic seeking immediate gratification with little regard for ultimate consequences.

Some of the erratic unpredictable behavior of depressed men is due to *diurnal variation*, a term that refers to the tendency many depressed men have to feel better and worse at different times of the day. Some depressed men (those we commonly call "evening people") feel worse in the morning than they do later in the day. They characteristically do not want to get up and out of bed to face the day, and as a consequence may be late for work. They improve as the morning wears on, only to wake up the next morning feeling just as bad today as they did the day before. Other depressed men ("morning people") get up and out of bed early and on time. They rise and shine—only to have their depression erode their good mood as they gradually wake up to their bad reality and fall back into a morass—sometimes as early as lunchtime. Some men with this pattern have alcohol for their lunch in order to be able to face the rest of the afternoon working at a job they despise, and with people they hate.

Antisocial Behavior

From time to time many depressed men display antisocial or psycho-pathic behavior. In this antisocial/psychopathic state they become as unscrupulous as they once were moral and honest, and act as selfishly now as they acted altruistically then. Some begin to use alcohol and illicit drugs to excess—both to medicate their depression and to seek pleasure in any way they can, no matter the cost to themselves or to those who do, or would, love them.

Agitation and Irritability

In my clinical experience, *depressive agitation*, an active form of expression, is more common in men than in women, who tend to favor more passive forms of expression such as weeping or withdrawal.

Agitated depressed men according to Cochran and Rabinowitz experience symptoms of restlessness, increased motor activity, and an inability to concentrate in a setting of "Type A behavior patterns."[6] Also according to Cochran and Rabinowitz they pace, and moan, but they rarely cry, and typically develop an "increase in intensity or frequency of angry outbursts"[7] often in the form of temper tantrums during which, as one depressed man put it, "I run off hatefully at the mouth and afterwards cannot remember what I said." Insomnia often occurs and takes the form of an inability to easily fall asleep, tossing and turning all night long, and frequently getting up throughout the night culminating in early morning awakening.

Depressive agitation is in part an interpersonal expression meant to convey two things: "How much I hurt inside" and "Look at how much you made me suffer." Some depressed men consciously or unconsciously moan and hand wring as their way to plead for the care and love they feel they are missing, and desperately need.

Dynamically speaking, agitation can represent a spill-over of bottled-up anger. Pressure builds, with the agitation a discharge mechanism offering partial release as the head of built-up steam breaks though in the form of vocalization and muscular movement. As will be noted throughout this text, men bottle up their anger in the first place because they feel guilty about feeling and getting angry, fear being flooded by too much anger, and are cowering in response to others who are making it clear that because they view anger as an abnormal and unacceptable emotion, they will punish and abandon any man who gets mad. Social sanctions against getting angry, for example, the biblical "turn the other cheek," are also powerful anger suppressants.

Somatic Complaints

Somatic (physical) symptoms and complaints can occur, and include: loss of appetite or increased appetite associated with weight loss or gain; hypersomnia or insomnia often associated with nightmares with themes of abandonment, loneliness, and isolation; and according to the *DSM-IV* manifest "psychomotor agitation or retardation"[8] and "fatigue or loss of energy nearly every day."[9] Many depressed men are prone to hypochondriacal worries such as cancer phobia, which can be indirectly fatal if it leads them to fear going to the doctor lest they be diagnosed with a terminal illness. Somatic symptoms are also discussed in Chapter 6 on atypical presentations of men's depression.

Selfish and Narcissistic or Excessively Unselfish and Altruistic Behavior

Some depressed men behave in an excessively *narcissistic* fashion. For example, they collar people and unload their problems on them, hogging the conversation, and showing little or no concern for anyone but themselves. Others are just the opposite of narcissistic. They are excessively empathic and altruistic individuals much too concerned about others' feelings to the detriment of their own. Such men fail to be adequately self-protective and self-gratifying, and give too much to others and take too little for themselves. They deprive themselves of what they need and long for—even to the point of giving away their most treasured possessions (a possible warning of a suicidal attempt).

Dependent/Regressive Behavior

Many depressed men display a kind of *infantilism* in the form of a constant searching for new and better caretakers. They expect or demand others put them first—before everything and everyone. One depressed man expected his wife to take off from work to hold his hand every time he went to the doctor, even for trivial complaints. Developmentally such men were often forced as little boys to prematurely renounce their attachment to their mothers just so that they did not become "mamma's boys." Now, never having gotten over their need for a mother, they continue to seek mother-figures to fulfill them, only to go into a depressive tailspin when their expectations, as predictably happens, go partially or even completely unfulfilled.

This said, many dependent depressed men hide their dependency because they fear that it is not manly to show it. Predictably those on whom they wish to depend even a little fail to identify, respect, and gratify their rational dependency—leaving the man rightfully feeling depressed over being ignored, and appropriately shattered over seemingly having been abandoned.

Vicious Cycling

Vicious cycling tends to be a feature of depression. In a common scenario, men cannot work because they are depressed, and they are depressed because they cannot work. Depressed men are depressed because few want to take care of them, and few want to take care of them because they are depressed.

Manipulativeness

A depressed man's behavior rarely takes place in a vacuum but mostly requires someone to register and respond to it. This can give the depression a manipulative quality as the depressed man means, almost consciously, to catch others up in his blackness, and to make them feel his hurt and pain. Such men often draw strangers into their orbit, pinning them against the wall, trapping them into listening to their tales of woe, and demanding that they offer them healing nurturance. With them the nurturance, however, only goes one way, for when someone asks for a payback they use their depression as an excuse to not return the favor.

Some men leave suicide notes as a weapon of vengeance—their way to make others feel guilty by implying, often in the very act of denying it, "See what you did to me." A patient left a suicide note saying, "I want you to know that I don't hold your divorcing me responsible for my taking my life"—his way to hurt his ex-wife by the very act of denying that that was his exact intent. Characteristically such behavior intensifies with affirmation and diminishes with limit-setting—but this is not guaranteed. I have devoted Chapter 4 to suicidal behavior.

Depression can also be manipulative in the sense of being an interpersonal defense against getting hurt. Many depressed men are in effect proclaiming that they are depressed as their way to offer up the tender underbelly in a passive compliant abdication meant to thwart an imminent attack from real or fantasized others believed to be their adversaries.

Acting/Acting Out

Many depressed men submerge their depression beneath a cloak of activity. This activity may consist of workaholism; food and sexual addiction or addictive gambling; rejecting others in order to abandon them actively before they are passively abandoned by them; and confrontational and even violent behavior toward a stranger, friend, or partner—for example, a raging over an imputed slight or insult such as found in road rage or walking out on someone as their way of punishing them. A man told his mother he wanted to get married. The mother felt that he should finish college first. She didn't like his wife-to-be because she was an excessively thin woman who hardly said a word to her or to anyone else. When his mother merely asked if he were willing to at least wait until he finished college, he felt she was trying to take away the little he could get in, and everything that he wanted out of, life. So he got his revenge by leaving home without leaving a forwarding address, and has not been heard from since.

SPEECH

Some depressed men deal with feeling lonely by muttering to themselves—self-stroking by humming, singing, or prattling, hoping that it will somehow lift their spirits. Once after I regretfully had to put my dog in a kennel in preparation for going on a long trip, I found myself constantly singing a little meaningless ditty over and over again, just because it reminded me of her and of home.

The content of depressed men's speech often consists of characteristic depressive preoccupations: a fear of abandonment, hypersensitivity to criticism, and the belief that the future holds nothing but disappointment and loss. Sometimes their speech reveals a characterological passivity via the use of compliant words and expressions packed with intimations of resentful submission—so that a man might say, "Okay, okay, sure, sure," but really mean, "That is not at all acceptable." Some depressed men favor thick moody words like "bitter," "sigh," and "alone." Others attempt to triumph over compliance with defiance by speaking in an excessively macho fashion to reassure themselves that they are strong not weak, and invulnerable not endangered.

Many depressed men brood aloud about imponderables or insignificant things. A neighbor got quite depressed because the hall of his apartment was a dark color. He thought about the problem continuously, and harangued his neighbors to agree to lighten the shade "before I go crazy."

Sometimes shame keeps the depressed man silent about his thoughts and feelings. The silence of depression can also be about control. Some depressed men will not speak simply because they have been asked to say something—or they will speak, but speak only monosyllabically in order to indicate their angry resentment about having been requested to talk.

Depressed men in the passive-aggressive mode favor indirect verbal attacks as they subtly but still effectively hound, harass, plague, and annoy others in an unpleasant, grating, intrusive manner. Some accomplish that goal by complaining about how angry and depressed they are. Others accomplish the same thing by flagging their anger as disappointment, for example, "I am disappointed in you" instead of "I am angry with you." Others couch their attacks on others in the form of manifest attacks on themselves, such as, "I guess I did something wrong, didn't I?—having angry words with themselves to hide their hostility in the guise of self-complaints they substitute for complaints about others. Others nonetheless do pick up on how they are the real targets of the so-called self-complaints. They sense that the depressive cry, "I am so stupid" really means "You are as dumb as they come," or "I am such a failure" really means "You have failed me completely." We now hear, "I don't like depressed men," when what people really mean is, "I don't like men who complain about themselves because I know who they are really attacking." Alternatively, some men couch attacks specifically meant for individuals as general complaints about society and the world. They omit any direct reference to their specific targets, while making certain that the message "You are the one in my sights" still gets through.

Depressed men who become hypomanic often display pressured speech. They simultaneously use, or overuse, many ego words—"I" in particular. They tend to fixate on unimportant matters and make them into recurrent leitmotivs to which they then attribute greater than warranted significance. One man became preoccupied with how an animal got into his wall and disturbed his dog, and how the heating system in his apartment made so much noise that he couldn't hear his TV. The obsessive depressive who focuses on minute personal imperfections (then gets depressed because he is not perfect) has as his counterpart the hypomanic man who focuses on trivial achievements (then gets depressed when he ultimately, and correctly, perceives that he has accomplished very little in life).

THOUGHT

Low Self-Esteem

Depressed men notably suffer from low self-esteem. Men with low self-esteem compulsively seek failure; have such sexual problems as impotence or retarded ejaculation; have occupational problems such as writer's block; find themselves indulging in excessive self-sacrifice in the form of compulsive and excessive altruism; or suffer from depressive paraphilias. In the realm of the latter, some become pedophiles because they question their value as adults. So they select children for sexual encounters because they can only relate fearlessly to someone dependent, helpless, small, and too weak to protest, complain, or fight back, and too needy or scared to break away and leave. Others become rough trade paraphiliacs—those who feel entranced only by people they consider to be low-life, as they favor people, such as prostitutes, who they can view as being beneath them. They feel attracted to such people because they do not feel entitled to seek someone on their own level, and that desperate losers is all they can get.

Self-esteem is often low because of a range of negative feelings about oneself. These negative feelings, and the resultant lowering of self-esteem, can occur:

- As the outcome of child abuse. In one case the child abuse consisted of being devalued for being an unwanted "change-of-life" baby.

- As the outcome of feeling or being currently hated, rejected, and disdained by sadists whose negative evaluations are allowed to rule.

- As an inner response to inappropriately high self-expectations that originate in the impossible dictates of an overly demanding ego-ideal. A man with this problem often goes through life assessing his achievements not according to who he truly is but according to the "someone else I might and ought to be." So he regularly sees himself as a failure, and feels and acts as if he has actually failed.

- As the product of anger at others turned around to become self-hatred, with anger introjected due to guilt and shame about feeling angry, and kept inside due to the fear of losing someone if the anger is openly expressed. Such men's complaints about themselves turn out to be complaints about others, so that the depressive cry, "I am worthless" often means, "You did not act worthy of me," or the depressive plaint, "I don't have what it takes" often means, "You don't give me what I want."

- As the product of personality problems. Low self-esteem often originates in a masochistic excess of empathy for and altruism toward others—that overly sacrificial global kindness that so easily turns to rage at oneself when it is not fully reciprocated, so that the man comes to feel that he is a big sucker who has once again allowed himself to have been taken.

Low self-esteem and in particular its origin in warped self-expectations is discussed further in Chapter 6.

Fear of Success and Survivor Guilt

Men who fear success may choose to lead their lives uncompetitively. They become overly giving, excessively self-sacrificial individuals paralyzed by the zero-sum belief that should they win something someone else will lose it all and perish. Such men are often, to their own detriment, all too willing to take the bullet meant for their buddy. These men tend to suffer from survivor guilt should they succeed where a loved one, or even a hated rival, has failed.

Hypersensitivity

Men often get depressed due to their hypersensitivity to rejection. They tend to take rejection both seriously and personally. For them every interpersonal loss, even a naturally occurring death, represents a personal slight and criticism. Moreover, where the injured woman accepts her rejection, and often does so in resentful silence, the injured man protests his, and often does so in acts of violence

Men are also especially sensitive to threats to their status. They hate being put down and often complain that others are treating them like nobodies. They are also especially sensitive to the possibility that someone is trying to control them. They long to be taken care of and to have others take over, assist, and guide them, but still they cling to their independence and need for absolute freedom. In double jeopardy is the man who acts depressed because he feels that he is too dependent for his own good *and* because he fears that he cannot be as dependent as he might like to be—because no one cares enough about him to want to make him dependent on them.

A hypersensitivity to symbolic castration is central to depression in men, as discussed and emphasized throughout.

A Tendency Toward Having Bad Dreams

Depressed men often suffer from recurrent nightmares. Some of these represent the breakthrough fulfillment of secret forbidden wishes. One patient was involved in a stable long-term marriage that should have made him happy except for the fact that he felt trapped. In his recurrent nightmares he expressed his discontent with his perfectly good relationship in the following wishful image: "My wife is getting on a subway train and the doors are closing on me before I can get on the train with her."

Hypomanic men do not tend to have nightmares but have pleasant dreams that remake an unpleasant past so that things come out all right. A hypomanic man dreamt that his wife who had in reality walked out on him without warning returned, apologized, and promised never to leave him again. He also dreamt that his deceased parents invited him over for dinner. In another dream an apartment he had sold, mistakenly as it turned out, was back in his possession, and now located in a town that welcomed instead of virtually exiled him. Also in the dream the apartment had been successfully renovated so that it had the perfect room arrangement, ideal view, and correctly sized terrace—not so big that he got lost on it, and not so small that he felt cramped out there.

Ruminative Brooding and Catastrophic Thinking

In some depressed men their blue mood swamps their thinking, creating a troubled inner silence and wordless suffering that is, however, nothing like inner peace. In other depressed men obsessional brooding takes over instead. The man may brood silently, or he may brood aloud in the form of worrying and complaining. Some men don't think or talk much about how they feel. Brooders-out-loud think and talk of nothing but. They are like my neighbor who regularly greets me on a sunny morning with a blood-curdling, "I feel angry all the time, like everyday I am just looking forward to killing the first person I see. Can all the news I get get even worse?"

Depressed men often brood about presumably insurmountable obstacles poised to bring their lives to a halt. They brood that their world is going under and that they are going with it. They think constantly about holes in the ozone layer, contamination of the rivers, or global warming—important issues which, however, they can never seem to stop fretting about. Sometimes their brooding leads to corrective action, but often they make little or no attempt to bring indicated changes about. They do not raise money for charity or become activists for a worthy cause. Rather they just continue to unproductively torture themselves with the sad state of affairs in which they find themselves and the world, and with how helpless they feel about the possibility of ever doing anything to change things.

Depressed men also tend to ruminate about how to assign blame and fault in their personal interactions. Unlike paranoid men who conclude that they are never to blame, depressed men conclude that they are entirely responsible for all things, and should therefore be thoroughly scoured for everything. Typically they readily accept equal amounts of blame for unimportant and important things, so that they come to see themselves as just as guilty for ruining a picnic by forgetting the salt as for causing a severe auto accident by driving when intoxicated. Such self-blame usually occurs in the context of an already guilt-laden proneness to withdraw self-love on the slightest pretext—a readiness to lower their self-esteem by retracting any self-congratulations they had previously extended to themselves. When asked why they do that, they often answer that high opinions of the self are morally reprehensible, representing the apotheosis of what, to them, is the sin of unpardonable pride.

Depressed men tend to torture themselves with what they believe to have been big mistakes they made in the past, are making now, and are about to make in the future. When I get depressed I begin to dwell on a practice operation I was assigned to do in medical school on a dog—and weep silently to think that she, a purebred black and white cocker spaniel, was no doubt someone's pet who had either escaped or was stolen from its owner. One idée fixe that invariably accompanies my brooding is, "Poor dog, she didn't need that surgery. I should have refused to do it."

They likewise torture themselves with what they consider to be their personal imperfections. They criticize themselves for not having done something the one right way even in those situations where there is no one right way, only different ways that are all more or less correct and acceptable. For example, a man regularly brooded, "My wife's secretary never puts me right though when I call her even when it is important. Should I just wait and call back, or should I give her the 'what for' until she begins to comply with my requests?" One man perpetually wondered, "What is the one right way to handle my passive-aggressive wife? If I confront and stand up to her, she only gets angrier, and her passive aggression gets worse. But if I don't confront and stand up to her I am giving her permission to continue in her passive-aggressive ways, and so setting the stage for her passive aggression to get worse. If I do confront her she might feel hurt and never speak to me again, and I will get even more depressed. If I don't confront her I might stew and get angrier and angrier, only to ultimately drive her away by blowing up at her, and then I will get even more depressed. If I say something I am giving her the satisfaction of a response, which will intensify her passive-aggressive provocation. If I don't say anything I am ignoring her and she will have to intensify her passive aggression to get through to me." Characteristic of men who brood about such dichotomies is that they have little or no interest in, or patience with, anything resembling moderation in the form of a compromise—for example, "I can say something, but I have to use the right words because she is so sensitive, and what really matters is not what I say but how I say it."

Ambivalent thinking, which often accompanies brooding, is the product of intensely mixed feelings that render a man unable to make up his mind, leading to the cancelled movement and even to the paralytic blankness and numbness of depressive *anhedonia* (lack of energy and inability to experience pleasure) and *alexithymia* (an inability to feel) translating into depressive *avolitional anergia* (a paralysis of the will). In a typical scenario a man cannot weep at a funeral because he cannot make up his mind if he loved or hated the person who died, and so he "doesn't quite know whether to laugh or to cry." Some men freeze for quite a while; others just freeze for a bit then go on to act impulsively simply to break the stalemate.

Dynamically, ambivalence often rests partly on a wish for success countered by a fear of achievement, so that the man climbs high then defeats himself just as he reaches the top, or cancels narcissistic stirrings with altruistic self-sacrifice. When guilt affects both an idea and its opposite, and desire and renunciation exist side by side, the man thinks that it is bad to want too much, and equally bad to want too little.

Ambivalent men torture not only themselves but also others with all their uncertainty. Commonly their plaint, "I cannot make up my mind," is mirrored in others' complaints, "Make up your mind already."

Splitting often accompanies ambivalence. Depressives who split either hate themselves abjectly and love others completely, or love themselves completely and hate others abjectly. In the first case, they belittle themselves and overvalue others ("I don't deserve wonderful you; you don't need or want someone as low-down as I am"), while in the second case they overvalue themselves and devalue others ("You don't have what I deserve in a woman"). Hating themselves more than they should, or loving themselves more than they warrant, they pull back from relationships—only to first feel, and then actually be, neglected by the significant others in their lives.

Underproductive Thinking

Thought is often underproductive because of two beliefs: "it is too much trouble to think" and (very characteristic of men) "my thoughts are just too embarrassing to acknowledge." In many men underproductivity of thought is also the outcome of stubbornness—for example, I refuse to think about something just because you want me to—with the man a wounded victim who stubbornly won't "move his thoughts" until some criterion, like an apology, is met. Sometimes blocking is accompanied by perseveration where the man gets stuck and becomes not underproductive but repetitive. With the onset of hypomania the repetitive stickiness can "blossom" to become racing thoughts. Now the man gets unstuck with a vengeance, as he thinks too much, and about things that are of very little importance.

Disliking and Devaluing Others

Depressed men are unusually angry people with a tendency to be as critical of others as they are of themselves. They often attribute negative motives to others' innocent actions. A woman puts her dog out on the terrace for an hour. The dog barks constantly, angering my patient. He, a psychologist prone to depression, says, "She is doing this because she is a hostile, careless narcissist." Another neighbor, a layperson not prone to depression, says, "Perhaps she is just trying to give the dog some air, and she doesn't even know it is making all that noise."

Depressive disliking/devaluing may develop in five steps:

1. Excessive anger at others appears
2. Excessive anger is bottled up
3. Excessive anger is turned inward
4. Excessive anger is taken out on the self in the form of self-critical thinking often accompanied by a fall in self-esteem
5. Excessive anger is projected outward (accounting for the close relationship between paranoia and depression) to become "Maybe I am not so bad; maybe I am not the one who is at fault. Maybe I shouldn't be angry at myself; maybe my problem is that you are doing bad things to me."

Anger and its tortured pathways are discussed further throughout.

INSIGHT

Generally speaking, women are more insightful about what causes their depression than are men. Men generally find introspection to be overly poetic and hence sissified. If they are introspective at all and develop any insight whatsoever they tend to feel ashamed of what they have discovered about themselves, and out of a sense of misplaced manly pride don't want to talk, or even think, about it.

This said, there are several levels of insight that some depressed men can and do develop. Some men sense that something is psychologically wrong but rationalize their difficulties as being nonproblematic or, if problematic, nondepressive. A visitor asked one depressed man to open up the blinds so that he could see the view from his apartment. The man responded: "They are big blinds and it's too much trouble to open them up, and I don't want to let the sun in, for it might fade the furniture." He ultimately acknowledged that he was functioning beneath his potential but not that he was so doing because he was depressed. He came to know he had emotional problems, only to go on to explain them entirely on the basis of being caught up in an existential mid-life crisis.

Some men mostly speak of their depression indirectly and euphemistically—by talking about burnout on the job, or about a physical ailment such as hypoglycemia or Epstein-Barr chronic fatigue. Others speak of their depression but of only a few of its aspects. Many report a vague sense of falling short when trying to live up to their potential; feel that they are going through a rough time; or feel somewhat incomplete, a bit lonely, or simply slowed down, or empty. Some complain not of being "down in the dumps" but of being uncontrollably irritable and hostile. They crack jokes at others' expense in order to keep their spirits up, only to have second thoughts as they wonder, "Was I really so amusing, or should I have kept my mouth shut?" For example, one man felt extremely guilty after he antagonized a friend by telling him, just after he had lost his wife, "Your loss inspired me to go into business— developing a full line of humorous sympathy cards."

Some men recognize that they are depressed but fail to connect the problems they acknowledge they have with a depression they also acknowledge. Instead of blaming their problems on their depression they blame them on bad luck, malignant fate, or unfortunate circumstances.

JUDGMENT

Poor judgment is a common and often serious complication of depression. It may be the product of a general sense of hopelessness that leads the man to prematurely give up on valid pursuits. He becomes an excessively conservative individual afraid to make a move because he believes that nothing he can do will improve his situation. If there is a swing into hypomania the poor judgment may be the product of a defensive denial intended to give the man a false sense of invulnerability. Now he makes rash personal and professional decisions in the belief that since nothing can go wrong for him he can get away with doing just about anything. In the depressed state it is "God hates me, so why bother?" In the hypomanic state it is "God loves me, so why worry?" Some of these depressed men seeking to have the bad feelings inside cut out of them develop a polysurgery addiction. Others develop an addiction to plastic surgery as they attempt to repair what is little more than a concrete manifestation of a poor self-image, possibly originating in a body dysmorphic disorder (the close-to-delusional belief that one's body is defective because it is physically distorted).

Of course, depressive judgment even when problematical can be deemed adequate or actually superior when a blind-luck bailout occurs so that the man who doesn't invest in a rising stock market because he fears success will be thought to have good judgment if the stock market subsequently goes down. However, behavior that is the product of depressive calculation still remains at least theoretically fundamentally ill-considered even when subsequent events vindicate the original judgment call. Indeed, so often the self-destructive aspect of the behavior will ultimately out and prevail—commonly because the behavior is compulsively repeated until the individual is at last successful in creating havoc for himself.

Often depressive catastrophizing of necessity creates distortions of reality that lead to repetitive excessive, unnecessary, and ultimately self-defeating attempts at prevention of, and restitution for, fantasized disaster.

MEMORY

In depressed men memory can be impaired should depressive preoccupations lead to inattention to anything that is not completely relevant to their disorder—that is, to anything that does not fit perfectly with their depressed view of themselves and of their environment. Exhaustion and an inability to concentrate due to a lack of sleep caused by insomnia can also take their toll on memory.

However, some depressed men suffer not only from *hypomnesis* (poor memory) but also from a paradoxical (selective) *hypermnesis* (memory that is too good and too exact). While they remain persistently unable to ingest, and recall, information that is outside of the sphere of their emotional mindset, they remain highly capable of assimilating, incorporating, and correctly and permanently filing and reviving those facts that suit their depressive purposes exactly. That theirs is a focus only on that reality that interests them is something that we typically discover when we touch on one of the real or imagined, past or present, injustices done, hatreds experienced, or sources of anxiety that have captured and fixed their attention—puddles of negative idea that attain further prominence as their depression causes the sea of contrasting pleasant and optimistic thoughts to dry up and disappear. Many have sharply distorted memories of a past they have retrospectively altered in order to make it bleak enough to fit in with their black view of their present. They deny a truly rosy past and instead create a bleak new one out of their depression in order to concoct a revised image of their past that fits in with their view of their troubled here and now. A possible outcome is false memories of childhood abuse. Those who say, "I am depressed now because I was abused as a child," may in fact really be victims of the opposite sequence: because they are depressed now they have come to believe, inaccurately, that they were abused as children.

Not surprisingly the capacity to remember waxes and wanes according to the depth and intensity of the depressed mood. Often depressed men can remember less of what happens in the morning, when they feel at their worst, than of what happens in the evening, when they feel better; and more when they feel calm, but less when they feel anxious, annoyed, threatened, rejected, or provoked.

ORIENTATION

Depressed men typically distort time, place, and person in an unduly pessimistic fashion, as in "It is late, I am old, and I have very little life left to look forward to." This is the opposite of how hypomanic men say, "It is early, I am young, and I have my whole life ahead of me." As the depressed man experiences time as moving very slowly, the hypomanic man experiences time as flying by. A depressed man on the fringe of the city says, "I hate it here in the suburbs," while a hypomanic man on the fringe of the city says, "I love it here in the country." Though average or above average, the depressed man thinks, "I am a loser," while though merely average the hypomanic man thinks, "I am the chosen one—a disciple, or even, moving up in the ranks, the new Savior."

✳✳✳✳

CLINICAL DIFFERENCES BETWEEN MEN AND WOMEN

Many studies have noted that women's and men's depression are clinically different particularly in regard to somatic symptoms such as anorexia and overeating, and weight loss and gain. Men tend to have more somatic symptoms than women for these are the symptoms for which, as Cochran and Rabinowitz note, it is "more acceptable for a man to seek help"[10] because "somatization functions as a defense against taking personal responsibility for life predicaments,"[11] and because somatization is a way to "avoid internal self-blame."[12] Too, most observers would agree with Cochran and Rabinowitz when they say that "the vast majority of perpetrators of violence are men."[13]

On the other hand, Cochran and Rabinowitz note that "the most frequently reported symptoms (e.g., dysphoria, death thoughts, changes in appetite and sleep, fatigue, [and] difficulties with concentration)"[14] do not differ significantly across the genders. Also according to Cochran and Rabinowitz, the frequency of occurrence of the first episode of depression might be clinically different but "once depression has developed, the nature of the disorder, except for a very few characteristics, does not differ at all."[15]

I have noted a different quality or "feel" to men's and women's depression that to some extent reflects the different presentation between the sexes based on the causal differences across the genders. The woman, stunned by loss, has an abandoned feel to her depression, while the man, stunned by a failure to achieve some ambition, an inability to feel in control, or the feeling that he is being castrated, exudes a wounded masculine pride that to the observer imparts a sense of abject defeat, often one of a sexual nature. Many depressed women remind us of a poor abandoned orphan who has just lost her parents, while many depressed men remind us of a crestfallen peacock or of a gladiator who has just been vanquished in the last battle he will ever fight. Gender-specific personality differences to some extent also account for some of the clinical disparities. In my experience men are more likely to be paranoid than women, and so tend to be more irritable and violent to others; while women are more likely to be masochistic than men, and so tend to be more all-suffering and violent to themselves.

Chapter 4

Suicidal Behavior

In assessing suicidal behavior I often compare the behavior of the man I am presently evaluating for suicidality to the behavior of my other male patients who actually made a suicidal attempt. I present two such men as examples.

A forty-six-year-old high school music teacher I was treating as an outpatient had entered therapy complaining of feeling suicidal. He felt that his life was over now because after he had merely suggested a trial separation from his wife she not only took him up on it but did him one better and filed for a divorce. He felt that he had nobody left in this world, and would never find another person to love, no matter how hard he tried, or how long he lived.

According to his history he had always been lonely, for he was an intensely aggressive man who found he was able to control his aggressivity by relating distantly and incompletely to as few people as possible—his way to make certain that others would not be around to provoke him to anger. He also had a history of being erratic professionally. He would take a job, do it well for a few months, start slacking off, then quit, almost always on a flimsy pretext and usually after starting a fight with the boss.

The patient's father had been a well-known composer and teacher. While my patient admired his father's professional work he felt that he failed as a father because he was overly involved with his job, but not involved enough with his family. As my patient put it, "He was a basically warm and loving man who, however, had the fatal flaw of putting his professional commitments first and his family responsibilities next." When my patient was nine years old his father, for no discernible reason, and without any warning, hanged himself.

The patient described his mother as similar to his wife: a difficult, shrewish woman who criticized him unmercifully, constantly rapping his knuckles over minor things. For example, once referring to a slipup he made when performing in concert, she called him a "dirty pianist" because he "played in the cracks." The patient went on to compare his wife to his mother as follows: "Both of these women constantly make me feel as if I would be lucky to be back in parochial school."

During our first session, the patient complained of chronic suicidal ideation in the setting of severe somatic symptoms such as headaches and stomach pains. In the last few years he had been drinking heavily to cope with the physical and emotional problems he felt had resulted from his wife's constantly henpecking him, or as he referred to it, "continuously castrating me." After years of living with this behavior he had suggested the trial separation. As he put it, "The straw that broke my back was when she complained for the umpteenth time that I put a wet towel on the bed, then said that she couldn't stand my doing that one more time."

Shortly after his wife responded by filing for a divorce, he moved out of their suburban home and into a studio apartment in the city. There he began to feel lonely, isolated, and his physical health began to deteriorate. For example, he developed even worse stomach pains and lost thirty pounds. He was in such pain and looked so sickly that his doctors seriously considered the diagnosis of pancreatic cancer—an illness from which a cousin had just died. A warning to me that he was thinking of suicide was that he started brooding about the content of his will, particularly about the disposition of his personal property after his death, wondering if he should leave everything to another cousin, the only relative he liked and the only one to whom he was still speaking. Or perhaps, he thought, he should leave everything to charity. Making a kind of dynamic sense was the charity he chose to leave everything to: one that cared for orphaned children. I became alarmed when next he started acting withdrawn, developed a severely melancholic look about him consisting of a facial droop and body stoop, said he had stopped talking to almost everyone, and had decided to take a few months off from work because he could no longer concentrate. It was then that I decided to hospitalize him at least briefly for evaluation and treatment.

At first he resisted hospitalization. He tried to reassure me during his session that things were improving and he would be okay. But the night after that session he called to say that he felt bad, was contemplating suicide, and was no longer wedded to the contract we made that he would tell me if he were going to make a suicidal attempt before he actually made one. He was now beginning to realize that our therapy was a complete waste of time and that he could use the money for better purposes. He complained that my pathetic attempts to reassure him that all was not as bad as he feared were minimizing his anguish, and that I was doing nothing at all to help him, but instead saying only stupid, unhelpful things like, "Get out of the house more, exercise, go to the gym, and do what you love even if that means doing it by yourself." So I called his favorite cousin to let him know that the situation was deteriorating, and asked him to go over there immediately, look in on him, and take him to the local hospital's emergency room for an immediate evaluation. When he arrived at the hospital, the doctor on call admitted him to the psychiatric service on an emergency basis.

When I saw him the next day in the hospital he complained that he couldn't eat or sleep. He was pacing and moaning, saying "ah, ah, ah" over and over again. But when I asked him what was troubling him he would simply reply, "Nothing." At first he would not take his antidepressant medication. But finally, reluctantly, he agreed to begin a course of Selective Serotonin Reuptake Inhibitors (SSRIs). After a few weeks he said he felt much better and denied being suicidal. The treatment team believed that he was no longer a suicidal risk. In favor of that conclusion they noted that he did not have a prior history of making a suicidal attempt; had never been violent; admitted to, instead of denying, being depressed; was generally open and honest about how he felt and what he planned to do; had been fully cooperative after initially refusing his medication; did not at discharge time appear to be angry or sad; and had a major "social resource" in the person of his cousin who was eager to help him out even if that meant moving in with him at great personal sacrifice. He had also reassured all concerned that he would call the hospital psychiatrist after discharge should he feel he was slipping and on the brink of making a suicidal attempt. So his doctors discharged him and gave him a month's supply of medication.

That afternoon he took a (nonfatal) dose of all his medication at once, and called his cousin to tell him that he was about to die. The cousin called the police and had him brought back to the emergency room for rehospitalization.

The depressive episode for which I treated my second patient was also precipitated by the breakup of his marriage. He had fallen in love with and married a woman to whom he was faithful even though he suspected, after she completely stopped having sex with him, that she was cheating on him. Yet he denied what was going on—until one day he came home to find her in bed with two other men, both handsomer and younger than he—among other things seriously calling his masculinity into question and bringing up new and old feelings of worthlessness and defectiveness. Soon he began repeating to himself, "Like my mother said, I will never be good enough for any woman," and "See what sex does to a relationship." He applied for a divorce and moved out of their suburban home into a city apartment, only to find himself "too lonely to breathe." After a year or so a serious episode of melancholia ensued and I had to hospitalize him on an emergency basis because he was threatening to take his own life since "what does it matter, it's not worth living anyway."

This man had a long history of temper tantrums and severe asthma, both of which he admitted he used as attention-getting devices directed toward seeking the ministrations of his mother, a remote distant woman who "had the bad habit of never taking my side against anyone who was abusing me." He complained that his mother met all of his desperate attempts to please her by becoming even more sadistic to him as if his trying to please her merely revealed his vulnerability and weakness. "Worst of all, she brought her mother to live with us in a small apartment, with only one bedroom for the two of us." Her mother was an elderly psychotic woman who spent hours telling him to look out the window to see if the kidnappers were finally coming to get him. This grandmother also "went on a campaign to stop me from playing with myself." Once, for example, "she showed me a picture of a harp whose pillar consisted of a man with air-brushed genitals, and told me that I would lose mine as he lost his if I continued to touch myself down there." He hated this grandmother, but his mother, predictably taking her mother's side, told him that he was a bad little boy with ugly feelings toward a woman whose only fault was being too concerned about him, and loving him too much for her own good. He was unable to grieve when his grandmother died. In response, his mother beat him with the back of her hand "for being the kind of uncaring kid you are."

As an adolescent he failed repeatedly in school because he hated his female teachers. Looking back, he called them "a bunch of slashers." During this time he began to act out by stealing trinkets from department stores, drinking heavily, smoking three packs of cigarettes a day, and becoming promiscuous—having developed a special fondness for orgies because "those made me feel like a real man for a change." Later on, in his twenties, he developed a series of severe depressive episodes. The first took the form of chronic fatigue misdiagnosed as mononucleosis due to the presence of a few atypical lymphocytes in a blood sample. Subsequent episodes consisted of depressive symptoms that were more overt than atypical. He felt flat and unresponsive and at times he felt as if the weight of the world were oppressing his chest. During such episodes he became preoccupied with having wasted his life, being a wimp who couldn't speak up, and feeling so guilty that he "couldn't say spit if he had a mouthful."

Throughout the course of his hospital stay, including the day of his discharge, he insisted that he was going to kill himself as soon as he was let go. His doctors, after many consultations with each other and with outside experts brought in to assist in his discharge planning, felt that he should be discharged anyway. Their reasons were that he had obtained maximum therapeutic benefit from his hospitalization and that no matter how long he was hospitalized he would continue to have suicidal thoughts, and there was little they could do to stop him from having them. Besides, his insurance had run out and they felt that having to pay out of his own pocket would depress him more than the help he would derive from staying in the hospital a little longer.

A week after discharge he killed himself by taking an overdose of sleeping pills—medication he had been secretly saving for months.

Levels of Suicidality

These two men illustrate aspects of what I call the four levels of suicidality: suicide equivalents, suicidal thoughts, suicidal threats, and the making of unsuccessful and successful suicidal attempts.

1. *Suicide equivalents.* Suicidality can be subtle, covert, and symbolic when it takes the form of one or more suicide-*equivalent* behaviors, such as

    - Taking inadequate care of one's physical health
    - Occupational block
    - Workaholism
    - Reckless hypomanic hyperactivity
    - Addiction, especially to alcohol, cocaine, and Oxycontin
    - A success neurosis consisting of defeating oneself at every juncture as well as defeating those who are trying to help, typically by stubbornly refusing to cooperate with potential helpers, instead devaluating their abilities, questioning their motives, and challenging their methods.

2. *Suicidal thoughts.* Suicidal *thoughts* are virtually universal in most everyone. However, all concerned must determine whether suicidal thoughts are or are not likely to translate to actual suicidal behavior—that is, all must distinguish between the thought, the revelation/threat, and the intent. There are, unfortunately, no perfect rules for making this distinction. Depressed men often hide what they are actually thinking and planning. They themselves are often unable to predict what they intend to do, because their plans change from moment to moment depending largely on their mood swings. Some depressed men (Abraham Lincoln, perhaps) think about suicide a great deal but never openly or actively attempt it (although some argue that Lincoln's failure to adequately protect himself from assassination was in part motivated by suicidal tendencies). Others make an unsuccessful or successful suicidal attempt to express exactly how they feel. No certain relationship exists between the apparent depth of a clinical depression and potential or actual suicidal behavior. Some men who seem mildly depressed (or who do not appear

to be depressed at all) successfully commit suicide. Others who are deeply depressed remain in good control of any suicidal impulses. Also, not all suicides are depressive. Suicide can occur in the setting of, and be the product of, other psychopathology such as schizophrenia or paranoia. It can, especially when socially sanctioned, also occur in individuals who do not have any apparent emotional disorder.

3. *Suicidal threats.* These are particularly difficult to evaluate in terms of seriousness. Many men utter them. Only a few see them through. Some are trying to get attention and provoke others to behave in a certain way, but others are just being punctiliously honest about what they intend to do. It is not true that the man who intends to kill himself will do it without giving prior warning. Indeed, so often an actual suicidal attempt is a response of angry disappointment to warnings that have been given, only to be ignored.

4. *Suicidal attempts.* These can be gestural (manipulative) or represent the living out of a real wish to die. True intent cannot always be accurately inferred from the nature of the action. For example, was a man making a serious suicidal attempt when he poured out 50 painkiller tablets into the palm of his hand and made a gesture of putting them in his mouth, without actually swallowing any? At the time I thought so and strongly recommended hospitalization, but now I am not so sure that that was the proper course of action.

Understanding Suicidality

In both cases presented, speaking psychodynamically the suicidality was overdetermined, consisting to varying degrees of many of the following trends:

- An ultimate form of self-hatred.
- A living out of low self-esteem, along the lines of "I don't deserve to walk the earth any more."
- An ultimate form of self-love (to spare oneself pain).
- An ultimate gift to someone one loves as well as hates (to spare them pain).
- A manipulative sadomasochistic act meant to hurt and get back at others through hurting oneself; for example, "She will miss me when I am gone," "I'll show that mother of mine what she did to me by treating me the way she did," or "That therapist pisses me off—I'll have her license and her house as part of a big malpractice settlement. I won't tell her that I am planning to attempt suicide, then I will try it, and she will look incompetent." Commonly found are vengeful sadomasochistic suicide notes that say exactly the opposite of what they mean, such as those that contain an attack in the form of an apology ("I don't want you to think that it was you who drove me to kill myself.").
- An identification with someone who hates the person (often, or especially, a parent, often one's mother).

- A way to take control of one's life along the lines of "I don't have to put up with this; I can always end my suffering where and when I want to."
- A way to get unpleasantness over with so that "I do something actively to myself to avoid having something happen to me passively—out of my control, and when I least expect it."
- The product of demoralization and despair, which can be either appropriate or excessive, or, selectively, both.

In other cases suicide is:

- A living out of a feeling with some basis in reality that one no longer has a compelling reason to continue to exist—so that the suicidal action is based on rational decision making that is in some respects an appropriate response to especially difficult, intolerable, and unalterable circumstances.
- A way to make an existential philosophical point, for example, self-immolation as social protest.
- A culturally sanctioned/approved/encouraged action such as hara-kiri.
- A product of social pressures, for example, "Listen up, we don't want old people around here any more."
- The product of a psychosis, for example, a response to voices.

Managing Suicidality

I manage suicidality both in and out of the hospital using an eclectic form of treatment that starts with developing a psychodynamic, interpersonal, and cognitive understanding of the suicidal thoughts and actions and goes on to responding with a judicious combination of support and affirmation, insight, cognitive/behavioral, and interpersonal therapy. When appropriate, I use total push techniques that involve urging the man to be more active with an eye to developing new, more satisfactory relationships and becoming more successful professionally. In particular I often use psychodynamically oriented psychotherapeutic techniques to soften a harsh punitive conscience that is making the man feel guilty in situations where he did no wrong and was not the victimizer, as accused, but the victim, as overlooked.

In both of the above-presented cases I tried to impress the men with the necessity of taking a positive view of the future. I suggested that while I understood how badly both men felt now, they would almost surely ultimately come to feel better. Since depression is often a self-limited illness I believed that they could profitably tolerate their present depression long enough to see it through into future remission. To abort catastrophic thinking I tried to have both men view their present situations realistically so that they could see that their plights, while considerable, were more modest than otherwise. For example, my second patient had become alarmed that his city apartment was on the market for two months with no takers. He said that he needed to sell it fast because it was a third-floor walkup and he feared that since he was getting old he might be stuck at home, unable to walk up and down stairs. I tried to make him realize that he did not have to respond as if he were dealing with an imminent catastrophe. He was unlikely to become physically incapacitated in the near future, and if he did become incapacitated he could always sell his apartment quickly by cutting the price and, in view of its price appreciation, still come out ahead with enough money left over to move to a new, nice, more accommodating place.

As I generally do with men who are depressed, I focused on both men's anger. I did that not to encourage them to get their anger out but to help them find ways to reduce the angry feelings inside. In each case I wondered if it would help if they put some distance between themselves and their wives. It was clear to me that constantly going back to their wives to try to gain their respect and hopefully get their wives to treat them better was only making matters worse.

In the first case I involved the family in treatment. I interviewed the patient's favorite cousin and asked him to watch out for him and report back to me if he thought things were getting worse. I recommended group therapy for both men. My goal was to help decrease their isolation and to hook them up with watchful eyes other than mine—other men and women who could sound the alarm should their disorder appear to be worsening. Throughout, I reassured both men that if they felt worse I would be available in an emergency and I could, based on need, increase the frequency of sessions. In the first case I contacted the man's internist to follow the progress of his workup for abdominal pain, which turned out to be a benign, treatable gastritis.

In both cases I began pharmacotherapy hoping to bring about some immediate relief and improvement. I chose SSRIs because they were less likely to be fatal if an overdose were taken. Since I didn't know that the second man was accumulating pills, I was unable to take measures to have his cache removed and destroyed.

As is usual I had to deal with both men's resistances to therapy, particularly those originating in the belief that a man should be ashamed of and not talk about his depression. We worked to dispel the myth that depression is a weakness that needs to be hidden—when in fact it is an illness that needs to be treated.

I also chose in these two cases to help deal with resistances to therapy by using the controversial technique of speaking of my own intermittent depressions, and how I triumphed over some of my life's burdens through effort and resilience. I had intended to present myself as a model. While this was minimally helpful in these cases, this technique must be used judiciously because it can backfire if the patient thinks his therapist too self-preoccupied and too little focused on him, or perceives the therapist's depression as his "weakness"—a perception fomented from the dangerous tendency many depressed men have to externalize their own feelings of inferiority. They then come to the conclusion, in the transference, that others are as inferior as they believe themselves to be, and in the case of their therapists, they should quit their current therapist and move on to find a better man for the job.

Chapter 5

Grief

Many observers believe that men do not grieve as openly as women. These observers remind us that the stereotype is of the grieving widow, and that men are not either figuratively or literally "the ones who wear black."

Men of course do grieve, if not so openly as women. However, men and women seem to grieve the most intensely about different things. In my experience, many men grieve the most intensely after an abstract, as distinct from a concrete, loss. Men, especially when already somewhat depressed, and additionally blessed, or cursed, with a poetical bent, tend to view abstract symbolic losses as being as significant, important, and devastating as "real" losses, or even more so. For such men losses that are particularly shattering include the loss of their youth, their self-respect, and their manhood. I was present when Eric Lindemann, an expert on grief, in 1961 interviewed a man who had become severely depressed after his pocket was picked. As it turned out, he was responding less to the loss of his wallet than to the emotional assault on his person. For what bothered him the most were the unacceptable sensations aroused when the male pickpocket, in reaching for his wallet, came on and touched his genitals.

Unfortunately, too many of us, including the depressed man himself, tend to minimize the significance of abstract losses, and to criticize the man who responds to them as a weakling, or as a "girly-boy," or "faggot." Too many of us equate a man's sensitivity with "a woman's oversentimentality," then speak with one voice to the depressed man responding to symbolic losses by saying, "You are getting depressed over nothing," forgetting that the proper response should be: "If you are getting depressed over something, for you, at least, it must not, by definition, be nothing."

Clinically speaking, many of the symptoms of grief, and especially the symptoms of impure or complicated grief (defined below), overlap with many of the symptoms of depression. In both grief and depression the sufferer may feel blue and cry or feel blank and be unable to weep. Often there is a degree of withdrawal. One man who had just lost his wife said, "My life goes on, but around me, like I am a stone in the river, lying there inert as the water just flows by." Somatic sensations like pressure in the chest or an empty gnawing feeling in the pit of the stomach are common, and in severe cases somatic preoccupations like an irrational fear that one has cancer can occur. Such somatic preoccupations often both hide and express secret wish-fulfillments, two common ones being, "I wish the one who had died was spared, and instead I was the one taken ill" ("Why, God, did you take my wife, and not me?"), and "I hope that this is fatal so that I can join my departed wife in the next life." As with depression, suicide can occur should the man become seriously demoralized after experiencing what appears to him to be a loss that is incalculable and overwhelming.

Grief exists on a continuum from *mild to severe*. Grief may be *mild* (or absent) when what was lost was predominantly a negative force in the man's life, so that "good" lessens the impact of "riddance." Paradoxically, grief can also be mild under just the opposite circumstance— when the relationship with the person lost was so predominantly positive that only good memories prevail (but see below). A grief reaction can *seem* mild when preceded by anticipatory grief. Here the loss was anticipated and the mourning process occurred in advance as a way to prepare for what is bound to be, so that by the time the actual event occurs, the grieving process is just about over.

Mild grief is merely somewhat distracting. It interferes only minimally with day-to-day function. It can last for months, or even years, but it usually ultimately resolves spontaneously, or in response to therapy. Should therapy be necessary all that may be required is a brief, supportive tiding-over in anticipation that it is the tincture of time that will do the healing.

Grief may be especially *severe* in older men because they are at heightened risk for many emotional disorders, and because they have less opportunity to make up for losses. The deepest grief I have seen was in an aging man who lost his beloved wife and had inadequate philosophical and spiritual/psychological defenses to fall back on, few or no supportive friends and family to help make his loss more bearable, and no chance to make up for the financial problems that resulted when he was left strapped without his wife's income. His relationship was a truly loving dependent merger, and, as often happens, when such mergers dissolve due to death, he as the surviving partner was left truly at sea and thoroughly floundering.

Grief also exists on a continuum from *pure to impure (complicated)*. Pure grief comes closest to unalloyed sadness. Impure grief, defined and discussed further below, and sometimes called "complicated grief," comes closest to depression itself, mostly because of anger held inside and taken out on the self, in part because the lost object has been internalized—a process that I will explain as we go through the four steps of complicated grief in the discussion to follow.

Impure or complicated grief, which is often severe, proceeds and resolves in a series of steps.

Step one of the impure or complicated grieving process involves the griever losing his self-support. Men often lose their self-support because they feel guilty and full of self-blame due to perceiving themselves as selfish. They hate themselves for welcoming their loss as if it were a gain, for example, "I am really better off without her." They discover that their grief is more for themselves than for their partners—so that the loss they are really grieving for is the loss of their status, or of the social life they had when their partner was still alive. For example, one depressed man felt guilty for not being able to do any better than complain: "Now that I have lost my wife, no one is going to invite me to their country house. As a single man I will predictably threaten all the married men in the group, who will think that I am about to steal their wives." He was also ashamed to find himself "foolishly" preoccupied with and bemoaning minor changes to his routine, such as, "Who am I going to go to the theatre with?"—and felt guilty that he was more devastated by those than he was by the actual loss of his wife.

Men also often lose their self-support because they feel guilty and full of self-blame over prior behavior of which they feel ashamed—behavior not stopped before the fact or adequately regretted afterwards. In one case the emotional self-flagellation started with the thought: "What kind of person am I to have bought her such a cheap casket just so I could use the money for an expensive new car?" That thought ushered in a spreading litany of self-complaints about what "I could and should have done," such as, "I am bad for not taking her to a doctor earlier, having that affair, being nasty to her all these years, and not even being there at her bedside when she died."

Men also lose their self-support due to feeling guilty and full of self-blame because of the reawakening, and surfacing, of anger, which they cannot manage in a healthy way. First, at times of grief anger toward the lost person often reawakens, surfaces, and prevails. It typically does so when the lost relationship was a particularly ambivalent one, and now the rage part of the ambivalence, rage that was previously kept in check, no longer needs to be contained out of a sense of decency, or in order to keep a relationship viable. Also the rage comes to prevail because the other person is no longer around to take the steam out of it by providing a reality check to runaway angry fantasies—say, by countering unfair accusations with considerations of reality, or by agreeing to improve in the future.

The griever now turns his reawakened surfacing anger around on himself. He does this for at least three reasons:

1. He can no longer get his anger out of his system by expressing it, say by starting a fight. Therefore with no outlet the anger wells up inside, has no place to go, and begins to spill back onto the self.

2. He dislikes himself for being angry with someone he is supposed to have mainly or only loved. We first hear such cries as, "I feel furious with you for going away and leaving me all alone. Why didn't you take better care of yourself and have that cancer check-up like I told you to?" We second hear such cries as, "How can I feel angry with someone who suffered so much and had to die so young. Poor thing, I hate myself, for I am a miserable wretch for getting mad at her."

3. He deals with his loss by resurrecting the lost object inside himself, doing so in an attempt to keep it alive—if only in fantasy and for a little while. Now he has in effect moved the target of his anger from out to in.

Finally, men often lose their self-support after retrospectively distorting the nature of the person and of their relationship with him or her, seeing things as more positive than they actually were. As one man put it, "my grief is making a new saint out of that old sinner."

One of my depressed men had a distinctly ambivalent relationship with his second wife. He had married her on the rebound after his first wife died, and as far as he was concerned his second wife was never as good as the first. Shortly after they got married his second wife developed severe heart disease and needed open heart surgery. Against his wishes she elected to have the surgery not at a major medical center but at a local hospital—just so that she could be closer to where her sister lived. She died on the operating table, in great measure due to the incompetence of the surgeon she had hired, also over my patient's objections. My patient felt for her and missed her but he was also furious with her for "abandoning him" now that he was old and, as he saw it, at age 58, too ancient to meet someone new. He next developed a severe impure (complicated) grief reaction during which he stopped eating and talking. He stopped eating in part because consciously he didn't want to buy food because he feared that he would run out of money and then not only be alone but also be impoverished at his advanced age and have to go on the public dole. He stopped talking in part out of an unconscious identification with his wife. He had reconstituted his relationship with his wife inside himself so as to never have to let her go again, at least in his thoughts. Just before she died she had become severely anorexic and fallen silent herself—except to bewail the fact that she would never be able to become independent enough again to be able to return to work and help support herself and her husband. Revealingly, when he began to speak after the prescribed antidepressants kicked in, he began to use the same expressions as she had used when she was alive—words and phrases which he had never uttered previously. Unfortunately, what was at first a positive attempt to hold on to his wife's memory ultimately worked against him to seriously hurt him and harm his mental health. For his inner anger with his wife right there inside of him led to his becoming agitated. He moaned and wrung his hands as his way to hurt himself and simultaneously discharge some of his anger. To make matters worse, his anger at himself escalated when he retrospectively distorted his view of the kind of person his wife had been—to the point that he came to see her as a woman entirely without flaws. So we heard, "I am a bad person for hating her. I am remiss for not realizing how good she was. Yes, there were things she did wrong, but the wrong things were not so bad, after all, and anyway they do not matter now. For now the only thing that matters is that she is gone, and I have lost a wonderful, wonderful person, the only true love of my life. We laughed before we went to bed, and we laughed when we got up in the morning. Now there is laughter no more—only tears, tears, and more tears."

Like this man, most grievers do not get to the point where their internalized anger leads them to attempt or commit suicide. Mostly they just flagellate themselves emotionally. But sometimes they attempt or commit suicide, an act that represents the ultimate form of the self-blaming and self-abusing process.

Step two consists of denial. Here the man, unable to sustain this level of self-blame and self-hatred, going into denial begins to think of all the advantages of being alone and going solo once again. He relishes the opportunity to have promiscuous sex, but forgets about the substantial and gratifying pleasures of his marriage or partnership, such as always having someone around to make plans with for the holidays. In denial he attempts, often futilely, to reestablish relationships with old friends, family, and in-laws, many of whom by now have closed ranks and extruded him from their lives—no matter what promises they previously made to stand by and take care of him in his moment of need. He may overshoot in a hypomanic way, rushing about trying to find someone new to make his life whole again. This is a particularly dangerous development, for during the hypomanic phase the underlying grief reaction can seriously compromise his immune system and his judgment. He badly needs his immune system to be at peak now that he is becoming sexually more active and his body requires maximum protection, and he needs good judgment to protect him from the emotional battering that often occurs in newly formed relationships, many of which tend to go nowhere and break up precipitously. This phase cannot last, and when it is over, he enters step three.

Step three involves a complete succumbing to his grief. Reality supervenes as he realizes how all told his life had been good up until his loss. Next he feels even bluer, cries a great deal, thinks all is lost, or, going beyond blue and broken, feels drained, flat, blank, and immobile. Everything seems to be too much of an effort. As one grieving man said, "While I look like an old man left to die in a nursing home, I feel like a baby abandoned to wither in an orphanage."

This, a penultimate phase, like a climax of fever, involves hitting bottom. But just when it appears to be the darkest time of all, dawn breaks and ushers in the final, or fourth, phase of grief.

Step four involves the beginning of improvement. Feeling blue begins to wane, hypomanic denial subsides, good judgment prevails, and remission, well under way, eventuates either in a complete recovery or, in less favorable cases, recovery but with minor or significant deficit.

Why is bereavement, whether complicated or uncomplicated, mild or severe, the self-limited process that it is? Mostly it is because the passage of time heals. Grief, however severe, is unsustainable for long for in a sense the body recognizes that, and, as it might heal a physical wound, heals the griever, by, so to speak, simply insisting that he once and for all put the grieving process to a stop, and get on with life.

But though it tends to be self-limited, grief, when it takes over, can be as or more severe than depression. Also for many men the process of growing from grief and mourning can be a difficult and somewhat lengthy one, for at least two reasons. First, it is often difficult to disentangle and resolve the complex mixture of love and hate that exists in any relationship. Second, the work of mourning is almost always done with reluctance, for not only is grief pleasurable in a masochistic way but there is almost always resistance to abandoning the lost object no matter how negative certain aspects of the relationship had been. As a general principle, grievers say they want to forget, but they act like they are reluctant to forgo remembering.

Group and individual psychotherapy can quicken the process of resolution of grief, although many men improve without these. Group therapy can be particularly helpful for the man left seriously down and out after a significant loss. However, if grief is complicated and severe enough to approach the level of a clinical depression, group therapy is often profitably combined with individual psychotherapy and perhaps pharmacotherapy, essentially following the guidelines of the pharmacotherapy of mild to moderate depression.

Chapter 6

Atypical Depression

Depression in men often takes an atypical form. Here it presents as depressive equivalents, that is, with the blue mood modified to become:

- Emotionally based somatic complaints suggesting physical illness
- Alcohol and drug abuse
- Irritability and anger perhaps associated with domestic violence
- Action-oriented symptoms such as agitation associated with moaning, wailing, and hand-wringing
- Characterological problems—particularly psychopathy
- Real's "failures in intimacy"[1] as manifest as a fear of commitment or in interpersonal distancing
- Occupational disorders leading to on-the-job problems perhaps with failure to advance professionally due to what Real calls "self-sabotage in careers."[2]

These depressive equivalents dynamically represent variously a defense against, a cover-up of, an alternative to, or a transformation of the underlying mood which as a consequence seems diminished or absent. Often the classic *DSM-IV* attributes of depression remain clinically manifest but are relegated to a halo effect and as a consequence become peripheral.

To illustrate, a man hated his life though it was in fact both good and full. This was partly because he believed that people who were actually neutral toward or felt positively about him were in fact rejecting him. Nothing seemed to satisfy him or give him much pleasure, while everything seemed to dissatisfy him and give him a great deal of pain. For example, he complained incessantly that his wife had parked her old beat-up car across the street from their apartment and refused to have it towed and fixed, "messing up" his view, and as a result seriously compromising his happiness.

He expressed his depression not overtly but as severe headaches that I believed symbolically referred to his feeling that his world was giving him a pain in the head; and as griping stomach pains that to me were symbolically expressing his need to bellyache—about his fate, his life, and all the people in it whom he believed had mistreated him. He hid much of his disappointment and rage in somatic symptoms because he was by nature a passive man who didn't like to meet challenging situations head on, and a fearful man who hesitated to get openly angry with others because of his concern that they would turn on and completely reject him. His somatic symptoms were also a venue by which he could passive-aggressively contaminate others with his black mood. This he could do guilt free by torturing them sadistically with complaints that brought them down when they were feeling up—something he did whenever he perceived that they felt good and were having that proverbial nice day he could ruin without appearing to do so, "because I was not attacking them, I was just telling them how bad I felt physically." Unfortunately, at the same time he was making himself miserable and punishing himself with his somatic complaints, for these were also a way to dull his own happiness by saying, "Look, I may have a lot to rejoice about, but I cannot possibly be a truly happy man, since I am not physically a well person."

What follows is a description of many common depressive equivalents found in men. Because most depressive equivalents have a differential diagnosis, a single sign or symptom should not be considered to be a depressive equivalent until and unless it is determined to be driven by and associated with other inferred or clinically manifest aspects of depression. In most cases, because true severe depressive affect has too strong a profile to "allow" itself to be diluted completely beyond recognition, if it were there in the first place its traces should remain as it continues to lurk in the shadow of its substitute. This is important, for as mentioned throughout, a corollary to how depression in men is too often missed when present is that in some circles it is too often diagnosed when absent—and the man given medication that he doesn't need, will not do any good, and can even cause him harm.

WITHDRAWAL

The withdrawal spectrum of depressive equivalents includes *anhedonia* (the relative or absolute inability to experience pleasure), *anergia* (energy depletion, a depressive "washed-out feeling"), *alexithymia* (a relative or absolute absence of the ability to feel, or to feel strongly), boredom accompanied by loss of interest especially in pleasurable activities, demoralization, some forms of fatigue, and a general sense of feeling debilitated.

Many so-called cases of Chronic Fatigue Syndrome and "burnout" are actually expressions of depressive anergia. Burnout on the job is dynamically often a way to pull back to avoid expressing job-related anger directly but to instead express it indirectly, in a socially acceptable, if passive-aggressive, manner. The man really wants to say, "I *hate* it, and everybody, here," but because he values his career and needs his paycheck he holds his anger in, and instead of blaming others for his plight ("My boss makes me nuts") blames himself for his not being able to tolerate his circumstances ("Maybe I could do a better job if I weren't so stale"), and so doesn't say, "I am fed up," but says, "I am burned out."

AGITATION

Some depressed men suffer from an agitated depression. They moan, pace, wring their hands, and cry out the same mournful "woe-is-me" wail over and over again. They seem to be expressing their desperation and anger nonverbally in a way specifically geared to drawing others (who cannot help but notice) into their plight. Additionally theirs are sad and truly heart-wrenching pleas for help, but wedded (however counterproductively) to a simmering anger at others: those they blame for causing their plight in the first place, and in the second place for not helping them extricate themselves from it.

HYPERSOMNIA AND INSOMNIA

Some depressed men experience hypersomnia. Typically they go to bed too early, sleep deeply through the night, and then take one or more naps during the day, only to awaken from each still feeling tired—longing to stay asleep or actually going back to bed. But many depressed men instead experience insomnia. Insomnia is often, although not necessarily, the product of depression. It can be one of its earliest symptoms. Many depressed men become insomniac because they have difficulty thinking the pleasant thoughts necessary to lull themselves to sleep. Also, some of these men are constantly angry individuals and as such too roiled-up to relax in or out of bed.

Depression-based insomnia may be either initial, middle, terminal, or all three. Perhaps the majority of depressed men develop middle awakening. They fall asleep easily but they wake up in the middle of the night and then toss and turn agonizingly as if in emotional pain, their mind full of racing worrisome thoughts such as "I will not be able to fall asleep again tonight. Therefore, all is lost, for I have a big conference tomorrow and if I don't get some sleep I am going to screw up my presentation and lose my job." When they finally do fall asleep, the sleep is often not restful. Instead they wake up and fall back to sleep over and over again. Often they finally fall deeply asleep just before they have to get up, have difficulty getting out of bed, and come in late to work.

Middle awakening is often associated with angry or fearful nightmares. In cases of mild depression the unpleasantness in the dreams comes out all right, and all is well. In more severe cases of depression things in the dream don't resolve themselves quite so favorably and the terrifying dreams end rudely in the familiar "waking up in a cold sweat."

For example, a mildly depressed patient had a nightmare that "all my old pots had been forcibly removed from the closet then lined up on the table, but I was putting them back, one by one, into the cabinet where they belonged." He associated to his dream as follows: "The day before the dream I had a bad time in my apartment complex. One neighbor pounced on me on a beautiful summer day to complain that my air conditioner was dripping on her window; another insisted that a new carpet be installed in our common hall before I had some work done around my apartment (she didn't care that the contractors doing my work were likely to ruin the new carpet and I would have to pay for its replacement); and my downstairs neighbor seriously abused me because my contractor didn't show up for an appointment for work that required getting to the pipes under my floor by going through his ceiling. I wanted to move to another apartment house, but circumstances made that impossible. So I stood up to all concerned and told them, 'All air conditioners drip'; 'No way are we going to do my work after installing a new hall carpet, because my construction people could ruin it and I would have to pay for it'; and 'Don't abuse me; I didn't stand you up; my contractor did.' Next all concerned got angry with and stopped being so friendly to me, and I saw that as just one more instance of having my knuckles rapped, as usual, when I stood up for myself."

In real life this patient had to take all the pots out of the cabinets so that some construction work could be done around his kitchen. In his dream, putting the pots back had several possible meanings: that he wasn't doing this work and so could avoid being beaten up emotionally by the neighbors or that the work was done and over with and the associated problems behind him, and with all his friendships still intact. Also, the dream said that he had come through all the knuckle rapping with his "cajones," his "pots," intact after having been removed so rudely—for now here they were, going back there in place, exactly where they belonged.

As Erman says, factors that start and perpetuate insomnia are "cognitive distortions with regard to sleep, making too great an effort to fall asleep (leading to paradoxical arousal), and use of alcohol or other ineffective sleep-promoting agents which may actually fragment sleep through the middle hours of the night."[3] It follows that treatment, again according to Erman, involves "attempting to maintain regular bedtime and waking hours ... engaging in relaxing activities in the hours before bedtime ... avoiding physical activity or exercise in the evening hours,"[4] and avoiding the taking of naps during the day because these "reduce ... sleep drive at night, making entry into sleep and sustained sleep more difficult."[5]

SOMATIC/VEGETATIVE SYMPTOMS

Common depressive somatic symptoms include abdominal pain, back pain, headaches, chronic fatigue, and carpal tunnel syndrome along with other hand syndromes such as motoric writer's cramp (as defined below). Asthma and other allergies can, if not be caused by, at least be intensified by depression. Motoric tics such as spasmodic torticollis (a compulsive twisting of the neck), or repetitive nervous movements such as restless legs, knuckle cracking, or cuticle picking, may be seen. While constipation is very common, diarrhea can also occur. Anal pain due to fissures from straining at stool might accompany the constipation, and pruritis ani might accompany the diarrhea.

Some men experience *emotional* writer's block. Emotional writer's block may be *motoric*, for example, typist's cramp involving a reduced ability to move the hands, or *ideational,* involving the inability to be "moved by" or think of anything to say.

Motoric block can originate emotionally in a depression poured into and transformed into physicality by neuromuscular mechanisms. In pianist's cramp, which can be a motoric cramp, the left, and almost never the right, hand becomes paretic (partially paralyzed). In singer's cramp, which also can be a motoric cramp, hoarseness can occur due to laryngospasm (which is often in turn due to or made worse by stage fright). Carpal tunnel syndrome can be the result of the hand muscles tensing up in a display of anger first manifestly experienced then taken back. In one scenario the unhappy worker first makes a fist at the boss, and at the world. Then, feeling guilty about that, he tenses his hand in a symbolic attempt to keep it from striking others, self-punitively injuring himself instead, not only directly but also indirectly, by hurting his hand as his way to hurt his career. When psychological factors contribute heavily to carpal tunnel syndrome, surgical intervention, such as an operation to free up tendons, is readily viewed as punishment, possibly leading to an unfavorable medical outcome.

In my experience, motoric writer's block seems to be found equally in women and in men but ideational writer's block seems to be found more commonly in men than in women. The dynamics of ideational block are also different across the sexes. Women often block in response to a significant "real" loss, especially the loss of their mothers. This was the case for Agatha Christie who according to her autobiography was unable to write for about a year after her mother died.[6] While men also block ideationally after a "real" loss (Maurice Ravel stopped composing for a few years after his mother died[7]), more often a man's block represents an emotional retreat in response to a symbolic event. Such symbolic events may involve feeling controlled ("You can't establish a deadline for my article; do you want it good, or do you want it Tuesday? I'll show you and not be able to finish it ever."); fearing criticism ("If I don't complete this no critic will pan it."); or having fantasies of being castrated ("If I say what is on my mind I'll get raked over the coals and lose my reputation, my manhood, my genitals, and maybe even my life.").

As noted in Chapter 3, some depressed men suffer from a *polysurgery addiction*, although that appears to be more common in women than in men. In both men and women polysurgery addiction can represent a misguided attempt at self-improvement—a way to elevate self-esteem by removing what are believed to be the "physical deficiencies" that form the basis of the lowly self-image. An addiction to plastic surgery can occur, although this also appears to be more common in women than in men. Sometimes a man requests a sex change operation not because he (as familiarly) wants to act in a way consistent with letting the woman inside out, but as his way to live out his belief that his genitals are ugly or defective, and as such create a blot on his self-image that needs to be removed.

Why do some classic signs and symptoms associated with depression take the form not of symptoms of the mind but of symptoms of the body? Depression can certainly *interfere* with bodily activities, as when generally slowed bodily functions lead to constipation. Or depression can be *converted* or *translated* into somatic complaints then somewhat lost in the translation, as when somatic complaints/symptoms like headache or back pain are the product of a channeling of anger—which in men is so often about the usual depressive triad of feeling or being overlooked, ignored, and rejected; feeling or being controlled; and feeling or being criticized—for example, feeling castrated. Or the depressed man is merely expressing alarm couched metaphorically in physical terms. An example is the complaints of the histrionic depressed man who expresses despair in the body language of cardiac disturbance where simple gastric reflux becomes, "This is it; I am finally having that fatal heart attack I always expected." Not unusually, somatic complaints simultaneously convey an attack on others ("look at how sick you made me"). Often depressed men use somatic complaints once established to try to get sympathy as they further elaborate a mild condition to make it appear more severe than it is, as when a depressed man works up modest back pain in his mind to become severe back pain, then calculatedly mentions it over and over again precisely to elicit a specific favorable response from his caretakers.

In the past clinicians have claimed that somatic symptoms could be reliably and literally translated back into their presumed unconscious meaning. Thus abdominal pain and colitis were believed to be somatic expressions of emotional griping or physical displays of such regressive fantasies as "my tummy hurts from hunger because you haven't fed me." Or symptoms of rheumatoid arthritis were interpreted as a depressive weeping into the joints. Headaches were believed to state another somatic metaphor, thus: "You give me a headache and this is the pain in the head you give me." Formulations like this have some validity to them for some men, and occasionally postulated links between specific emotions and emotional states and specific bodily symptoms are indeed persuasive. However, in many cases the manifest equivalency is likely to be in part, if not strictly, metaphorical.

Certainly somatic symptoms can dynamically speaking represent an identification with someone else who is, or was, suffering—for example, the terminal pain of a loved one who died of cancer. Such morbid identifications may be part of the grieving process—a way to become like the lost object to hold on to the departed in fantasy, if only for a little while longer. They can also be empathic manifestations, as are sympathy pains arising out of an identification with the painful birth experience that a man's wife or partner is going through, or as are in some cases the symptoms of postpartum depression—in men.

Neurochemical, vascular, and hormonal mechanisms often mediate mysterious leaps from the mind to the body. Emotionally based headaches are often the product of muscle tension or vasodilatation, and stomach pains are often due to a neurochemically mediated increase of stomach acid produced as a response to stress.

HYPOCHONDRIASIS

Depressive hypochondriacs may overelaborate mildly negative somatic sensations, such as winter itch, into issues of serious and potentially fatal import, such as terminal lymphoma. Or they may develop a delusional perception about their bodies, such as the delusion that they smell bad or a pianist's delusion that his left hand has turned to stone.

Dynamically speaking, hypochondriasis is often a way to self-punish with painful worries that give the individual the fodder he wants and needs to salve his conscience by destroying his happiness. A regressive component often takes hold as well: many hypochondriacal depressed individuals basically want to give up and let other people assume the responsibility for running their lives. Some of these men are making excuses for their reluctance to take responsibility for themselves along the lines of, "If I am personally ineffective it is because my body is physically defective."

Depressive hypochondriacs typically communicate with us not only verbally but also nonverbally, that is, with their bodies. Our emotional reaction to their bodily complaints can offer us a good clue as to the exact meaning of their hypochondriacal communications. We sense: they refuse with a headache instead of saying no; they attack with a chest pain instead of saying "get lost"; and they withhold with an abdominal cramp instead of saying "I won't." Hypochondriacs also use their physical symptoms to speak to themselves. Often they first tell themselves, "I need to do better." Then second they take this back, telling themselves, "But I cannot, for I am a very sick man."

APPETITE/EATING DISTURBANCES

Two forms of appetite and eating disturbances occur in men who are depressed: overeating leading to excessive weight gain, and semi-starvation leading to inordinate weight loss (perhaps more common in women than in men).

Depressed men who overeat may do so in an attempt to treat their depression chemically by giving themselves an endorphin high, and to treat it emotionally by "feeding themselves a little pleasure" and/or by enhancing their self-esteem by being "sophisticated foodies." In the realm of the latter, one depressed patient in his forties gushed that a ten-course dinner with eight bottles of wine and dessert served at the very fashionably late hour of 1:00 A.M., was without a doubt the highlight of his entire life. Some are overeating in response to the depressive delusional belief that any weight loss signifies cancer or HIV—and their gaining weight means that they are out of the woods and not about to die. Sometimes their overeating is the product of the increased appetite that signals a *recovery* from deep depression as they get a rush of relief over how their burdens have finally lifted. Overeating with excessive weight gain is a possible side effect of antidepressant medication. On a more positive note, overeating can be part of a deliberate plan to gain weight—as when it involves the fulfillment of a personal aesthetic for the man who believes that being hefty makes him look and feel desirably zaftig, or even "motherly." Weight gain due to overeating has to be distinguished from weight gain that is the result of exercising, where the laying down of muscle increases weight by increasing the ratio of heavier muscle to lighter fat.

Excessive weight loss can also occur. It can be due to anorexia. Here the man eats too little because he no longer feels hungry because his blue mood has diminished his appetite; because while he does feel hungry he is too self-punitive to fully slake his hunger; because he is self-punitively going on a hunger strike; because he wants to be attractively very thin in order to compensate for feeling unattractively very fat; or because he has a body dysmorphic disorder and as he looks in the mirror imagines that he is fat and so does everything he can to get thinner—because to him any fat fold whatsoever represents a significant deformity which does not fit with his own idealized self-image. It might also be that he is involved in a power struggle along the lines of "see if you can make me eat; I dare you to try" and is punishing others by starving himself; or because he has swung into hypomania and is now manically starving himself and working out in the gym to get the perfect body—as did the man who worked out three times a day, every day of his life, so that he could "finally get some woman to marry me."

SEXUAL PROBLEMS

Depression is associated with a number of sexual problems. Many of these arise out of sexual guilt. The sexually guilty man might simply condemn himself for what he considers to be his oversexed nature, saying to himself, "Men are supposed to want sex, but they aren't supposed to be thinking about it all the time like I do, in the way I do, and to be constantly on the prowl like I am." Some depressed men actually lose their sexual drive—like the husband who gives his wife five children then moves to the next room, and never touches her, or anyone else, sexually again. In other instances, sexual activity continues but with little interest or involvement. We see a relative inability to be aroused sexually possibly accompanied by impotence marked by a general alubricatory joylessness, erectile dysfunction, ejaculatio tarda, or the inability to have or to feel orgasm. Dynamically, such men may believe that enjoying sex, like enjoying anything else, is shameful. Some have lost the self-confidence they need to get and hold an erection, while others cannot enjoy themselves because they fear getting a disease or performing inadequately and thus displeasing their partners, who will presumably get back at them by leaving them.

Paradoxically, sexual guilt can also take the form of *hypersexuality*. Such hypersexuality is meant to create suffering—the suffering that arises out of deliberately opening oneself up to the crushing rejection that predictably comes from repeated attempts to make contact with people one hardly knows, or that is the upshot of the man cheating on his partner in a way that is certain to be discovered. Such men are often unconsciously planning a bleak future for themselves by avoiding commitment in any form, doing so precisely to guarantee that they will be lonely forever and ultimately die alone.

Sometimes hypersexuality is less the product of guilt than of a demoralized hopelessness, as when the man says to himself, "Life stinks; I'm going to die soon anyway, so I might just as well go to my grave in style, and with a smile on my face." It can also be a hypomanic defense—a way for depressed men to deal with and defeat depression along the lines of, "See, all those people want me, so how bad can I be?" Here the hypersexual man is dealing with his devalued self-image by using the pseudopod of sex to reach out and relate to others on a personal level, ratcheting up his exposure to increase his chances of connecting, hoping to strengthen his self-esteem through a series of sexual triumphs that presumably will repair his damaged self-image. He feels alone, unloved, unwanted, and like a "big nobody without somebody." He feels unlovable because he feels that nobody loves him. So he seeks multiple conquests and then displays them as trophies for self-approval and for the admiration of others. While some of these men are truly unloved, many only feel that way because they are unduly needy or demanding, to the point that for them no love is ever enough. Men like this tend to get depressed after experiencing just one night without a phone call, one day without a visit, or one weekend without a sexual encounter.

Not a few men become sexually hyperactive as a way to deal with the real disappointment involved in being caught up in an unloving relationship with an uncaring, negative, critical, rejecting, depressing partner. They are both trying to get some satisfaction out of life and trying to get revenge on a partner for real or imagined harm. Some accomplish the latter by being contemptuously unfaithful with a third party and making certain that the encounter is discovered.

Some *paraphilias* are depression-based, as when depressed *pedophiles* choose children as sex objects for the following (highly disturbed) reasons:

- They believe that children represent a purity and innocence that they themselves have permanently lost and need to regain (via merger).
- They believe that they are too defective and personally deficient to be able to relate to someone their own age.
- They need to reestablish and retain dominance and control, and require a weak and submissive object.
- They wish to avoid being ridiculed and humiliated by a critical parental transference figure, so they choose children, who by definition are likely to be, can be seen as, or can actually be made to be passively, compliantly "nonparental."
- They are regressing to infantilism, and to a remembrance of times past, perhaps once again playing the childhood game of "doctor."

- They experience an antisocial rage where they do exactly what society finds most abhorrent, deliberately or unconsciously acting in a way meant to embarrass their parents or resented late-life parental substitutes such as the Mother Church or God the Father.

Foot fetishes can be found in men who are basically deeply depressed. In the psychoanalytic view to which I subscribe (even though it doesn't explain everything), some men view the foot as a phallic symbol—and develop a foot fetish as a way to say, "I search constantly for the perfect foot/penis in others to make up for the feeling that my own is defective or has been removed." For parallel reasons some depressed men *flash*, doing so in order to impress a victim into thinking, "Look what he has; isn't it grand?" This is, of course, self-defeating, because the victim usually is not only unimpressed but also frightened, displeased, and apt to call the police.

MARITAL PROBLEMS

Marital problems are often considered to be the *cause* of depression. But just as often they are only one of its *symptoms*. Many men blame their depression on their divorce when they might instead profitably blame their divorce on their depression.

When depression appears in the context of marital relationships and relationships with significant others it often takes the form of infidelity or spousal abuse. In some of these cases the man has turned the depressive, "I am not good enough for you" into the paranoid, and often subsequently abusive, "You are not good enough for me." This said, men who abuse their spouses are too often unfairly singled out by their families, their society, and their therapists for being fully responsible for the abuse when in fact they have been somewhat provoked to hit their wives by wives who first hit on them—making them angry and depressed to the point that they can no longer control themselves. There is no excuse for violence no matter how much provocation there has been. There is, however, often an explanation, and in perhaps more cases than we acknowledge the full explanation needs to include the role that each participant, the woman as well as the man, plays in the ongoing process.

I once gave a lecture on how couples can work out problems with intramural violence in their relationship. I recommended minimizing confrontation and overlooking minor sources of aggrievement, for example, not having big fights about such little things as putting wet towels on the bed. Several women in the audience, women who had been hit once or multiple times by their husbands, disagreed with my approach. For example, an attorney said that she thrived on being confrontational both in and out of her marriage. Another woman hostilely spoke of the serious disadvantages of having her mattress soaked by wet towels and noted that for her having a dry mattress was as or more important then having a "soggy" relationship, especially since "what counted was the principle of the thing." These thoughts crossed my mind:

- Are such women propping themselves up by putting their husbands down, and making them depressed and angry by constantly confronting and harassing them about petty things?
- To what extent could some of these women have avoided being emotionally or physically mishandled by avoiding being so provocative?

I have seen cases where a therapist by taking sides one hundred percent with the woman against the man furthered the man's feeling abandoned, controlled, and castrated—making him more depressed and more violent. No wonder men in such a position, feeling first castrated by their wives, second by a society that does not back them up, and third by a therapist who misunderstands and mistreats them, get depressed, contemplate suicide, and even become violent because they feel frustrated by not finding a sympathetic ear, emotional backup, or personal or professional validation, seemingly no matter where or to whom they turn.

VIOLENCE

Violence in depressed men of course occurs not only within but outside of marital relationships. It can be a sign of worsening depression. Or it can be a sign that depression is not worsening but improving, where it signals that the depressed man is becoming once again energized, although hardly along healthy lines. The energizing can occur either spontaneously or as the result of treatment. For to some extent depression is the man's bastion against anger—his way to hold back the onrush of raging waters. So when the man becomes less depressed he no longer has the depressive defense in place to control his violent impulses. These break through, doing so sometimes with devastating consequences.

ON-THE-JOB DIFFICULTIES

Men's depression accounts for significant on-the-job difficulties. Men who are depressed often come in late to work, leave work early, drink at lunch, get into fights with coworkers as they rage after taking a colleague's or an underling's minor peccadilloes too seriously, play computer games instead of working, and send e-mails flaming the boss even though he or she is the very person who is paying their salary and providing them with the computer. Not surprisingly, such men often have difficulty dealing with the public. In this realm is the comment of a plumber I recently hired to fix my sink: "I hate faucets; they suck." Once I was having a new bathtub delivered. The truck driver looked me straight in the eye and asked me if he had to bring it upstairs. When I asked him what the alternative was, he suggested taking it back. When we straightened that out, he could do no better than complain how heavy it was and how hot it was outside—those problems, according to him, were only the beginning of a long list of reasons why he was right to hate his job (and ought not to be particularly guilty about taking it out on me).

These and other on-the-job work-related disordered behaviors often originate in one of several depressive emotional distortions:

- I do not deserve to accomplish much.
- I fear being successful so I convince myself that what I accomplish is not good enough to be shown or promoted, or should even, after being finished, be destroyed.
- I believe, in an almost paranoid way, that my (in fact kind and supportive) boss is actually a castrative bitch/ball-busting bastard.

Often such depressed men change their jobs when they should be instead changing their attitude. They might profitably stop blaming their job and start looking to their personal problems, especially their paranoid blaming attitudes such as, "No one can ever do anything right with a boss like mine" or, "The only reason I am stuck in this dead-end position is that I am completely unappreciated and thoroughly unloved."

Depressed chief executive officers (CEOs) may make professional decisions driven not by corporate need but by the need to adjust their mood. A CEO with an affective disorder can in a state of compromised judgment make business decisions not for valid financial reasons but to feel personally more worthy, potent, and complete. A boss with an affective disorder can make his employees' lives horrible. I well remember one of my patient's shriek of pain when he needed to close on a house on a certain day, but his boss simply refused to give him a few hours off to meet with his lawyers, even though he gave his boss adequate notice, arranged coverage for the few hours he would be gone, and promised to come back to work that very afternoon to finish the day's chores. This boss may have been a narcissistic bipolar man who didn't want any other man around him to have a big house, and particularly not one that was bigger and better than his. He had what I call an "Edifice Complex," consisting of a need to have the biggest structure of anyone in the company. So he felt particularly threatened by any male employee who might be rising to the top and closing in on him with a superior "erection." Fortunately, my patient didn't yield to his boss's attempt to control and castrate him. Instead he went over his boss's head, to his boss's boss, and got permission to be gone for the few hours he needed for the closing. The closing went well, but he got very depressed because when he returned he found his own boss fuming—almost literally frothing at the mouth in anger—and making (empty) threats to fire him because he had defied him.

Another time the same boss further depressed my patient by harshly criticizing him unjustifiably over a passing comment he made. A hospital designer had ordered new chairs for the waiting room. When the chairs came, though they were beautiful, as often happens when you redecorate partially they made everything else look seedy by comparison. My patient spoke to his boss about that problem, saying: "The beautiful new chairs make the wallpaper look old and tattered." His boss, extending his criticism beyond the realm of work-related matters into the personal arena, went on a rampage, harshly rebuking him, telling him not to be so critical of the designer "because it would make her feel bad." My patient was deeply hurt and as a result became quite depressed. He felt his boss had gone beyond his mandate to tell him when he did something wrong on the job and had moved on to criticizing him for something entirely unrelated to his work. During his next session he revealed how he felt, "I'm so glad to be here this evening to at last see, and be able to speak to, a friendly face."

I suffered from a mini-on-the-job depression on a psychiatric service where almost all the patients, regardless of the true nature of their pathology, were diagnosed, usually incorrectly, by a staff of doctors who almost literally made only one diagnosis: Major Depression with Psychotic Features—then routinely prescribed a combination of antidepressants, antianxiety agents, mood stabilizers, and major tranquillizers. It took me a while to understand why so many patients were being misdiagnosed and mistreated this way. I had my eureka response when one day I looked down at my boss's hands and noticed that he had a fine tremor—to me, a possible sign that he himself was taking lithium. I naturally wondered if this was a case of projective identification where he was universalizing his personal problems onto his patients. I was able to quit, but if I had been stuck there I almost certainly would have become depressed over feeling unappreciated, controlled, and emasculated—no matter what I did, and absent consensual validation from anyone, no matter to whom I turned.

Of course, on-the-job problems are sometimes not the cause but the consequence of depression. For example, a boss gave a worker a raise, presenting it, in hindsight perhaps insensitively, as a generous gift made out of the goodness of his heart, for he knew that the worker needed the money. Unfortunately, this depressed worker, picking up the wrong cudgel, responded not with a "Thank you," but with a thankless, "You know you didn't have to do that just because you felt sorry for me. In fact I can't stand it when people feel sorry for me. Your feeling sorry for me makes me feel even more like a charity case."

In conclusion, depression in men differs from depression in women in its greater tendency to camouflage itself as specific somatic and behavioral symptoms, some of which I have detailed. These are not invariably depressive in nature and origin, but all concerned should be able to recognize these "depressive equivalents" in order to determine if a man is depressed and ought to be diagnosed and treated accordingly.

Chapter 7

Hypomania

Hypomania is the obverse of depression, replacing depressive shortfall with hypomanic excess that undercuts, smoothes over, and denies depressed mood, low self-esteem, and the demoralized feeling that one is a big nobody with little reason to self-affirm and no ability to freely and healthily self-realize. In hypomania depressive impoverishment and slowing of ideation yield to pressured thoughts; a worrisome obsessiveness leads to firm but often misguided goal-direction; and social passivity, isolation, and a lack of engagement in and enjoyment of pleasurable interpersonal activities yield to social and interpersonal hyperactivity as the once shy, remote, and reserved caterpillar becomes the newly hatched social butterfly. A fear of failure becomes a certainty of success; guilt becomes an extreme loosening of the reins of conscience; and scrupulosity becomes a relative or almost complete lack of concern for morality and the possible consequences of one's own immorality. In short, in their relationships with themselves and others, their spending, studying, work, sleep, eating, and sexuality, hypomanic men exceed normal standards just as depressed men fall short of them.

AFFECT

Hypomanic men feel elated—not merely good, but too good, in ways epitomized by the expressions "in seventh heaven," "on cloud nine," and "on top of the world." They may even go so far as to become delusional as they come to think of themselves as a king, or a god. Their good, or excessively good, feeling is, however, typically shot through with irritability, which often appears when they feel or are actually thwarted even in some minor way. Now flashes of anger take over and they become explosively nasty and personally hurtful. As I was talking to a man who was rushing about happily on his way to take a train that didn't exist, my dog jumped up on him and licked his face. His expansive, euphoric mood was temporarily interrupted by an anger flash: "You fool, how could you let your dog lick me like that? Can't you see that I just finished squeezing my zits?"

APPEARANCE

Hypomanic men often look too bright, and overdone. One man said that one of his goals in life was to dye his hair pink so that he could look like a roadside diner with many mirrors and plastic flowers. His look was at one and the same time strange, funny, and tasteless, but it was not bizarre, spooky, or angry, for his intent was not to frighten others but to amuse and entertain them. His clothes were not costumes created in their entirety from bizarre inner fragmented mentation but stylish-glitzy exaggerations of outfits that were currently in vogue and in some circles even highly fashionable.

BEHAVIOR

Hypomanic men speed up in part because they feel that if they slow down at all they will sink completely into the mire. They often do several things at once, like the man who works out in the gym with a power shake in one hand, a personal stereo in the other, and a book on his lap, as he reads, drinks, and listens—doing all these things while working the Cybex machines.

Hypomanic men are not withdrawn. They require an audience, and preferably one that is appreciative. They wish to catch others up in their gaiety, not to offend or provoke them. They are generally not antisociety, for they want to maintain relationships with, not to alienate themselves from, others. They do not pretend to the often remote, distant throne of the individual who is avoidant, paranoid, or schizophrenic. Rather they wish to remain part of a group. They are not loners. Instead they are having themselves a party, and they want to invite the world to it.

Hypomanic men are exhibitionists who enjoy making others laugh. As the depressed man wants to produce anguish in us, the hypomanic man wants us to experience riotous joy. A laughing, clapping audience is his proof that he is desirable and loved. He *is* often actually funny, partly because he draws good humor from his depression-based talent for cynical caricature—spotting others' foibles, zeroing in on them, and going in for the kill. However, often his ancillary or main goal is not to make us laugh but to shock us and render us uncomfortable. For many hypomanic men have an antiestablishment-oriented streak in them, leading them to derive amusement from shaking the bourgeoisie up and out of their conformity. As such they often become amateur cynical practical jokesters with an iconoclastic aspect to their humor. For some the stage is set for them to become professionally successful as insult comics or "shock-jocks."

The hypomanic man often lives the glamorous life—in the fast lane, quick, flashy, uproarious, unsubstantial, and pleasure-oriented. He seeks joy as much as or more than accomplishment, for he can be primarily out not to get somewhere but to relieve the emotional agony that derives from his depressive pain, and especially from the angst he feels about being a big nobody.

Work inhibitions can also exist, but these differ from those found in depressed men. The hypomanic man usually goes in to work, but once he gets there his euphoria can make him an unreliable and inconsistent performer. Also he is often chronically exhausted on the job due to a constant wakefulness that drains his energy and interferes with his ability to concentrate. Sometimes he has trouble working not because he can do too little but because he does too much. He is also easily distracted from his job by outside diversions, so that a world that needs another clerk or doctor instead gets another lothario, compulsive gambler, substance abuser, or other twisted, extravagant, and grotesque version of the self that can be immediately appealing and effective but contradicts his true nature and belies his full potential by making him into a superficial, flighty, unreliable, selfish, self-centered person whose ephemeral values predictably lead to merely trivial accomplishments. Often he relinquishes transcendental motivation/goals to instead become uncompromisingly dedicated to visceral self-indulgences supported by earnings as he aggressively devotes himself to acquiring material things. While the depressed man uses material things to create a positive self-image dependent on order, precision, perfection, completeness, and balance, the hypomanic man uses material things to create a positive self-image predicated on impressing others. But too often things become more important than people, and the value of personal relationships diminishes. When that happens he first abandons others, and then others abandon him.

This said, some men do work effectively, and even more effectively than otherwise, in the hypomanic phase. This can happen when creative disinhibition replaces uncreative work inhibition; when activity replaces inactivity; or when a drive to be successful no matter what covers a fear even in some minor way of being a failure. Now the once diffident worker, becoming unable to rest, puts in long hours, takes on new responsibilities before discharging old ones, and even holds down two or three jobs instead of one or none. Not surprisingly, he comes to do things he otherwise might not and ought not to do, while denying the possibility that any of his actions could lead to potentially painful consequences. The above-described man with the zits signed up to take an experimental drug for which he was paid $5,000—money he didn't need because his wife was a high-earning, successful physician. His wife warned him: "Don't do that. These things can cause kidney and liver problems and other serious side effects." His response? A typical hypomanic, "Yeah, but what's a little dread for a lot of bread?"

SPEECH

Hypomanic speech may contain gentle sound (clang) associations (such as "dread" and "bread," as above) as the hypomanic man strings thoughts together as much by rhyme as by reason. Hypomanic speech is often pressured. There is logorrhea consisting of increased production of verbiage, with the speech also bombastic, empty, and full of filler such as the repetitive "Hell-lo! It's like, you know, awesome!" We also find circumstantiality—talking around a topic without ever getting to the point; tangentiality—a gradual wandering away from the main point; and overinclusiveness—inserting so many details that it becomes difficult for a listener to grasp the gist of what is being said.

Hypomanic humor may consist almost entirely of making smart remarks and cracking wisecracks. Very little that is even potentially amusing gets by hypomanic men. Rather they note, frame, enlarge, and distort most things to make them larger than life. They are often truly funny, but they are just as often offensive as they seize on even the most innocent of remarks and turn them into double entendres, or crack hostile, cruel, unfunny jokes to make fun of people, or to slaughter sacred cows to make antiestablishment, often hurtful, attacks on society's treasured institutions. A chef for a hobby show host showed the audience that he could sing as well as cook, only to have the host retort, half jokingly, but half seriously, "Well, now I know what you can do for a living after I fire you." A patient looking at a friend's winter hat noted, without prompting, that "You remind me of a demented smurf" and otherwise took great pleasure in making jokes about his weight, age, and ethnicity. Then after he completely devalued his friend, he attempted to excuse his obnoxiousness by saying, "Don't take offense: You know I was just kidding." A hypomanic man told a long, crude, and offensive shaggy dog story about how he was not sure whether or not he was a virgin, because he did have sex with one woman, but she was a seventy-nine-year-old prostitute with diabetes who had so much water retention that she sloshed when they were doing it, and so many fat folds that he was ultimately not certain if he penetrated ground zero or just sunk it into a pool of liquid or a fold of fat.

THOUGHT

Hypomanics have racing thoughts characterized by a flight of ideas consisting of a kind of pressured thinking for the sake, and joy, of thinking, and by associations that are both too rapid and too rich. The hypomanic man's need to express his true inner self takes precedence over his need to collect and organize his thoughts into something meaningful. He abdicates to feeling and mood, and even wallows in the allure of his disorganization. He makes little effort to be understood, for he feels entitled to be well-received just for being himself. While the depressed man thinks about outside constraints both primarily and constantly, the hypomanic man thinks mainly of "being me"—developing his identity to the fullest and expressing all his emotions without constraint, convinced that he alone is free of the consequences of so doing.

Hypomanic men often think grandiosely, but short of becoming delusional. Their semi-delusional thinking approximates how normal people would think if freed of inner inhibitions and external constraints. Typically they are braggarts, like the man who announced to an entire restaurant that he had just rejected the two-hundredth woman vying for his attention because none of them made his toes curl up. They concoct grand and wild schemes, many of which are potentially doable, and some become creative men and great leaders. Their success often derives from their ability to blur a distinction others maintain between what is possible and what is likely, and their talent consists as much of the absence of shame as of the presence of ability. Theirs is a self-certainty that enables them to succeed through sheer self-confidence and braggadocio. They permit themselves to move forward no matter what—by going to those proverbial places where only fools rush in. Brooking little or no interference from themselves, their critics, or their rivals, they let their ideas flow freely without censorship, undue reflection, excessive scrutiny, or stultifying revision, in favorable cases leading to a breakthrough of "smart" rushing along on the coattails of "speed." Even when they give up stable jobs in the pursuit of elusive goals, they may succeed beyond their own wildest imaginations. Their success, however, is not always measurable in positive terms. Some employ their charisma to form dangerous cults. Many are equipped to acquire but not to effectively sustain power, and fail when the first mood swing into depression comes along and does them in, as it does in others in their lives. Because their narcissistic beliefs lead them to see themselves as infant kings entitled to all they desire—either as their birthright or as a reward for their achievements—because of who and what they are or because of who and what they believe they have become—they think themselves immune from all the possible negative consequences of their ill-conceived behavior, along the lines of,

"It cannot happen to me." Not surprisingly when things don't go their way or others balk, they develop angry persecutory ideas along the lines of "You are out to spoil my fun" which too readily shifts over to become "You are out to get me." Just recently a neighbor, who seemed to be on a hypomanic high, told me that he was rushing to make a train that ran from our home town in New Jersey to Atlantic City, New Jersey. He was going to meet his mother who was having "an emergency" at the gaming tables. I had no success convincing him that no train ran between these two points, and that if he wished to take the train to Atlantic City he would have a long and tedious journey. Instead of thanking me for the information, he became furious with me because he wanted that train, and I was telling him that it would not be there waiting just for him ready whenever he wanted to spirit him away to his very personal destination.

As this neighbor's thinking illustrates, hypomanic grandiose ideation is often mood congruent—that is, it is the product of, and therefore makes sense in the context of, the elevated mood. However, when irritability appears the grandiosity becomes stained with anger, and the thinking begins to border on mood incongruent persecutory ideation, for example, not "I want that train" but "That lousy railroad should have run those tracks where I wanted them to go."

INSIGHT

Hypomanic men in the throes of their hypomanic "experiences" tend to have little insight. They feel at peace with their illness. The worrisome, brooding depressed man who formerly overanalyzed himself now becomes the hypomanic man who is not at all introspective. Also, since hypomania is pleasurable, Bipolar II men tend to see their mood disorder solely in terms of the depressive state and do everything possible to avoid the bad and perpetuate the good feeling. The depression that goes unidentified because it is hidden becomes the hypomania that goes unidentified because it is fun. Sometimes a significant amount of insight surfaces, or resurfaces, just as recovery from hypomania begins. Insight can also peak just before a relapse—a feature of the man's trying to talk himself down to prevent the advent of another attack.

JUDGMENT

A hypomanic man's judgment is often negatively affected by his expansive grandiosity. Hypomanic men may have good ideas but fail to implement them. They often compromise their best notions by being hedonistic, acting in a random fashion, and focusing on what is more illusory and symbolic than real. In the realm of acting in a random fashion, they pursue diffuse goals as they typically take on too many projects at once, and fail to complete what they started. While few become completely disorganized, many become "merely" inefficient as they head in several directions at one time. In the realm of focusing on the illusory and symbolic, they might bet at the casino less for the money and more to feel powerful and in full control of their lives. As they rise to symbolic more than to real challenges they naturally focus away from the meaningful and on to the superficial. They might, for example, spend too little time on the job creating the ideal career and too much time in the gym sculpting the perfect body. If they collect gewgaws it is not so much because they want the things they collect, but because of the challenge of having a complete collection: of something, just about anything, so that "mine" can be bigger than "yours."

Many men when hypomanic retain much of the stubbornness that is at the heart of their depression. They can be pigheaded, wrongheaded, sophomoric individuals who think they know it all when what they possess is mainly intellectual not practical knowledge. As such they fail to properly buy into feedback from others that they are headed in the wrong direction. So they do not adequately assess the difficulties in their paths, but instead irrationally see themselves as more effective, and the potential obstacles in their way as less significant, than they actually are. As a result they anticipate success even when failure is virtually assured. They may perceive that a negative outcome to their outlandish schemes is possible, but they get into serious difficulty because they fail to heed their own warnings and instead irresponsibly throw caution to the winds. In typical fashion, too giddy to properly look at a possibly dark outcome of their actions, they literally as well as figuratively gamble to excess because they feel too lucky to ever lose. They keep up their gambling even in situations where they know that the odds are clearly against them and even when they dimly recognize that if they continue along the same lines they will not make up for the shortfall but will instead lose even more.

They tend to be all inspiration but no perspiration. When they are depressed they are unable to work because no ideas come to them. But when they are hypomanic their inspiration flows freely—they fall short only in the realm of sifting, editing, and revising. As a result they become less like functional designs and more like intriguing, and fantastic, but cumbersome, or completely worthless, contraptions.

Suicidal thoughts or behavior may occur during hypomania. Here killing oneself, perhaps as part of a suicide pact, represents a joyful climactic act accompanied by fantasies of merging into the warm and welcome embrace of death. In some cases antidepressants seem to spawn suicidal ideation not because they are ineffective but because they work too well: relieving the depression that keeps the ecstatic suicidal hypomanic state from developing and emerging.

Hypomanic poor judgment and associated ill-conceived behavior elicits a specific, often diagnostic response in others. We secretly envy how they can get things without having to pay for them; take long vacations with little or no concern for their professional commitments; charge limousines even though they cannot afford to take a taxi; get drunk and take a plane for a joyride; or when irritable drive their lemon cars through the plate glass window of the car dealership. Who would not want deep down to do what one man did on several occasions: scoop up a goose or duck from the nearby lake and take it home, to quote him, "completely oblivious to the poop everywhere," and put it on his terrace or in his bathtub, and pet and love it for a little while (before releasing it unharmed). Similarly afflicted men take in scores of seagulls with injured wings and try to fix them, or take home a transsexual prostitute to set her on the right path to personal salvation—out of a surfeit of expansive love for humanity that some admitted began to uncomfortably take on the proportions of a Savior Complex. Not surprisingly, these are the people who get into the news, and make the headlines. We like to read about hypomanic men because they do what we would like to do—if only we could get over our inhibitions to just go ahead and do it.

PSYCHODYNAMICS OF HYPOMANIA

Hypomania typically results when a depressed man deals with his depression by employing the anti-depressive defense of denial. Also characteristic of hypomania are two other defenses: identification with the aggressor and projective identification.

Denial

Hypomanic men deny the components of their depression one by one. For example, guilty self-deprivation denied becomes guilt-free hedonism, and selfishness denied becomes excessive altruism and selflessness. In the realm of the latter, a patient was mugged by a homeless man who spewed pejoratives at him. Instead of complaining that he could no longer walk the streets without fear he gushed that he felt he deserved what he got for making eye contact with a stranger. Then he downplayed the impact of the man's actions by convincing himself that his being mugged was all for the good—for "it was better that it happened to me, who could take it, than to someone else, who might not be in as good a position as I am to handle it." Hypomanic men counter feeling controlled by feeling completely free, and counter feeling oppressed by acting as if they do not care one whit what other people think, say, or do. They force themselves to be happy as their way to deal with a pervasive inner sadness, and obscure feeling low by forcing themselves to become high. The hypomanic man is the anhedonic, withdrawn depressive attempting to revive himself, becoming alive, active, and productive through whistling in the dark to deny physical and emotional vulnerability. He also denies the possibility of rejection by trivializing serious relationships—by ridiculing them so that they no longer appear to count for much. He denies feeling alone by figuratively throwing confetti to have his own private party to make up for the feeling that he has not been invited to someone else's—his way to feel appreciated and loved instead of feeling as if no one actually likes him. He is often hyperactive sexually, but this hypomanic hypersexuality does not constitute a healthy, nonmasochistic attempt to stop renouncing pleasure and start having fun. Rather it involves a restitutive attempt to create the illusion that for him meaningful relationships exist, and to express the hope that a committed relationship will come by chance if only he can meet enough people. He is also substituting quantity for quality—multiple superficial relationships for one deep one—attaching himself to anyone available and then thinking that even the most modest of positive responses from that person means that he is truly and completely loved. He often commits to relationships after denying incompatibility, without paying attention to what commitment means, or to the responsibility entailed in beginning and maintaining a long-term liaison. Not surprisingly, he often loses interest in a relationship after getting the initial jolt he wants out of it. Sometimes, however, he stays in a flawed relationship, denying its problematic aspects just to have any relationship at all so he will not have to go through another breakup and be all alone again. Within the relationship itself he often forces intimacy to deny how much he fears closeness.

He denies feeling weak and defective by taking on only the difficult challenges and fighting only the hard battles. So he approaches complete strangers, sexually approaching them in inappropriate places like sleazy bars or family events. To deny vulnerability and mortality, he often takes on extreme danger with the express intent of triumphing over the most difficult circumstances. For example, by design he picks up a hitchhiker just so that he can fly in the face of the possibility that he is picking up someone who might try to rob or murder him.

He deals with his low self-esteem by installing a superiority complex to counter his inferiority complex. He basks in the glory of the reflected light of who he knows, name-dropping to announce how he socializes with famous people to make himself feel as if he is integral to their world and they an important force in his. He denies feeling personally bankrupt by impressing others with his money, possessions such as a beautiful house or apartment, or his professional triumphs, as when he becomes one with his publications or comes to believe his press releases.

He brags about what he has in an attempt to convince himself that having beautiful things means being a beautiful person and occupying an important place in the cosmos. He collects things not to acquire a large meaningful collection that he might enjoy, but to be able to brag about his big collection to compensate for how small he feels personally. Dynamically speaking, to many a hypomanic man having a big house or a big collection means having a big intact phallus—and that often signifies getting back the one he feels that he just lost to the abandoner's whim, the controller's machinations, or the castrator's knife.

Denial defenses are, however, unstable and brittle. This instability partly accounts for the bipolarity of the disorder, as hypomania reverts to depression when the denial no longer works and what was denied breaks through and hits home. Then another mood swing back to hypomania occurs because the depressive pain that takes hold demands a fresh denial. Denial defenses become particularly ineffective should they create many of the difficulties that they were originally intended to relieve. Trying to meet many people brings on a number of rejections. Clowning gets laughs but not respect, and people who roar in appreciative laughter to one's face snicker behind one's back at silly, frantic attempts to ingratiate, please, and impress. Sometimes it is society that breaks through the denial defense, as when the CEO who acts illegally, with a grandiose disregard for consequences, gets caught, loses his job, and winds up in jail.

Identification with the Aggressor

Hypomanic men comfortably identify with the aggressor in one or both of two ways. Some become vengeful people who turn the tables on others to hurt them exactly the way they feel they have been hurt by them. Hypomanic men want to shock and appall the establishment to pay it back for all the pain they believe it has caused them. Unfortunately for the hypomanic individual, establishments have their own need to feel in control and intact, and have their own ways of retaliating for the retaliation.

Alternatively, the hypomanic man may become a submissive person who turns the tables on himself in the form of self-demeaning actions meant to soften the blow of, or hold off attack from, others via the mechanism of presenting the vulnerable underbelly. This submissiveness often takes the form of self-demeaning humor consisting of self-abnegating, self-deprecating jokes made on the self to get there first and to send the protective message, "I am not to be taken seriously enough to be worth hurting." Simultaneously they get jollies by telling others, "I win points for being modest." However, they lose points for leading with their bad side, thus devaluing themselves unnecessarily and in a way that assures that others will devalue them even further.

Projective Identification

Hypomanic men use projective identification to deny feeling deprived. They do that by gratifying themselves through gratifying others the way they would want to be themselves gratified. This way they gain the illusion of personal value through what they consider to be admirable altruism. In a typical scenario involving excessive altruism, they become the perfect host just to feel like an invited guest, or, as many anorexics do, feed others sumptuously even while they starve themselves unmercifully.

POSITIVE FEATURES OF HYPOMANIA

Hypomania like depression has positive features. Like depressives, hypomanics can be creative when their pervasive mood collects and unifies diverse concepts under its spell—connecting disparate ideas in new and original, and often creatively idiosyncratic, ways.

The depressive's ability to carefully calculate what is important to you based on a sensitive self-perception of what is meaningful to me survives in the hypomanic's ability to employ insightful empathy to achieve his goals through spotting others' vulnerabilities. This insightful empathy, while somewhat pathologically manipulative, remains a valid and often very effective tool for achieving personal gain and social success.

Some observers believe hypomania is an illness and as such should not elicit an overromanticized response from others, from society, and from the world. It is true: the positive aspects of hypomania fall easy prey to the negative. But it is also true that the hypomanic man, like the depressed man whose creativity springs from the fount of his sadness, can squeeze a lot of benefit out of his excessiveness, turning a self-defeating liability into a self-enhancing asset.

PART II

CAUSATION

Chapter 8

The Psychodynamics of Depression

In Chapters 8 to 14, I focus on the main causes of depression and high-light those that seem to be more frequent, most important, and most highly poignant in men.

Depression is a destination, or final common pathway, that is reached not by one but by many often convergent routes. The depressed man interacts simultaneously with himself, with others in his environment, and with that environment itself. In turn, a complete understanding of the causes of depression in men requires that we look at all potential and actual trouble spots and then create an integral picture of causality that considers, includes, and weighs the significance of each. In other words, I believe that we can best understand depression from a holistic viewpoint that includes developmental, psychodynamic, cognitive-behavioral, interpersonal, and biological perspectives. For some of my depressed male patients, early developmental problems (as discussed in Chapter 9) seem to have had the most impact. For others their depression appeared to have been mainly due to later experiential factors, and was in a sense learned or conditioned, often in a setting of interactive interpersonal difficulties (as discussed in Chapter 12). For still others their depression appeared to be mainly, if not entirely, of biochemical origin (as discussed in the Appendix.) But for many men their depression was the product of a number of simultaneously operative trends. As is often the case, one condition or a single occurrence was not enough to trigger the depression. Rather it took a confluence of developmental lag, unresolved inner conflict, and unfortunate past and current circumstances to ignite their depression. In the realm of current circumstances, some men can tolerate one or two negative events, but no more.

Thus a man with much adversity in his life resisted depression until all at once his mother died, his wife retired, and his household income dropped just when his youngest daughter got married, moved away, and lost her first child. Many depressives say that bad news comes in threes. This may seem to be so because the man who can manage one or two setbacks cannot deal with more. Before three the bad news is manageable. With three it becomes notably overwhelming and depressing. Of course, as mentioned throughout, for depressed men bad news is relative, for as is often the case truly malignant situations have very little effect on some men, while seemingly benign situations have deep, extraordinarily noxious meaning, import, and impact.

As an example of news that became bad strictly because of its deep extraordinary personally noxious meaning, a patient got seriously depressed each time his wife sat on the sofa with a dog who took up all the remaining space to the point that the patient could not sit next to and watch television with his wife. He felt completely excluded, and brought to the point that he could almost see the veil of depression—a black curtain—coming down over his eyes and his life. I traced these depressive flashes seemingly over nothing to a mixture of factors that for him were quite something. Together these constitute a microcosm of what causes depression in many men:

- Feelings of being unloved, rejected, and abandoned
- Panic about feeling/being alone
- Simmering, resentful anger
- Painful disappointment, as if he were being betrayed
- Fear of competing unsuccessfully—in this case with both his dog and his wife (the dog likes my wife better than he likes me; my wife likes the dog better than she likes me)—accompanied by personal (and, when this occurs at work, professional) jealousy
- Remembrance of and association to previous bad things ("now" is just like when ...)
- Fear for the future (the hopeless feeling that "what is going to happen to me is all bad," and the fearful anticipation of disaster, as in "What will happen to me if ...")
- Fear of expressing oneself and one's complaints out of a fear of being criticized for asking for what one wants—because one is terrified of acting like a baby, of hurting and insulting people one needs, or of opening the inner emotional sluice gates and becoming flooded by, and losing control over, one's feelings
- Self-condemnation for normal acceptable thoughts and feelings as if they were abnormal, unacceptable, and forbidden

The following are discussions of the more significant psychodynamic causes of depression.

EXCESSIVE GUILT ARISING WITHIN A PRIMITIVE PUNITIVE CONSCIENCE

At times the guilt of the depressed men I treated was an *appropriate* response to how they had not lived up to their reasonable self-expectations and so ought to be disappointed in themselves—but still weren't correcting their past mistakes or trying to do better in the future. Some were right to believe that they ought to feel somewhat guilty over using their depression to manipulate others into giving them something they wanted but might not be entitled to have. Such was the case for the man who made suicidal threats to force his caretakers to take notice and respond in a gratifying way to what he himself recognized were the unreasonable demands he was making on them.

But mainly the depressed men I treated all tended to be *excessively* and *inappropriately* guilty. They were excessively and inappropriately superego-oriented individuals who were too moralistic for their own good. Often these men had internalized those who aggressed toward them and in turn treated themselves just as aggressively as these others had treated them. Perhaps, too, such negative passions as exploding primitive rage were emerging out of primordial instinctual ooze and unpleasantly and unfortunately boomeranging back on them. Or perhaps intense unacceptable sexual feelings were bursting forth, leaving them feeling sheepish and ashamed—as if they wanted to hide from the world. Perhaps they simply could not let go of the little wrongs they did, or think they did, earlier in life. Such men were dwelling on and ruminating about how awful they had been, and believing they could not improve in the here and now, or do better in the future.

Sometimes such men feel their guilt poignantly. At other times they go to extremes to suppress it, such as by developing a reactive Savior Complex characterized by being excessively good and becoming overly empathic and altruistic toward others in a way that greatly exceeds any empathy they might have toward themselves. Serious judgmental errors can occur as they masochistically put others' rights over their own, giving others those very rights, liberties, and other good things of which they deprive themselves. An example is the patient who accepted taking a big loss when his sports car was stolen because, as he put it, "I don't want to report the guy who took my car, and still has it, since a jail sentence might ruin his life."

ANGER ISSUES

As emphasized throughout, depression in men is often partly the product of an excess of anger kept inside then taken out on oneself, then discharged on others who the man condemns much as he condemns himself, so that others abandon him, making him even angrier than before.

Many depressed men are especially angry people. Their anger is both of the *appropriate*, or provoked, and *inappropriate*, or overreactive, kind. In either event, depressed men stifle their anger, and its expression, keeping it in because:

- They feel that if they get angry others will not like them.
- They believe that feeling and getting angry means being at odds with a self-image that to be positive depends on being peaceful—and anger goes against the grain of their personal preference and individual philosophy.
- They believe that if they let themselves feel a little angry they will let loose and become emotionally flooded because all their anger will emerge at once.
- They are too highly attuned for their own good to the many extant social prohibitions against feeling and getting angry.
- They are too highly attuned for their own good to other people's negative attitudes about their anger, especially the attitude of partners who find their anger unacceptable, and even appalling, and threaten to dislike, criticize, and abandon them out of retaliative angry feelings of their own.

Men who keep their anger inside find that the anger builds and soaks them through emotionally, leading them to take their anger out on themselves. Then their anger seeps out to be expressed indirectly and passively, or bursts out figuratively leaving blood on the floor. Anyone who is the victim of angry depressive fallout will attest to the truth of what Real says: depressives "inflict ... their torture on others,"[1] making the depressed man as aggressive, or passive-aggressive, to others as he is "auto-aggressive,"[2] that is, aggressive to himself.

However, it is an oversimplification to view depression exclusively in terms of anger held in then taken out on the self and subsequently discharged, covertly or overtly, on others. For one thing, while anger held in creates depression, depression already in place creates anger. A man gets depressed because he is mad at the world. He also gets mad at the world because he is depressed. For example, a man's mother is dying of Alzheimer's disease. His sister is taking care of their mother. The sister's attempts to move her mother to a nursing home are thwarted by problems she is having with handling her mother's cat, which is a real tiger in every sense of the word. The sister calls up her brother to grouse that the cat keeps getting in her way as she tries to move her mother's things out of the house. The brother's reaction is: "I cannot believe that my stupid sister doesn't know that she has to handle the cat first, and the move next, not the other way around. When will that idiot finally get a clue?" This man was already depressed because he had to put his mother in a nursing home. It was his depressed mood that in great measure fomented his anger with his sister—as is typical in such situations, over little, or nothing.

SEXUAL PROBLEMS

Men often get depressed over their sexuality. Some try to suppress their sexual feelings and actions because they see them as morally condemnable and personally or socially corrupt. For example, one of my patients got depressed because "I constantly have to face and struggle against my racing thoughts—about wanting to see, touch, and fondle a woman's silk panties."

GENERALIZED FREE-FLOATING ANXIETY

Depressed men typically get anxious as they worry about the possibility that new disaster is just around the corner, along the lines of "what will happen if ..." After they anxiously worry that bad things *might* happen, they become depressed because they convince themselves that bad things *will inevitably* occur.

Men typically get anxious and depressed in double-bind situations—where they can't win with others who make them feel that nothing they ever do is right. One patient described the following anxiety-creating dilemma: "If I sit idly by as my parents leave everything to my sister in their will I will have little or nothing, but if I complain to my parents, who favor her over me, I will be cut out of their will entirely and end up with even less." Here is an example of a personal double-bind situation which caused me to become anxious and depressed: A local man constantly insults me; however, because he is an important local political figure, I have to tread lightly so that I avoid getting into hot water around town. Therefore I feel stuck swallowing my rage and accepting his putdowns, taking guff from him the same way a man takes guff from his wife because he is afraid of being lonely or from his boss because he needs the job. Is it so surprising then that each time I see this man coming I feel my mood lowering—and my blood pressure rising?

Men often also become anxious and depressed in situations where they believe they are being controlled to excess and where they feel castrated—for example, by a wife who plutoes her husband by joking to others, speaking about him, "Don't take his advice; it will only get you into trouble"; by a mother-in-law who tries to break up his marriage because she wants her daughter back; or by a boss who fires a man after pointedly implying that he deserved it and this is his punishment.

In a bi-directional way depression can be a defense against anxiety. Depression reduces anxiety as the man thinks, "Why worry? All is lost anyway" and "I feel less anxious about what little I have after I convince myself that I don't deserve much." In such cases depression functions as a protective learned helplessness, a comfortable flight, where the man crumbles and puts his tail between his legs and sneaking off to be by himself feels better because now he is in hiding—and while in hiding comforting himself by licking his wounds.

EGO-IDEAL DISSONANCE

Ego-ideal dissonance results when there is a split between lofty self-expectations and actual accomplishment, as unattainable lofty self-expectations create the familiar plaint, "Maybe I have set my sights so high that nothing I ever do can satisfy me completely." It also results when the man has lowly self-expectations which he decries because he realizes that he set his sights too low just to avoid being disappointed in life—only to discover that all he has accomplished is to guarantee that he can never be anything but disappointed in himself.

REGRESSION

A man's current depression can be profitably viewed as a regression, occurring when current circumstances bring him back in time to an early depression thus reviving early emotional, interpersonal, and cognitive pre-depressive fantasies and behavioral patterns. In men depression often starts with the baby boy getting depressed because he cannot distinguish between big and little disappointments, so that he wails pitifully over nothing. That baby becomes the boy who cries over a candy bar he cannot have, then becomes the man who has difficulty distinguishing between "small potatoes" and "big deals"—to the point that he cannot stop sobbing over trivialities that become a lot more than just spilt milk. Often it is people who fail to succor and nourish the man today who bring him back in time—to that time long ago when his thirst was not slaked because his mother both literally and figuratively pulled away her breast before he was sated. However, as noted throughout, depressed men do not create their present illness only out of a remembrance of past shabby conditions. They also create their negative view of past shabby conditions out of their present illness. Many depressed men come up with memories of depriving parents even when their early succoring was entirely adequate—at least as adequate as nurturing ever gets.

LOW SELF-ESTEEM

Almost every one acknowledges that depression is a condition involving low or at least lowered self-esteem. But what exactly is that?

Low/lowered self-esteem is a dismaying, self-denigrating, demoralizing self-evaluation characterized by a loss of the positive sense of self, so that the self is viewed as valueless, insignificant, and unimportant, and the individual as too weak and ineffectual to improve his self-view, his self-image, his behavior, or his circumstances.

What are the *causes* of low/lowered self-esteem? The following sections discuss some of the origins of low/lowered self-esteem.

A Lack of Approval from Critical Significant Others

Here others' disapproving guideposts become one's own, along the lines of "If you don't approve of me, than I don't approve of myself." Once I gave a modern style of chair to a shop owner to sell on consignment. One night this shop owner was also the maitre d' at a restaurant I entered. At first he greeted me with a respectable joke involving his dual role: he didn't ask me whether I wanted an outside or an inside table but whether I had come to the restaurant to offer him yet another chair on consignment. Shortly afterward, however, the joking turned hostile. Giving an exact description of my chair, he continued, "I have a great modern chair that I got from this old codger. He wanted to get rid of it because he could no longer get in and out of it." I got angry first and depressed next, as I asked myself, "Do people really think of me as an old codger?" and told myself, "If he thinks of me that way, that is the way I must be." I took his slight seriously even though while I am not young I am not decrepit. His suggestion that I was decrepit was enough to create a dissonance in me between my ideal and actual self, forming and enhancing a defective self-image based not on what I thought of myself, but on what he seemed to think of me.

Self-Criticism

In the depressed man self-criticism originates in primitive guilt with roots in an overly scrupulous morality. The self-criticism often tends to be inappropriate, but also, as just mentioned, it can be appropriate when based on a realistic assessment that the man has in fact not lived up to his own reasonable self-expectations and others' rational dictates.

Warped Self-Expectations

The warped *self-expectations* that lead to depression in men and to the fall in *self-esteem* that characterizes that depression can be either *too high* or *too low*.

How can *too high* self-expectations lead to a fall in self-esteem? Too high self-expectations can lead to low self-esteem due to a depressing dissonance between "how great I ought to be" and "what I am and can ever become." "How great I ought to be" consists in the man of gender-specific idealistic self-messages involving being independent; being the provider, not the one provided for; being active, not submissive; being the powerful one in authority, not the weak one whom everyone bosses around; successfully competing with and crushing one's rivals; and always keeping a stiff upper lip—especially not responding to loss by grieving long and hard but by rebounding quickly, easily, and without a scar.

Where do such too high self-expectations that lead to a fall in self-esteem come from? They tend to evolve in a number of ways. They may evolve *developmentally* in one of two ways. The first is directly. Here the man has been coddled as a boy and as an adult continues to expect the same coddling from everyone else. He has in effect become the apple of his own eye, and as such a man who always expects to discern the same glint in the eyes of others. The second is indirectly and defensively. Here the man has been overly deprived as a boy, by devaluing parents who sided not with the boy but with his tormentors; who invalidated the boy's gifts and personal strengths such as his musical talent; who criticized the boy for being active when he was just being a boy; who shamed and humiliated the boy by broadcasting his peccadilloes to others; or who offered the boy little parental love or actually physically abused him and then told him he deserved it—particularly devastating to passive impressionable boys who are additionally isolated from potentially supportive peer groups and such supportive adults as a simpatico scout master. The response here is a defensive, "I'm not valueless, I'm great, and as such should expect nothing but the most from myself."

They may evolve from current *parental and social expectations of what it means to be a man*—consisting of a litany of which stereotypical personal and professional attributes to be proud of and display, and which to be ashamed of and hide.

They may evolve innately *as the product of characterological problems.* This is often the case with competitive, rivalrous, histrionic men who are on an unceasing quest to see themselves as and to be better than everyone else—especially people they secretly envy or are openly jealous of.

Conversely, the self-expectations that lead to the fall in self-esteem can be *too low.* How can too low self-expectations lead to a fall in self esteem? When self-expectations are too low, they can lead to low self-esteem due to being prophetically self-fulfilling, creating demoralizing disappointment with oneself as the man who doesn't expect much of himself goes on to live his life inadequately: beneath his capacity and often to please deserving others as distinct from his undeserving self. For example, a patient got depressed because he was gay, which he believed to be a mortal sin. He did not expect himself to be happy. Therefore he willingly gave up a happy, successful relationship with his male domestic partner and married a woman he didn't much care for, abandoning the lucrative restaurant business he and his partner had built from scratch. He had permitted himself to capitulate to his mother by tailoring *his* life plan to *her* expectations, doing so in the hope that she, a woman from the old school, would admire him for his heterosexuality. So he married to give her the grandchildren she always wanted and on more than one occasion even made clear that she expected. Not surprisingly, a few years into the marriage things deteriorated and he got seriously depressed, feeling that his life was ruined because of his own stupidity. Now he sought a divorce and ultimately had to be hospitalized for a severe suicidal attempt, "the right thing for a stupid schmuck like me to do."

Where do such too low self-expectations that lead to the fall in self-esteem come from? They tend to evolve in a number of ways. They may evolve *developmentally* in a setting where nothing much was expected from the boy.

They may evolve *interpersonally* as the result of a *direct identification with nonsupportive devaluing critical others*—especially parents who created and reinforced the boy's or man's hate-filled guilty relationship with himself. Such parents are like the mother of one of my patients who reported to me, "As a physician I once suggested that my mother, suffering from a depression-related back pain, try Elavil, a medication known to have both analgesic and antidepressive qualities. Her response to me was, 'Really, now, how would you know?'" Another example is provided by my cousin who said, "I am taking pills for ringworm." I asked, "Griseofulvin?" She replied, "How could you possibly have known that?" I reminded her of something she did or should have known well: "Maybe it is because I am a doctor."

They may evolve *innately* as the product of *characterological problems*. These may consist of

- *Paranoid* conviction—that since one is being accused of being inherently unlikable, or detestable, one deserves to be so accused, such as "assumed attacks leave me no choice but to attack and hate myself." A competitive man I know cannot accept that he is a minor talent. He cooked several times with Martha Stewart on her television show. At a party we both attended I made what I thought was a decent little joke. I asked him, referring to Martha Stewart, if he had brought along that neat little assistant of his, that underling who helped him out on his television debut. I had intended to kiddingly imply that he was her mentor, not the other way around. I was surprised, however, to discover that I had hit a nerve—a sore point of his: his belief that no one favored him outside of his relationship with her. To my bad little joke he did not reply with a smile but with a complaint: "I don't ever expect to go anywhere in life, because you, like everyone else, always have to taunt and attack me by reminding me that it's all about Martha and never about me."

- *Obsessive perfectionism* where the obsessively perfectionistic depressed man comes to expect little of himself because he views his minor transgressions as major human failures.
- *Masochism* consisting of a need to self-punish, with low self-expectations a way to tyrannize oneself and submit to the tyranny of others and to one's tyrannical society.

They may evolve as the consequence of an *unfortunate reality*—as in "So far I have had nothing but bad luck in my days, so why should things be any different now"—when bad luck has in fact been the story of one's life. Such a man thinks, "Alas, I have learned from past experience that I really ought not to expect much more out of my life than what little I have gotten until now."

Losses (Perceived and Actual)

Low self-esteem can be a direct response to real or symbolic losses when these foment self-blame. A bank turned down a patient who applied for a home equity loan to rehab his apartment. As a result he felt like a big nobody because he took it personally when the bank said his credit wasn't any good, which meant to him not that there was something wrong with his credit but that there was something wrong with him. That night he dreamt that his apartment had sprung a number of serious leaks. In the dream he tried to call the managing agent but couldn't dial the phone because there was something wrong with his phone and his finger. Then, still in the dream, the next morning he tried to convince the bank to give him the loan but was still unsuccessful, and that, as he saw it, was because he was not enough of a man to be trusted with the bank's money.

✳✳✳✳

DYNAMIC DIFFERENCES BEWEEN MEN AND WOMEN

Many women tend to be more relationship-oriented/dependent than many men. As a result depression in women tends to be more about relational abandonments than depression in men, which is often about relational rejections. In other words, not "Alas, she is gone," but "She really fixed my wagon when she left me and told me she did it because she despises me."

Depression in men more than in women is the product of feeling controlled by others and losing control over one's life. We hear, "Everyone tries to push me around and tell me what to do, when I would prefer to be free to make up my own mind," and, "My boss tries to keep me down to the point that I no longer have a say in my job or have a life outside of my work."

Depression in men more than in women also tends to be a response to losing out in competitive situations. Here the loss involves not the loss of a person or relationship but of one's dominance and status. Such loss leaves the man feeling emotionally bereft and worthless. He criticizes himself for losing out to those he admires or envies, and for coming in second, or worse. Then he thinks of himself as, and sometimes actually calls himself, such things as "chopped liver," "an amorphous blob," or "a sissy."

Depression in men is in particular a response to being in the arena with castrative others. Men are particularly sensitive to being under the thumb of a critical partner, like a wife who henpecks or sasses him ("You always put my things where I can't find them; that really annoys me"); a critical boss who savages him; a critical doctor (or psychotherapist) who demands more and more, setting the stakes for approval ever higher each time he meets the last challenge ("losing those 30 pounds isn't going to be enough; now we have to turn our attention to your whole unhealthy lifestyle); and a hostile critic who lambastes who he is, what he stands for, and what he does, such as the literary critic who savages his latest and greatest production—not because it deserves to be savaged but because the critic is personally a savage. It is for this reason that Cochran and Rabinowitz say, "Men ... tend ... to have higher levels of depression in relation to issues of self-criticism [while] depression in women tend[s] to be related to issues of dependency."[3]

Men generally tend to have more problems than women with their own aggression. In my experience women tend to be less aggressive than men and less guilty about their aggressivity. So often men find themselves feeling more aggressive than they would like to be, and out of a sense of guilt deal with their aggressivity by becoming "Mr. Nice Guy"—only to later regret that and condemn themselves for being a "wuss." For example, a patient complained to the owner of his gym that the machines were old and rusty. The owner looked uncomfortably embarrassed and even angry. The patient next thought, "He is going to throw me out of here for complaining" and so decided, "I'll put up with it, because I know how expensive it is to buy new machines." Later he had second thoughts about being so passive, and began to ask himself, "What kind of man am I anyway?" and felt troubled about whether he was a real man or a sissy. A neighbor who refuses to speak to me because I got angry with her after she complained too many times about a leak that was supposedly coming from my floor—when it was in fact coming from her ceiling—not only refuses to speak to me, but when she sees me coming crosses the street to get away from me, and when there isn't time for that, makes a big wide swing around me as if to say, "I don't want to get anywhere near you." It is insulting, unpleasant, and depressing to be treated like a pariah. So I decided to turn tables on her and do the avoiding myself—to get there first by being the one to obviously cross the street to get away from her. Alas, I began to feel very uncomfortable about my puerile behavior. I began to have fantasies that she would get mad at me and sue me for harassment. So I went back to being a wuss—saying and doing nothing when she continued in her obvious attempts to avoid me. Even though I found it painfully depressing, I gave up protesting and just accepted being shunned, and in such an obvious way.

Generally speaking, women seem more accepting of their homosexual inclinations than men. Women are rarely exceedingly self-homophobic. In contrast, men often find their homosexual leanings appalling and depressing and go to great pains to hide them from themselves and others, in the process suppressing all tender feelings and along with these a great deal of their humanity and much of their relational ability. Distancing is a symptom characteristically found in depressed men. It is also the reason why many men get depressed in the first place.

Chapter 9

Developmental Origins

The depressive mindset can originate developmentally in persistent effects of early trauma and a response to problem parents. These are discussed in the following sections.

THE PERSISTENT EFFECTS OF EARLY TRAUMA

Many depressed men have a history of having been traumatized as boys. Their traumatization may have been one of omission: involving a lack of support and neglect, as it was for the boy with a hypochondriacal father who constantly worried about his son's health when the son was well, but was so anxious about the boy getting sick that he went into denial and failed to act when his son actually fell ill and needed medical care. Or the traumatization may have been one of commission: taking the form of tongue lashings, emotional knuckle rappings, or even physical abuse.

For purposes of clarity of exposition, in the following discussion I divide a boy's psychic development into three phases and note some characteristic traumata associated with each. This division is a simplistic one, however, because the three phases overlap, and other significant events occur simultaneously.

Childhood traumata can involve:

- Oral-level abuse in the realm of inadequate succoring and caretaking of the boy, or, the opposite, overwhelming the boy, thus fostering his dependency by killing his independence with kindness.
- Anal-level abuse in the realm of excessively rigid, controlling regimentation or, its opposite, abuse by a paucity of needed supervision by parents

who let the boy run too wild for his own good and for the good of all concerned.

- Phallic-level abuse in the realm of lack of support of, or put downs for, boyish assertion, manly competition, and budding masculine sexuality.

In a typical scenario involving *oral-level traumata*, a man as a boy was criticized and punished for being excessively demanding when he was simply asking that his legitimate needs for love and attention be met. His parents treated his natural, native childhood neediness as a weakness and called him a sissy for showing his feelings, as if he was signaling a vulnerability that was strictly feminine.

In the realm of the latter-day sequelae of persistent oral-level traumata, many men who were thus traumatized as boys go through life in a state of self-induced deprivation meant to ensure that they will maintain their relationships, which they believe they can only do if they don't ask for too much. Such boys forevermore hide in the shadows of painful personal renunciation to avoid feeling the worse pain of overwhelming deprivation and loss. As men such boys tend to get depressed because they have become overly passive, accepting, and self-denying adults out of a fear that complaining and standing up for themselves is counterproductive since it will certainly lead to the rupture of relationships they need and want. When I was in psychoanalysis, I wanted a nighttime job to pay for my analyst's fee so that my parents didn't have to put out money they really didn't have for my psychiatric care. So I pushed hard to get a spot on a rotation working nights at a hospital covering the inpatient psychiatric service. Perhaps I pushed a bit too hard, or perhaps I was just a threat to others who wanted to keep all the paid time for themselves. In any event, the doctors already on the rotation chastised me for being much too pushy and aggressive. Then I got depressed because I was having a "here we go again" reaction since I was reminded, rightly or wrongly, of earlier times when my parents first deprived me of something I was legitimately entitled to, then put me down as spoiled when I complained, rebelled, and decided to go after it whole-heartedly anyway.

Many such boys were prematurely forced to renounce their dependency on their parents, in particular on their mothers, because "it is good for you to do so." Some of these boys as men go through life as lonely individuals who think that it is wrong for them to ache for closeness and right for them to view splendid isolation as the default position and manly norm. Such boys, having been encouraged to prematurely renounce close maternal bonds to not become a "mamma's boy," tend to develop the habit of depriving themselves of close committed relationships, only to then get depressed because their relational detachment leaves them without affection and desperate for love, resentful that they don't have or cannot get it, and feeling that others are rejecting them out of hate, although they have been the ones doing the rejecting of others out of fear.

In a typical scenario involving *anal-level traumata,* a man as a boy was punished by being straitjacketed for being normally rebellious at the first sign that his nascent masculine independence was developing and fully flowering. His parents warned him in essence that no one could tolerate him unless he completely disavowed his manly aspirations, strength, and independence. He was ultimately misdiagnosed with Attention Deficit Hyperactivity Disorder just for acting like a normally active boy, then in effect controlled, reprimanded and punished by his doctors, with the complicity and consent of his parents, by being over-medicated with Ritalin.

In the realm of the latter-day sequelae of persistent anal-level traumata, many men who were thus traumatized when they were boys go on to become men who equate growing up with being put down. These men do what they are told by those who want to put them down. Only they regret it later as they come to feel sorry that they did not stand up to the people who tried to regiment them. Predictably they get depressed because they yielded to people who acted like they were their boss when they were in fact their equals or even their underlings. They often take this yielding to the extreme and feel that even appropriate suggestions are inappropriate commands. They then come to feel depressed because everyone they know pushes them around or throttles them. They also often paradoxically respond to the *absence* of control by getting depressed. They feel needy and empty since they feel that everyone leaves them floundering because, as they see it, no one wants to guide them, which to them means that no one is out there today to remind them of how pleasant it was at home yesterday, under their parents' controlling—yet still warm and protective—thumb.

In a typical scenario involving *phallic-level traumata,* a man as a boy was chastised for being competitive with other boys and his father and for his emerging sexuality. His parents, and the rest of his family, did so both with veiled and with overt threats of emasculation. In a typical instance, his little sister told their mother that she and her brother showed each other "theirs." The mother punished the boy but not the girl, telling him that if he kept that up his "thing" would fall off.

In the realm of the latter-day sequelae of phallic-level traumata, many men who were traumatized this way when they were boys as adults come to feel lonely and depressed because they connect their sexuality with painful, frightening punishment, as if they will be beaten for even thinking of taking pleasure in the warmth and love of another person and her or his body. The boy who was punished for showing his sister "his" vowed that he would never do anything like that again, only to go on to become an adult who rarely sought sex—and when he did was barely able to enjoy it. However, in other similar cases parents are innocent as charged of traumatizing the boy over matters relating to his budding sexuality. They punish him for something else, which he then perceives to be a punishment for his sexuality, and carries that misperception through to his adult life. A man who as a boy was severely beaten with a horsewhip for leaving home for a few hours to play "doctor" with a neighboring girl became an asexual adult who spent day after depressing day scrupulously confessing sexual fantasies that wouldn't go away to priest after priest in the (vain) hope that he could find one or more priests who would *not* forgive him, but would instead damn him to the hell where he felt he legitimately belonged.

In conclusion, early oral-, anal-, and phallic-level developmental traumata tend to persist and affect the developing adult male. Traumatic memories resurface when current events bring back old stuck-in-the-craw traumatic experiences and the man gets depressed because he feels totally rejected, controlled, or criticized for being assertively demanding, excessively independent, or for his normal, and entirely acceptable, sexuality.

As a general rule, men traumatized as boys tend to develop a depression with prominent *masochistic* features. Rather than express their needs, they suffer in silence. They punish themselves and they make certain that others will also punish them for being too demanding, competitive, or overly sexually preoccupied. They do this by repeating the scenario of early traumatic abuse with a series of adult abusers. As Real puts it, they form "pathological attachments to those who abuse and neglect them, attachments that they will strive to maintain even at the sacrifice of their own welfare, their own reality, or their lives [having imprinted on] abusing objects,"[1] a practice that even "supersede[s] self-preservation."[2] They seek out and tolerate those who abuse them in an attempt to master their early traumatic experiences through repetition, something they do in the hope that this time things will turn out better and their abusers will come around and treat them more kindly. These attempts to seek a reversal of fortune in situations where it is quite unlikely to occur—simply because they seek it from the very people who are most like their early abusers—can only prolong and fix their inner sense of badness.

An example involves a nurse I work with whom I tolerate and keep going back to in the hope that she will be nice to me. I once told her, "I am allergic to everything, including my allergy pills." To this she replied, "What you are is such a mess." Then turning to a colleague I was with, she said, "And I feel sorry for you, having to put up with him 9–5 day after day."

A RESPONSE TO PROBLEM PARENTS

The Depressed Parent

A boy with depressed parents is often a long-term victim of the parents' depressive fallout. They blame him for their woes, as in, "If it weren't for your school expenses we could have afforded to go on vacation," and they do it so persuasively and continuously that he feels he deserves it and goes on to blame himself as well. They rage at him and he assumes that he merited it so he rages at himself, sending himself the same hostile messages his parents sent to him. He also models himself directly on his parents and thinks and behaves toward himself just like they do toward him, a practice that intensifies his self-abusive attitude toward and negative guilt-laden view of himself.

This said, many parents are not the bad people that their sons, retrospectively through the lens of a current depression, perceive them to have been. All boys view their parents as ogres. It is part of growing up and becoming independent to want and have to "get outta there." But it is those men who later go on to get depressed who are especially prone to resolutely and selectively focusing on and remembering only the bad things about parents who were also good.

The Difficult, Unfair Parent

Many parents criticize their boys more than they criticize their girls. Possibly that is both because boys can be more difficult to handle than girls and because many parents think that brothers can take it better than sisters. Particularly severe emotional problems occurred in my male patients' families who preferred a girl to a boy. A father liked his five girls better than his one and only son, for the girls were passive and did not sass or compete with him. The girls got all the attention and all the loot, leaving the boy to nurture himself—only to figuratively, and at times literally, starve to death. As an adult, this boy, like many boys with similar backgrounds, would first expect little from others and from life, only to get depressed over not having and never getting anything at all—anywhere or from anybody. Some of these boys develop a protective acceptance of and insensitivity to being overlooked and ignored. But others, like this patient, never give up on their unrequited longings for a little attention, some affection, and their portion of the spoils, and instead get depressed because they constantly bewail the absence of such things.

Just recently I consulted on the case of a man who was a neglected boy like this. He got depressed when, for his fiftieth birthday, his (wealthy) parents sent him a card and gave him fifty dollars, saying he was getting one dollar for each year of his life. When he asked them right out, "Why such a cheap gift?" they told him, "Son, we are broke.

We have a ninety thousand dollar debt to pay—on the house for which we just spent a half a million dollars—to buy it for your sister."

This sister was a sickly child who had visual problems that required many corrective operations. So the parents gave her most of their attention and spent all their money on her—not only on her medical expenses but also on generous gifts meant to help her get through her sad little childhood. In contrast, the boy got little attention and affection. As a result he became a virtual toady throughout life out of the fear that if he spoke up at all, especially to complain, parental figures like his boss would tell him that his services were no longer required, then fire him without even giving him a chance to explain himself or apologize. For this man any expression of negative feelings threatened his self-preservative instincts. He finally became so demoralized that he gave up and retreated from a world where he would always have to re-experience feeling shunned and neglected over and over again by everybody's constantly turning away from him, and onto someone else they seemed to prefer over him.

In other, even more unfortunate, cases, such boys become men who do not retreat but go on to batter others, especially their wives, the way they felt, and perhaps actually were, battered by their parents. Not surprisingly here the battering starts when they feel a wife, or someone else of importance to them, has overlooked, rejected, or abandoned them in favor of another person. One such man called his wife names like slut and whore and hit her repeatedly for her most innocent of actions. Once he even beat her rather unmercifully—for, as they were walking down the street, she merely glanced in passing at an attractive man strolling by.

In conclusion, almost all of the depressed men I treated claimed they had a difficult early childhood. It was not always clear to what extent they only saw it that way as they looked back on their early years from the perspective of their current depression and its tendency to distort the past the same way it distorts the present.

Chapter 10

Social Causation

Society induces depression in men through its stereotypical tenets of what men ought to be if they want to be considered to be real men. Men who do not comply with the following four debatable but nonetheless widespread depressogenic social postulates tend to feel defective and as a result get depressed over their supposed inadequacies:

1. *Anger is a male thing—and you are not a man unless you feel irritable, act angry, and even become violent.* Society calls men who are not irritable, angry, or violent names like "wimp," "wuss," or "faggot"—in effect telling them that unless they act testy they don't have testicles. Society calls angry women "castrative bitches." Society calls angry men "heroes."

2. *Toughness is a male thing—and you are not a man unless you are tough enough to deny your emotions.* Not surprisingly, many men minimize the significance of their emotions and what triggers them to appear strong and intact, as distinct from vulnerable and sissified. Men who express their feelings condemn themselves after the fact for being crybabies—the same way society condemns them for being soft simply because they do not match up to the ideal of the Spartan soldier and other strong men of legend who can endure all misery without flinching or weeping.

3. *Distancing is a male thing—and if you pretend to closeness and commitment you are a sissy.* Society condemns as "mammas' boys" those men it perceives to have deep relational needs and expectations and who shun remoteness in favor of seeking interpersonal closeness and commitment.

4. *Being ambitious professionally is a male thing—and you are not a man unless you are out there clawing your way to the top over mounds of the dead bodies of the competition.* Many men cannot be happy on a good job because they condemn themselves for not having a better one and for not having gone as far as they could possibly go up the corporate ladder. Unfortunately,

society places men in a double bind in this arena. It encourages them to push hard to succeed, as in "The rule of show business is: when someone is down, kick them." Then it cuts them down afterward for having trampled on others to get ahead. It thrusts them into performing competitively, and then it knocks them for being cutthroats. It encourages them to go out and create only to expose them to unmanageable professional jealousy and serious critical abuse, or, completely turning away, simply doesn't pay them a living wage. Society has a one-two punch for men: it eggs them on, so that it can cut them down.

This said, society, doing a balancing act, simultaneously *protects* its men from getting depressed. Fewer men than women develop a mood disorder in part because society offers men the protection from depression it doesn't offer women, leaving the woman in the position of having to fight harder than the man if she is going to survive in this, "a man's world," without getting seriously depressed.

Society respects men more than it respects women and devalues men less than it devalues women. A "man thing" is a good thing. Rarely do we hear of a "woman thing," good or bad. Commonly we hear of "masculine" but rarely of "feminine pride." Society tends to view a woman as a lesser man—as just one of his ribs. (This is a double-edged sword, for ironically one so-called positive effect of this double standard is that women don't suffer as much as men from "social castration anxiety." For in a very unfortunate sense, many women have come to accept their social inferiority, and so might be said to have no further reason for concern, and thus no longer any reason to get depressed about their supposedly "one-down" status.) Society expects women to envy men, and to get depressed from a surfeit of "penis envy." For some extremists in our society having a penis is the grand default position, and not having one properly a source of anguish. Some women seriously buy into that postulate. Women who mistakenly do that tend to put themselves at great risk for developing a serious depression.

Society tends to go much easier on the man's than on the woman's sexuality. Men who are hyperactive sexually are called Casanovas. Women who are hyperactive sexually are called sluts.

Society protects men from loss by encouraging them to become independent individuals who go through life more solo than attached. Society encourages men to leave the house, and allows them out, but it tells women that their place is in the home. Men rarely feel resentfully unfulfilled because they have to be the ones who run the house and have to stay home and take care of the children while the women go to work. They don't birth babies they don't want, generally don't find they have to put up with a partner's affairs because they feel too old and tired to care or leave, and aren't always the ones who are assigned the task of taking care of aging parents. They feel justified in protesting when their wives attempt to shift home-based burdens and responsibilities onto them—because they feel good about leaving home to go to work—protective, like a knight of old, not submissive, like a slave of yore. They feel that they are not tied to child rearing but living their lives to the fullest—by going out into the world.

Getting out and going solo can help men avert a depression through activity. A man can handle marital difficulties by plunging himself into his work, or even by having an affair—and he can do that without all the socially induced guilt that many married women might feel. A man's acceptable independence also protects him from the grief reactions many women seem prone to develop. Many women have fewer opportunities than men to replace what they lose. Many men have a number of options to avoid losses or to make up for any they might incur.

Society also demands that a man not get depressed. Society makes it clear that it considers depression to be a feminine malady, not one suitable for men. Wryly, society says, "If you must have an emotional problem, at least become a psychopath." Men, especially those who already show a tendency to get depressed, tend to comply, for they recognize that they will get no sympathy if they allow themselves to become sad and blue or, even worse, admit it openly. In a round-about way that helps protect them from actually getting depressed.

Society does not reinforce a man's depressed state. Society openly encourages men to fight their depression gloriously while subtly encouraging women to yield to their depression ignominiously.

In conclusion, society helps decide who will and will not get depressed in the first place and in the second place who will get overtly depressed and who will instead hide it and express it indirectly and in an atypical way. If men fall silent about their depression it is because they are told to keep it in. If men repress their emotions and don't cry even when they feel like weeping, it is because society tells them that dry eyes are macho. Society has its stereotypes, fortunate and unfortunate, about who and what men and women should be and how they should act. Men and women buy into these stereotypes and follow them blindly. Men follow them out of depression; women follow them into it.

Chapter 11

Cognitive Causation

Cognitive therapists do not emphasize the process of uncovering the past to explain and resolve symptoms in the present. Rather they mostly seek to explain present symptoms strictly in the here and now. They do not deny that there is a continuity between past and present. They simply focus on another continuity: the one between irrational (dereistic) thinking and its inherently illogical and often negative formulations and the development of a psychological disorder like depression. Thus cognitive therapy of depression in men consists of revealing how men process information erroneously so that these men can begin to challenge the illogical formulations that create the low self-esteem and pessimism that characterize their depressive mindset.

Some specific cognitive errors that create blue mood (and therefore need correcting through cognitive therapy) are discussed in the following sections.

Polar thinking. Men who think in a polar way tend to see everything in a positive *or* in a negative light, absent shades of gray. They evaluate life, and themselves, in an all-or-none fashion so that they come to either love or, more likely, to hate themselves fully and completely. In *absolutistic dichotomous thinking,* a type of polar thinking, the man gets depressed after seeing himself as entirely imperfect simply because he sees himself as not "all perfect," or sees a world that is not completely perfect not as imperfect but as completely bleak, and therefore believes life to be not at all worth living. One patient got depressed thinking, "I am not any good because I am not all good." Either he had a great job or was fully unemployed. Of course, his was a seriously rigid and inflexible definition of "great job" and "unemployment." For this man, a writer, the only great job was a "real" job that involved going to the office, having set hours, receiving a fixed salary and benefits, and doing simple, concrete, action-oriented, immediately satisfying, goal-directed, money-making things such as "churning the copier." As he saw it, the job he had as a writer was not a job at all because it involved his staying home, working odd hours, freelancing, and wallowing in matters that were abstract (philosophical) instead of concrete, eminently practical things that were geared to bring in a steady income and provide him with a cushy retirement plan.

Making cause into effect (figure-ground distortions or "the tail wagging the dog" thinking). Depressed men tend to blame themselves (as cause) in situations where their actions were provoked (as effect). For example, a man thought, "I'm depressed because I'm not working," when in fact he was not working because he was depressed. He thought himself incompetent because he was having difficulty working on a project, when in fact his project was so difficult that nobody, however competent, could have ever hoped to complete it.

Symbolization. Men who symbolize tend to attach excessive meaning to neutral events and hence extreme importance to circumstances that others view as merely part of life's give and take. Thus for one man a damaged car symbolized mortality, such as the transience of all things, and human perfidy, such as the carelessness of whoever did the damage. Men who overdo "It's not the thing itself; it's the principle of the thing" are especially prone to getting depressed, because they are especially likely to view mere abstractions as the real thing.

Magnification (a common response to which is "Spare yourself the dramatics") is a typical consequence of symbolization. The man draws conclusions based on scant but highly symbolic reality, creates a completely new negative reality, then blows the importance of this new reality up way out of proportion, having taken this "neoreality" too far and too seriously. As a result, he creates a depressive catastrophic reaction out of a minor occurrence so that it is as if every day becomes the day he is going to fail his final exam. Now anxiety and depression are simultaneously his forte, his constant companion, and his ultimate undoing.

Symbolization and magnification are often at the core of depressive manipulation of others—where the man almost consciously "cries the blues" over very little to gain sympathy and to get others to do his bidding. Some men turn their depressive disorder itself into a manipulative tool, as when a man uses the learned helplessness characteristic of some depressions as a way to spare himself effort, and leave the hard work up to others.

Overelaboration of a specific negative detail. Here the man gets depressed when he focuses on a single negative detail, or multiple negative details, thereby excluding the positive aspects of a totality.

For example, my neighbor complained to me that his life was being *completely* ruined by all the junk mail he had to plow through, and by the increased traffic on his street and the unavailability of easy parking spaces due to his neighborhood having become gentrified. He also complained about the patrons of the outdoor tables of the restaurant downstairs who threw cigarette butts all over the sidewalk and placed their chairs in front of his door blocking his exit and forcing him to ask them to move. He forgot not only that the gentrification had enlivened the street life, made his street safer, and caused his property values to soar, but also that it would have been easier to overlook the detritus of city life and just say "excuse me" than to make a federal case out of someone temporarily blocking his entryway.

In overgeneralization, a phenomenon related to overelaboration, the man creates a global-level formulation out of a provincial-level occurrence, then develops a depressive catastrophic response to what are merely the annoyances or reverses of everyday life. This overgeneralization is the soul of hypersensitivity and that hypersensitivity is the soul of the low self-esteem that can go on to become the core of the depressive mindset. In many such cases the depression that results tends to have a noticeably paranoid tinge.

In selective abstraction, a type of overelaboration, the man gets depressed due to a part-to-whole syllogism in which he justifies an overly critical view of himself by generalizing from those aspects of himself he does not admire while suppressing his more favorable aspects. A selective view becomes the whole picture and the baneful side of his life becomes its essence. A selective inattention to his positive aspects is typically accompanied by an equally selective inattention to other's negative sides. The man now begins to feel envious and even jealous of everyone—often to the extent that he begins to envy and be jealous of both a given individual and his or her opposite. For example, men with a tendency to get depressed can induce despair in themselves by at one and the same time envying teachers for their considerable time off and doctors who, admirably consumed by their profession, work constantly and without a break. They can envy all lawyers for being rich, though tied down, and all artists for being poor, but free. They can envy all government workers for being tenured, and all free-lancers for being mobile. They can envy all successful people for having wide exposure, and all unsuccessful people for maintaining their privacy. Their goal—on which their self-esteem too often entirely rests—is based on expecting the impossible from themselves: to be at both extremes of all continuums at once, and to be all things to all people, including themselves, at the same time.

Part=whole is another form of depressive thinking related to over-elaboration. Part=whole thinking men are driven perfectionists who become paralyzed miniaturists after focusing on single unimportant details, and instead of viewing the big picture (the whole) resolutely try to get the minutiae (the part) exactly right. Such men condemn themselves completely for minor infractions that would be unnoticeable or unimportant to others. Off-putting, isolating, paranoid anxiety can be the result when such men focus excessively on others' minute annoyances with, and nascent negativity toward, them. Now even a compliment can become a criticism, as when they read "You are doing really well" as a statement that their past behavior left something to be desired.

Personalization. Men get depressed when they take random or impersonal negative events as planned vendettas meant just for them. This self-oriented, narcissistic perspective leads them to develop a bleak view of the world due to the belief that all negative but neutral external events happen primarily with reference to them. For example, one man got depressed because he saw a billing error as reflecting the exasperation and ill will of particular persons within the billing companies, and the general layoff in which he lost his job as a personal attack by the boss—so that, as he saw it, he was not laid off, but fired.

Arbitrary inference. Many depressed men simply jump to their woeful conclusions without considering much or any evidence. "Murphy's Law," if something can go wrong it certainly will, is one such arbitrary, illusory formulation that turns statistical nonsense into illusory evidence—with a very depressing effect.

Similar things are the same thing. Men often become depressed after viewing constructive criticism as a destructive attack on and hence a castration of them; seeing their being active and manly as being unacceptably aggressive; viewing their quirky originality as disrespect toward and defiance of the establishment; and seeing their being alone even for a moment as being lonely for a lifetime. Many such men fail in life because they confound effort with accomplishment. For such men hard work too regularly becomes its own reward, as trying becomes succeeding, good intentions become significant accomplishments, and losing the battle becomes acceptable as long as they did what they consider to be their one and only job: fighting the good fight, and doing so bravely and well, whether or not they actually even came close to winning the encounter and garnering the prize.

Chapter 12

Interpersonal Causation

DEPRESSOGENESIS

Depression in men often originates in stressful interpersonal relationships that the man allows to continue without taking corrective action. In my experience, men are no less sensitive than women to the fallout from relational disputes and disruptions. But while many men accept and integrate big relational catastrophes, such as a divorce, they let little ones bother them a lot, such as their wife criticizing them over nothing or their mother overlooking one of their significant achievements. One of my patients got depressed because his wife didn't let him watch television in their vacation home, using as her reason that it was inappropriate to watch it in a country house. Then, as he put it, she made him even more depressed when she joked, "It's okay that we don't have a dishwasher in our mountain cabin—for after all, we do have you."

To some extent the man's character structure determines what exactly he will find interpersonally depressing. For example, dependent men thrive on positive feedback and feel stress when the feedback is anything less than one hundred percent favorable—something that does not necessarily bother independent men who don't care what other people think. Men who are dependent care about others' opinions and readily get depressed due to being vulnerable to feeling overlooked, ignored, and disdained. Such men are at risk of developing a major depression in situations where the negativity toward them is minor, constituting no more than the usual irritants of everyday life that all of us experience, have to live through, put up with, and find a way to cope with.

Of course, some men go beyond being hypersensitive to interpersonal stress to actively generate the stress they believe they respond to only passively. Some depressed men masochistically seek out abusive people, and others are perfectionists who demand the impossible and then feel blue because they find nothing they desire is just the way they want it.

This said, some individuals in our lives seem capable of creating depression in almost any man, even those men whose only meaningful characterological problems consist of being too good, patient, kind, and loving to people who do not deserve it. I felt blue when after I used an example from my personal life to clarify something a cousin was saying she responded with, "It's always all about you, isn't it." A neighbor caused me to get depressed by epitomizing my greatest interpersonal fear—that I would be rejected if I stood up for myself and put my foot down. This neighbor constantly complained to me about the sorry state of our apartment complex—to the point that I couldn't listen to one more word without feeling a griping pain in my stomach. One day this neighbor locked himself out on the roof (through no fault of his own, because the locks had been changed without his knowledge). He then called me on his cell phone asking me to open the door to the roof for him. I did open the door, only I merely stuck my head through the crack to say that since the door was now unlocked I was leaving. I got out of there fast because I was working and didn't have the time (or the desire) to hear the details of what had actually happened (and the usual griping about how badly run the building was). But as soon as I waved goodbye, my neighbor started screaming and cursing at me. Later he called the management to report me for being a sadist, for, as he put it, I came to the roof, opened the door a crack, just said "Hi," then chortled about his plight and once again locked the door leading from the roof, leaving him stuck out there. I stood up for myself by saying, as tactfully as possible, that I did not want to be cornered and have to listen to any of his complaints just now (or ever). But his response contained the elements of the things I feared the most: "no good deed that I do goes unpunished," "extending myself for another just risks my being abused for not extending myself enough," and "all that ever happens when I stand up for myself is that someone just shoots me down."

Here is an example drawn from an interaction I had with another neighbor, a depressingly nasty woman:

She: "They are putting that exhaust fan from the restaurant up on the roof of my condo. They aren't going to get away with it. It looks terrible, and it makes noise."

Me (trying to consensually validate her pain): "I know; it's awful; you are going to smell the food odors, too."

She: "What do you mean? I'm not going to smell anything; I just told you that they aren't going to get away with putting it there."

Me (trying to change the subject by referring to her recent return from vacation): "Well, anyway, welcome back."
She: "What do you mean by that? Are you accusing me of being stupid enough to actually want to return to a place like this?"

The examples to follow are of individuals who in my personal and
professional experience tended to be particularly depressogenic to
vulnerable, and sometimes even to relatively invulnerable, men.

Double Binders

Depression often occurs in the interpersonal context of "no matter
what I do it's wrong, and there is nothing I can do about that." Double
binders first issue contrary messages/orders that put men in a no-win
situation, and second issue a stricture to keep them there. The victim
feels that with escape impossible, depression is the only way out.

Four types of double bind are:

1. *Duty without protection from adverse consequences.* For example, a therapist
   has a duty to report a patient's dangerousness but is also given inadequate protection from the consequences of breaching patient confidence. A stricture is that therapists want to keep on working to help
   people, and have to keep on working to make a living.

2. *Assault with justified defense too costly or time consuming.* For example, an
   attorney started a vengeful frivolous lawsuit that a patient could win,
   but without coming out ahead overall. When this patient sold a house
   with a pool the buyer had him put money in escrow to assure the funds
   were there to pay for a new pool liner. After the closing the buyer
   demanded the full replacement value of the liner. In response, the
   patient offered him the liner's depreciated value. The buyer had a
   brother who was a lawyer willing to take the patient to court pro bono.
   The patient wanted to fight, but he thought better of it and decided to
   pay up after discovering how much it would cost to mount a defense.
   But the lawyer, full of resentment, wouldn't give up, and started looking
   for other reasons to give my patient a hard, and expensive, time for
   "causing me and my brother all that pain and suffering."

3. *Assault where self-defense is impossible or only inspires further assault.* For
   example, the woman who lived below me who kept insisting that my
   pipes were leaking down into her apartment—when the leak was coming not from my floor, but, as it turned out, and was obvious all along,
   from her ceiling—seriously upended my life for a few months by constantly calling the management and demanding that I let in one plumber
   after another to fix the problem, disrupting my schedule to repair a leak
   that was in fact not mine but hers. After months of this one day I was
   out on my little terrace watering a plant. Apparently a few drops of
   water leaked down onto her terrace below. She climbed the staircase to
   my terrace, and soon from behind I heard the distinctive wail of her

complaining voice passive-aggressively beseeching me to stop splashing her. In an exasperated tone, without, however, blowing up, I pointed out that I was trying to be as good a neighbor as possible, only it seemed that I never did anything right or good enough to please her. Apparently she took that as a serious verbal assault on her person, and as a result stopped talking to me completely. It was then that she started harassing me—by obviously giving me a wide berth when our paths crossed on the street—and even crossing the street to avoid me. I ultimately squelched my anger and instead stewed inside, but that left me feeling depleted and anergic. The stricture was that the only way to get out from under this unpleasantness would have been for me to move, something that I was in no position to do, or had any intention of doing.

Some of my depressed male patients complained that they responded particularly negatively to women who made it clear that they hated them, and all men; then, in self-defense, claimed their right to say so freely based on their right to free speech. Many complained to me about professional critics who dealt with their own low self-esteem by reducing the self-esteem of their victims—then, the stricture, countering complaints by stating that they had an inalienable right to speak freely (even if wrongly) in a free country with a free press. Several patients who wrote for a living complained to me that what they hated the most was being misquoted in circumstances where they couldn't defend themselves, especially in irresponsible negative reviews on the Web site Amazon.com (which double binds authors by publishing unwarranted tirades and rants and not accepting authors' replies in self-defense).

4. *Making constant unfulfillable demands in an unyielding fashion.* I know of a writer who is currently in agony because his agent wants him to revise a book proposal, but won't say how (because "you are the writer and I am only the agent"), and then complains that he keeps changing the good things and leaving in the bad. At a conference I gave someone asked me for advice on how to handle an emotional problem her father had. I respectfully begged off because I hadn't actually seen her father professionally. The woman then complained that I was not meeting my responsibility to her as a physician—and she complained so loudly that I yielded and offered her what I considered to be a harmless bit of advice just to give her something to do (and to get rid of her). She tried my suggestion, found that it didn't work, then wrote me a long e-mail saying that because I was responsible for hurting her father, she was considering hurting me by suing me.

Selfish Individuals

Seriously selfish, self-serving, narcissistic individuals ignore a man's legitimate needs in favor of pursuing their own illegitimate goals. Often such individuals burden the man with their own depression—a process especially bothersome to men who are themselves already on their way to becoming depressed. I asked a friend many times to call me after I stop working at about 3 o'clock. Yesterday she called me at 12:15 P.M. just to chat, said she was at the end of her rope about something minor, then complained that I didn't seem to be paying much attention to what she was saying. When I reminded her that I was working, she shot back, "But I have to call you when I remember to, otherwise I forget." The next day she called me at 8:45 in the morning to ask me a question—then reassured me that she didn't need my answer until after 3 o'clock.

Misguided Therapists

Misguided therapists make men more depressed when they blame them first for getting into their depression and then for not getting out of it. Some of my male patients who felt angry with and even had violent fantasies directed toward their wives tried to explain that their wives provoked some of this anger, only to have their therapists hold them one hundred percent responsible for their angry response, while holding the wife one hundred percent blameless, and considering their wives to be innocent victims. These men had therapists who viewed domestic violence as one of those rare difficult interpersonal situations that only takes one, not two, or if it does take two, saw any attempt to understand the man's violent fantasies as working against and undermining the need to just stop having them.

Ungrateful Patients

Some of my patients who were dentists got depressed because few of their patients thanked them for what they did for them. They complained, "They remember that I hurt them physically, but forget that I save their teeth." Many mental health workers find their patients' predominantly negative transference responses to them depressing. Some medical doctors get depressed when their patients ask too many questions, and ask them not because they want the answers but because they are challenging and trying to "one up" the doctor. Recently a dermatologist blew up when a patient merely called to demand that he give him real Benadryl, not a prescription for the generic kind, telling him, "You will take what I give you, or you will clear out of here and find another doctor." Then he confided in me: "It's so depressing to have every patient of mine so noncompliant."

Mothers-in-Law

According to legend men have more difficulty with their mothers-in-law than women have with their fathers-in-laws. In one typical scenario a mother-in-law of a patient resented him for marrying her daughter and taking her daughter away from her. So she set about to destroy the marriage. The patient could handle her, but he became depressed when his wife sided with her mother. He felt excluded and abandoned, then he felt angry, started coming home late from the office, and started having an affair at lunch.

Children

Sometimes a father's hyperactive, shiftless, thankless, and critical children cause him to get depressed. This said, many men cannot just accept a child's normal adolescent rebellion. They take it personally and blame themselves for being an inadequate father unable to stop the rebelliousness—even though, as they know, their son or daughter is just going through a stage of normal, healthy, rebellion, and they should not attempt to regiment him or her just because they feel put off by his or her flight into freedom and desire for liberation.

The following exchange between a father and his daughter, who left home and refused to see her parents ever again because they supposedly didn't approve of her marriage, illustrates how hurtful and depressing can be the serpent's tooth of a thankless child.

When my daughter's minister called me last night, he said she was "in a bad way" and he thought she needed family. She was pregnant, neither she nor her husband had jobs, and they both had to move in with the husband's family (the husband's father had been out of work and they had quite a few of their own to support). He said she was caught up in astronomical credit card debts. This is probably true because I get threatening phone calls all the time from creditors looking for her and they still have our address on their records.

So the minister gave us the number and we called. The first time she wouldn't take our call, then we called again and she took the call but was hostile, belligerent, and abusive—more toward me than toward my wife, but she made it clear she despised us both. The conversation went something like this:

S: We love you, Jean.

J: Don't give me that crap or your patronizing voice.

S: I've been sick with worry; are you all right? I want you to know you have a family here and whatever happened is past. We want to be part of your life and support you in whatever you do.

J: A little too late for that isn't it, you bastard. Maybe if you had said that a year ago I would have invited you to my wedding. And don't put that guilt trip on me of you being sick; it's not going to get me to come home.

S: I will always be your father and will always love you.

J: Your fathering days are over; I'm twenty-two in case you haven't noticed.

S: We'd all love to see you. And your husband is welcome too. Will you come for dinner?

J: No. I'm not taking any more crap from you and the old lady, and I don't feel like an inquisition.

S: We won't ask you anything. We just want to hug you and tell you
we love you.

J: Too late for that. No.

My self-esteem as you can see is nonexistent at this point. Failing as a
father is like nothing else, and clearly I failed. I keep thinking of what I
could have done differently or better. But I did the best I knew how and
loved all of my kids very much. I never dreamed I would end up one of
those fathers who are hated, but whatever her perception, to her it is real.
I couldn't sleep all night. I have this pain in my belly, and the pain of
knowing she has no intention of ever speaking to me again. She did speak
to her sister and told her she missed her very much. Her sister asked why
she hadn't called her because they used to be so close. She said it was
because of the "bastard and the bitch."

I don't know what this all means yet for me, but I only hope I can pull
out of this with a thicker skin.

The Politically Far Left and Far Right

Some of the more conservative members of society depress selected
targets by unfairly demonizing those helpless individuals who are innocent victims of fate and bad luck, saying that they simply brought their
own problems down on themselves. Others who are more liberal
depress selected targets by claiming they themselves have been victi-
mized passively when in fact they played an active, major role in their
own victimization.

Bad Bosses

Some men blame themselves for being burned out on the job, as if they
are at fault for allowing their jobs to get to them. But many men are not
so much burned out as burned. A bad job with a bad boss would depress
anyone. Many bosses become bad bosses when their emotional problems
create havoc with their employees' mental health. Some bosses are sadists
who enjoy inflicting pain on their employees, for example, by showing
favoritism. One boss let a friend off extra-hour duty that she assigned to
others, giving as her reason that her friend's husband didn't like his wife
being on call nights and weekends. Particularly depressing to most men
are bosses who are psychopaths—individuals who run their companies
strictly for personal gain and without regard for the well-being either of
the company or for those who work there.

Critics

Some of my male patients got depressed after their critics put them
down, or "plutoed" them, shattering their pride by not taking them and

their good works seriously. Francis Thorne, a successful contemporary American composer, once said in a speech given at the American Composers Orchestra concert on December 5, 1993, that he got depressed and completely withdrew from composing. He became a naval officer and composed nothing for almost twenty years because of what the composer Paul Hindemith, his teacher at Yale, said about, and did to, him. Whenever he brought a work to Hindemith, the composer would rip it up, then sit down at the piano with a red pencil and sometimes a blank page, and rewrite it, saying, "*This* is the way it should go." Then, at the end of each lesson, Hindemith would tell Thorne, "Yes, you should compose, but not professionally, only as a hobby."

Critics have a particularly devastating effect on those men who are sufficiently impressionable and field-dependent to buy into their negativity. They also devastate men who are so hypersensitive to anything even approaching negativity that they have difficulty distinguishing constructive from destructive criticism and professional supervision from personal criticism, and so see even constructive criticism and meant-to-be helpful supervision as demoralizing and rejecting. Particularly vulnerable are the men whose self-esteem is so low and whose masochism is so pervasive that they go back for more, trying to undo the hurt at the hands of others whom they already know will not change their minds, but will instead almost certainly traumatize them even further.

The following are some of the most depressogenic critical types I have run across. Each had personality difficulties, and so I classify them accordingly.

Paranoid critics criticize men, often vitriolically, for something to avoid blaming themselves for the same thing. They decrease their own guilt in direct proportion to how they increase the guilt of others and enhance their own low self-esteem by diminishing the self-esteem of their targets. They condemn men for flaws they themselves have but overlook, hold a man to loftier standards than the ones to which they hold themselves, and expect the man to do what they say even though that is not what they do. They willingly turn reality around to fit into their irrational blaming scheme of things. The wife of a patient of mine is always late for engagements. Her husband tries to get her to leave on time, but she always manages to be delayed by about an hour. Almost incredibly, along the lines of a formulaic paranoid "it's not me but you," she blames not herself for her unacceptable behavior but her husband for his irrational attitude. One day arriving for a luncheon at 1:30 P.M. when she was due at 12:30 P.M., she proceeded to chastise her husband for being a stupid man—because he left too early for every engagement. As she put it, in essence, "If it were up to you, you would leave at 10:30 A.M. just to be on time for a 12:30 P.M. appointment. What a ridiculous excuse for a man you are."

Many paranoid critics treat their own depression by provoking one in others—in effect putting others down to make themselves feel more up. They are like the woman who calls a man a caveman for expressing his sexual feelings to her simply to make herself feel better about her own guilt-ridden sexual feelings for him. Another example is the patient of mine who ran a soup kitchen in an upscale neighborhood. The neighbors didn't mind the many hungry homeless men lined up outside, but they did mind, and got depressed about, these men's postprandial behavior consisting of urinating on and sleeping in their doorways, and even breaking into and entering their houses. When a coalition of neighbors asked the man to hire guards to control the hordes, all he could do in response was to demonize others so that he himself could feel even less like a devil and even more like an angel—as he scoured them for being bad people who should share what they had instead of complaining about those in their midst who were needy. A patient could not forgive her husband for having an affair with a married woman—even though the affair occurred before they were married. She instead sadistically taunted him, constantly throwing his past behavior up in his face, leaving him depressed enough to have to take medication. She was criticizing him to avoid criticizing herself: for her desire to have homosexual intercourse with the woman with whom her husband had had the affair, and for her desire to cheat on him by having her own affair with one of her married male friends.

Hypomanic critics are motivated by the conviction that they are innately superior to their victims, who don't compare to them in any way. *Dependent* critics are motivated to obliterate their rivals in dependency so that they can be number one in others' affections. *Borderline* critics too readily feel disappointed in those they supposedly love dearly but abandon without warning, with very little provocation, and with much blaming—like the friend of a patient who refused to see him ever again because he had had dinner with a former friend of hers, someone with whom she had recently fought and had herself stopped seeing. *Avoidant* critics reject a man personally so as not to have to get close to him. *Passive-aggressive* critics get under skins and inflame wounds in a way that is subtle enough for them to later deny. They express their rage indirectly so that they can brutalize others then claim they did nothing to cause their victims to feel so attacked. For example, the board in the apartment building where a patient lived was having new windows installed. For years the building had used one company, Sky Windows, with great success. This time the building chose another company to do the job, with disastrous results. My patient, wanting to know what had happened, asked a member of the board, "Why didn't they use Sky Windows this time as well?" She replied that Sky said it was too small a job. He then replied that they did a very small job for him—just two windows—just a few months ago, so that something else must be going on to explain their refusal to do this job, which was a relatively big one. He wondered aloud what that could have been.

He had hoped for an explanation. Instead he got a veiled personal attack, in the form of a question. She replied, "You—here you go again. Why do you always have to make trouble?" He asked her if she was upset with him for some unfathomable reason. "Not at all," she replied. "I was simply asking you an innocent question."

Passive-aggressive critics like her know how to subtly foment guilt. They remind me of the woman who looking at my dog on a leash told me, "Let her free, you shouldn't own a dog, for no one creature should ever own another." Or they play the interactive game of "now I've gotcha" by giving a man enough rope by which to hang himself, such as by failing to provide him with the information he needs to respond the way they want him to and think he ought, so that they can later complain that he is acting inappropriately, and being thoroughly unresponsive. Some subtly encourage grief because they enjoy seeing men unhappy, and certainly no happier than they are, and no happier than the saddest person in the room. So they remind the grieving man of how much he has lost, how it can never be regained, and encourage him to mourn intensely, even deliberately attempting to add to his burdens by suggesting additional reasons to grieve, while also attempting to prolong his grief on moral grounds and simultaneously discouraging improvement on the same grounds. In the realm of the latter, we might hear, "How can you enjoy yourself so soon after your wife died?" or "How can you, twelve months after your husband died, even think of taking a pleasure cruise?"

Narcissistic critics, thinking mostly, or only, of themselves and not of others, give men a hard time for supposedly imposing heavy burdens on them. A patient gave the CEO of a gas company a hard time for trying to move its offices near his apartment: "Because that will ruin my neighborhood by bringing in riff raff trying to pay their bills directly to save on the postage." These critics are needy individuals who, however, never feeling succored enough, constantly criticize others for depriving them of something they long for. They become especially critical of you should you need *them*, at which time they show their true colors as self-preoccupied individuals who condemn others' needs and generally humiliate and hurt them by their lack of empathy for them—and for anyone but themselves.

Obsessive critics are rigid people who condemn those who do not willingly participate in their ritualistic behavior. One wife, a vegetarian, criticized her husband for touching her plate with a fork that once had had meat on it. These individuals ask for advice only to obsessively countermand all suggestions and come up with supposedly better alternatives of their own. They are also perfectionists who without letup focus on others' minor miscalculations or personal peccadilloes to the point that they become ritual harassers constantly harping on trivialities. They also passive-aggressively criticize others subtly and indirectly in the form of continuous worry, like the wife who constantly worried about her perfectly healthy husband's physical condition and criticized him for only going to the doctor yearly because "unless you go more often you might get sick, die, and leave me."

Histrionic critics are seriously competitive people who put men down in order to enhance their own self-esteem and status. They are castrative individuals out to lift themselves up by humiliating the man, depriving him of his manhood by deflating manly pride by invalidating it, besmirching a man's masculinity by failing to recognize his true worth and actual achievements. One patient flashed in order to handle a depression that began when his wife started regularly putting him down for being a wimp. Though he knew the women he flashed would be rattled, he hoped against hope that at least once things would turn out differently and he would get the admiration and praise he longed for from his wife, rather than the familiar call to the police he dreaded from strangers.

A friend, speaking of a patient's professional writing career, made it clear that she put down his life in comparison to hers for being one of excessive ease and relaxation. She described a typical writer's lot as follows: "You have it easy. I have it hard. When I retire I will do just what you do—take it easy and not have to work. I know you write but that's fun, not work, for you work at your own pace, and in your easy chair." She enhanced her sympathy for herself by invalidating the intense, often painful concentration involved in his work and the sometimes extraordinary distress associated with his having to meet impossible deadlines.

Histrionic critics are particularly prone to strike when they cannot be dominant. They even long to be dominant in situations that call for cooperation, such as where the issue of inequality is not being tested. They particularly go for the kill in zero-sum triangular relationships in which there is only one prize, and either they take it and you are defeated, or you take it and they are the ones to lose.

Psychopathic critics depress men for self-serving purposes. For example, they put them down to avoid paying a fee to a therapist, paying a restaurant bill, or giving a tip to a waiter. Or they do it to seek self-promotion—like the critic who hiding beneath the skirts of a pseudonym savaged one of my books in order to make his competing book look better.

As will be discussed further in Chapter 18 on self-help, the therapeutic implication is that men who are victims of criticism can help themselves heal by recognizing that their critics have their own agendas, and criticize them out of the font of their personal problems that often have very little to do with the targets of their criticism. Depressed men should recognize that the competitive histrionic boss who knocks his workers to enhance his self-image or the manipulative psychopathic co-worker who deliberately criticizes a colleague to lower his self-esteem to get ahead of him at the office is not offering valid criticism, to be taken to heart, but is instead behaving in a validatably neurotic fashion, to be taken with a grain of salt.

✳✳✳✳

CLINICAL DIFFERENCES BETWEEN MEN AND WOMEN

Raeleen Mautner, a psychologist and author, commenting on the above case of the child who hurt her father, spoke as follows: I think there is a fundamental difference between how a mother handles certain family rifts and how a father handles them. A husband for instance may get extremely depressed about it, but is much more willing to move on, and refuses to blame himself. A woman on the other hand keeps ruminating over what she might have done better or differently when raising her child. In so many cases a mother questions whether she should have just kept her mouth shut and not said certain things, for example. Instead of giving advice she should have said, "Just do what you want and we will support you in it"—especially when she has a sensitive child prone to seeing advice from a parent (who just wants her child to succeed) as a command to do this or that. In contrast a husband will often defend his parental actions as "just the right thing." A father will think, "That's her problem," but a mother will keep thinking, "I don't really care whether what I did was 'right' or not, if the bottom line is that my daughter blew up, cut us off, and is lost forever."

Chapter 13

Stress

Sometimes a depressive episode occurs without an obvious precipitant—that is, it appears *endogenously*. At other times a depressive episode seems to be the product of ongoing stressful circumstances or the response to a distinct identifiable stressor, that is, it occurs *exogenously*. The distinct identifiable stressor may be severe in actuality or objectively mild and only subjectively severe. When severe enough, objectively or subjectively, we call the stress traumatic, and the stressor a trauma.

In men it is especially difficult to differentiate endogenous from exogenous depression because men believe that confessing to being traumatized means confessing to being weak and soft. Also men tend to respond even more to traumata that are symbolic than they do to traumata that are "real," so that they respond as much to trauma to their egos as they do to trauma to their bodies. As a result, as Real suggests, "the most obvious injuries are not necessarily the ones that do the most harm."[1] For as Real goes on to say, in men a "relatively delicate injury [can often do the most harm with] males ... appear[ing] if anything [to be] even more sensitive than females to injury or deprivation."[2] Men often respond as much to traumas of omission (that often go unnoticed), such as mother's failure to validate her son, as they do to traumas of commission (that certainly register), such as mother beating her son with a horsewhip or a father dying when the boy is only a few years old. Many men can handle the big but not the little negative events in their lives. For them what is generally considered to be big stress, like a death, can produce little depression, but what is generally considered to be small stress, such as a lost wallet or a broken cell phone making all their stored phone numbers inaccessible, can produce a major depressive response. I have seen a number of men who tolerated well the death of a parent but got significantly depressed after the death of a pet.

To a great extent a man's individual philosophy, personality, and circumstances determine the impact a given stressor will have on him. For example, a divorce is intolerable for men whose dependency leads them to read a sense of finality into it, but tolerable or even welcome for the independent man who reads his wife's departure as a newly opening door to a better life. The departure of a wife who is both a companion and a dictator elicits mixed feelings, softening the blow of despair with a countervailing sense of relief.

It is particularly difficult to evaluate the response to stress/trauma when that response is delayed. Recently I spoke to a man whose mother died twelve years ago from Alzheimer's. He is just today—now that he is getting older and becoming more needy himself—beginning to feel the impact of her loss and starting to integrate it. Previously he recognized the loss intellectually, but only now is he emerging from denying its serious import and feeling its full impact emotionally.

An important caveat is that trauma that at first appears to be passively experienced may in fact have been actively created. Depressed men, and particularly depressed men with a masochistic bent, tend to inflict one trauma after another on themselves. They readily assume the victim position and go down. Then they find someone to kick them: to give them the pleasure in pain they have come to expect and even begun to long for.

Losses can be severely threatening traumatic life events in themselves or take on the most significance due to the guilt that can appear in response to the loss. Fenichel along classical psychoanalytic lines suggests that losses are generally followed by "identification with the [lost] person."[3] However, if "the relationship of the mourner to the lost object was an extremely ambivalent one ... the incorporation [or identification] not only represents an attempt to preserve the loved object but also an attempt to destroy the hated object. If a hostile significance of this kind is in the foreground, the introjection will create new guilt feelings."[4] I have treated a number of men who after a loss resurrect the ambivalently loved or actually hated lost object inside virtually so that they can continue to beat up on it for various real or imagined misdeeds and failings. Then they feel guilty about all the hatred in their hearts. These guilt feelings turn them into their own worst enemies, and all the self-blame changes their sadness into depression, so that the man not only loses someone, he also loses his positive sense of self.

Men who view a loss as abandonment and the abandonment as a rejection are also quite likely to respond to a loss less with sadness than with depression. In such cases the resulting depression often has posttraumatic features where the man tortures himself over how he erred and experiences recurrent nightmares which constitute flashbacks to the loss—only here the flashbacks occur not when the man is awake but when he is asleep. One of my patient's wives said she divorced him because he was abusive to her when in fact her divorcing him was essentially unprovoked and mainly consisted of *her* being abusive to *him* and ultimately rejecting and abandoning him. After she left he began to have recurrent depressive dreams of feeling lonely and being abandoned. He dreamt that he could not find anyone to have lunch with. In the dream he kept trying to call up former friends who rejected him in the past. However, he was unable to get their number from the phone book or from information, or if he got their number he would call them up but get no answer because nobody was at home or the phone had been disconnected. This man had a large supportive family and a new girlfriend who adored him. Nevertheless, he became extremely depressed because he blamed himself for his divorce. As he put it, "There is hell to pay for bad people like me who hurt innocent people like my wife. No one will continue to supply me and I will starve to death, and no one will want me and I will never find anyone to have sex with again."

As noted throughout, depressed men have a tendency to create their own losses. So often guilt over being successful propels them to leave a partner or situation and seek a new one, only to discover, as they could have anticipated, that the new one has few or no advantages over the old one.

In conclusion, I believe that many cases of depression in men can be profitably viewed as a form of *Posttraumatic Stress Disorder*. The two disorders are closely related conceptually and clinically. In both, anxiety is a feature as well as a misguided and usually futile attempt at mastery consisting of preoccupation with and even flashbacks to the original traumatic occurrence. These flashbacks are consciously frighteningly unwelcome, yet unconsciously "purposively" installed, and reinstalled, as part of a well-intended but ultimately futile plan for healing that smacks, in the most unfavorable cases, of being part of an ill-conceived plan to punish oneself.

If we look at the implications for treatment and the specific therapeutic method used, we note that many physicians feel that it is appropriate to give medication with or without psychotherapy for an endogenous depression, while they recommend psychotherapy alone for a depression that is exogenous. I believe that when a man's depression contains a significant component of posttraumatic stress/anxiety, benzodiazepines, although not ordinarily considered to be a cornerstone of the treatment of depression, may be a helpful therapeutic adjunct.

The nature of the traumatic life events will often dictate the specific therapeutic approach. For example, a man who gets depressed after the death of a significant other might require and respond to grief counseling, while a man who gets depressed because his wife has just left him might primarily require intensive insight-oriented therapy meant to determine why exactly his wife went away—and if in any way his personality problems drove her to leave him. Hopefully if the man remarries, his next wife will not leave him for similar reasons.

✳ ✳ ✳ ✳

CLINICAL DIFFERENCES BETWEEN MEN AND WOMEN

Women and men respond very differently to *early* stress. Many women who were traumatized as children tend to go through life repeating their traumatic experiences with new people. In particular they select abusive men to flagellate them in much the same way that they were emotionally beaten up when they were children. They also find reasons to feel that they deserve to be beaten up emotionally, and come up with a number of rationalizations such as, "I was a bad child and here's how." They often blame and criticize themselves in lieu of blaming and criticizing their parents, something they want to avoid so that they can continue to love them and in turn be loved by them. In contrast many men tend to respond to early childhood traumata by fighting back. Many men, instead of abjectly retreating, or repeatedly traumatizing themselves and allowing others to traumatize them, instead identify with their aggressors, become aggressors, and become angry violent men who avoid being traumatized themselves—by instead traumatizing others.

Chapter 14

Personality and Men's Depression

There are at least five ways in which a man's depression and his personality, personality problems, or personality disorder can be interrelated.

1. *A man's personality problems can predispose him to feeling depressed.* Some personality problems tend to foster a depressive mindset. For example, excessive perfectionism can create the pervasive depressive feeling that "I have never lived up to, and can never live up to, my self-expectations." Problems with avoidance can lead to a fear of relating to other people that can in turn lead to a depressing state of isolation.

    Men with different personality types and personality problems tend to develop clinically distinct depressions. For example, histrionic men talk more about their depression than do men who are schizoid. While the histrionic man often cries out of sadness, the obsessional man, as one of my patients put it, is more likely to "cry wolf out of anxiety."

2. *A man's depression can give rise to his personality problems and personality disordered behavior.* Depression often leads to a withholding of intimacy that can become the first step on the way to developing a comorbid *Avoidant Personality Disorder*. Or depression can be manifest as restitutive psychopathic acting out as the man, no longer able to tolerate all the self-deprivation, throws caution to the winds and instead lives care- and guilt-free—with little concern for others, and so ultimately equally little basic concern for himself.

3. *A man's personality disorder can defend against his depression.* Obsessive brooding about how all *may be* lost can ward off the depressive conviction that all in fact *has been* lost. The magical wish-fulfilling thinking characteristic of many histrionic men can ward off depression by reassuring the man that he is in full control of, not being completely controlled by, his environment.

4. *A man's depression can defend against his personality disorder.* Feeling down can paralyze a man enough to keep him from acting out psychopathically in a way that he will later regret.

5. *A man's depression and personality disorder can coexist and present simultaneously or cycle one with the other.* Both depression and personality disorders can represent alternative ways of expressing similar or the same inner psychic turmoil. For example, anxious men can handle their anxiety with both depressive despair and interpersonal avoidance, while guilty men can handle their guilt with both depressive self-punitive tendencies accompanied by self-condemnation and painful obsessive worry that amounts to a form of self-torture.

I have divided the main personality styles/disorders associated with depression in men into five basic types. Few men fit these types exactly. There is a great deal of overlap between the different personality styles/disorders. In my experience mixed personalities/personality problems are the norm.

TYPE I: EMOTIVE

Histrionic

Histrionic Personality Disorder can predispose a man to depression via the histrionic propensity to catastrophize so he responds to routine minor events as if they were major disasters. Some people pejoratively call histrionic depressed men "drama queens" based on their tendency to make sad plays out of playlets and steep, unconquerable mountains out of molehills. Often these men come to feel negatively about themselves and life after intensifying every emotion, thinking in hyperboles, and valuing symbols to the point that they exaggerate the importance of minor setbacks and overreact to trivial interpersonal occurrences, such as rejections, that have very little true meaning or significant import. They are like my histrionic depressed patient who would become anxious and depressed when his wife was a few minutes late coming home from work and didn't call to tell him that she would be delayed. This man would cry, pace, moan, feel abandoned, and develop distorted cognitions along the lines of "Finally, just as I expected, all is completely lost. She died in an automobile accident and I will be alone for the rest of my life." For him, even a bad haircut was symbolic of castration. He reminded me of myself as an adolescent, and like most adolescents, somewhat histrionic. I went to the barber for a crew cut, hoping it would make me look more masculine and so help me fit in with the gang. The barber, alas, cut off too much hair, almost down to the skin. As a result I felt defective, and was depressed for a week thinking I was disfigured both now and permanently, resulting in the gang never accepting me as one of them—because I was no longer a real man and therefore not qualified to belong to their really macho group.

Histrionic men have characteristic developmental problems that predispose them to getting depressed by making them unable to find true love, sometimes for the whole of a long, sad, lonely life. Some such men have an *erotic mother fixation*. In one possible outcome they develop an isolating dependency on their mothers that leads them to avoid intimacy with others because they feel that outside relationships take them too far away from home—as one man revealingly put it, "I am too attached to my family to ever be able to marry someone who is a stranger." In another possible outcome, they can form relationships with women but only distant ones with older women who represent mother figures. But they then go on to reject these women as wrong for them, doing so for two seemingly disparate reasons: first, they feel these women don't match up to their real mothers, which disappoints them, and second, they feel these women are too close for comfort to their real mothers, which, because it raises the specter of incest, frightens them. Such men often protect themselves from becoming overly intimate by forming compromised relationships with women—relationships that predictably go nowhere, such as one night stands with pickups in singles bars or anonymous acquaintanceships with devalued women, like prostitutes.

For some histrionic men the mother fixation is less *erotic* than *traumatic*. Such men go through life attempting to undo their mother's disdain for them both as a person and as a man. In these men the process of forming adult relationships is truncated because it is restricted to resolutely overcoming a woman's neutrality or hostility. Unfortunately the women they choose predictably give such men not the acceptance they long for but the rejection they fear. This is not surprising, because in seeking a bad mother to remake into a good one they doom themselves—for by looking for a woman just like their own mother they predictably select a woman who is going to reject them just as their own mother did. They then become progressively more frantic to find love and to be loved, only to attach themselves to even more women who don't love them back. Instead of accepting them as a whole, satisfying person, and an acceptable and desirable lover, they depress them by treating them like big nobodies, and demoralize them further by treating them like complete nonentities.

Some histrionic men have more of a *father* than a *mother* fixation. These men compulsively form triangular "oedipal" relationships with women to live out their rivalry with their fathers (and siblings) for their mother's exclusive attention. Such men's relationships are truncated because they are really looking less for a loving woman than they are looking to best all rivals for a woman's love. So they focus not on love but on triumph—the triumph that comes not from getting the woman they want but from emerging on top after vanquishing those suitors who are keeping them from making that woman their own, alone. These men predictably get depressed because, as Cochran and Rabinowitz note, "of [the] narcissistic injury [that predictably is the result of the] activation of envy and rivalry.[1]"

Speaking clinically, histrionic men are especially prone to the more dramatic forms of depressive somatization. These men build depressive bodily complaints (conversion symptoms) from fantasies that traverse the mysterious leap from the mind to the body to become physical sensations and symptoms. These often have a characteristic depressive woe-is-me quality to them. The man feels as if he is doomed, as in, "I just know I have cancer throughout my whole body, and I am certain that I am about to die."

Narcissistic

The narcissistic mindset acts as a fiery cauldron for generating depression. Men with this mindset famously have an inordinate sense of self-pride coupled with an equally inordinate amount of self-concern, leading to self-indulgence. Together these trends constitute what the layperson charitably calls *egocentricity*—or uncharitably might call selfish, demanding, self-preoccupied, self-centered, ungratifiable, and malcontented behavior, marked by very little or no empathy or altruism and even less humanity. Men with this problem personalize events and view them in a highly self-referential light, to the point that they become overly sensitive individuals whose feelings are easily hurt. They also expect or demand too much from others, to the point that they are left vulnerable to easy disappointment and demoralization at the hands of almost everybody. Too, their self-esteem is overly dependent on getting a full measure of care and concern from almost everyone. Therefore, their self-esteem predictably droops when their demands for desirable positive feedback and necessary supplies are not immediately met. Paradoxically, it also droops because they misinterpret the intent of those who do actually give them what they want. They see these others' actions in a negative light along paranoid lines, such as seeing a giver as condescending, so they view the gift as demeaning. For example, a boss gave a man a raise and told him he did so because he deserved it. In response the man said, in effect, "You are diminishing me by giving me a raise, because I just know this is your roundabout way of telling me that I need the money, and a sneaky way of telling me that I am, and your treating me like, a charity case."

I divide narcissistic men (along psychodynamic lines) into oral, anal, and phallic narcissists.

Oral narcissists are those men who were either undergratified as boys and so go through adult life trying to make up for everything they lacked as children, or who were overly gratified as boys and so as grown men become what I call *Pollyanna Depressives*. In the latter group are the men whose primary problem as adults is that they always expect to be as completely fulfilled as they once were as children, and hence respond catastrophically to minor, which they predictably come to view as major, deprivations. They expect that things will always go well for them, and that all tragic events will bypass them. They find themselves surprised, shocked, and disappointed when circumstances, as inevitably happens in our lives, turn against them. As workers they become hypersensitive to criticism and respond to a boss who assigns them a menial task by thinking that they are menial people. They also tend to confound constructive with destructive criticism, and come to feel that any suggestion about how they might do better amounts to a tongue lashing for their having done something completely wrong.

Anal narcissists are those men who always feel that they ought and deserve to be in control of every situation and everybody. They view anything less than full control and dominance on their parts as a complete loss of control and painful abject submission to others. Some of these men were physically abused as boys. Now as adults they respond to anything that smacks of the loss of complete mastery over their environment as if once again they are boys being beaten. At work these men, unable to separate their work from themselves, their professional from their personal ego, typically become depressed after confounding being appropriately supervised with being unnecessarily and rigidly straitjacketed, and see all legitimate requests their bosses make of them as part of a plot on the part of the higher-ups to regiment them completely and quash them thoroughly.

Phallic narcissists are intensely competitive men who devote their lives to being "numero uno" and standing out from all the rest. As a result, they become easily disappointed when they discover, as they invariably do, that they are only one face in the crowd; that they compete with many others for the finite amount of rewards available in this world; and that they clash with other people who also feel entitled to get something for themselves—and especially with psychopaths who deal with the fear that they can never have all they want by stealing anything that they can get. Such competitive narcissistic men feel that it always has to be all about them, become angry when others show any inclination to want to share their spotlight, and get depressed when they feel that others have, even in some minor way, hogged the stage that they have become convinced belongs only to them.

Phallic narcissism can seriously disrupt personal relationships, leaving the man without deep, meaningful, sustaining attachments. For so often such men routinely ignore people who are good for, and hang out with people who are bad for, them, as they align themselves solely with flatterers who prop up their self-esteem, as if that were the only thing that could possibly make them feel like a force in the world. In contrast, they feel little attraction to simple, virtuous people—who may not idealize them aloud, but who love them quietly.

Generally speaking, the self-indulgent quality of narcissistic men is characterized by an infatuation with themselves readily carried over to become an infatuation with their depression. They come to view their depression as an admirable gift and a valuable asset to be retained as one that enhances, rather than interferes with, their overall functionality, and often more specifically, with their creativity.

In a bi-directional way, *Narcissistic Personality Disorder* can defend against depression. Men often install excessive narcissistic self-love as a way to cope with feeling unacceptable, as a way to deny self-loathing, and as a way to improve their self-esteem by thinking and acting as if they are better than everyone else. They also devalue others to avoid being devalued by them, getting there first with criticism and rejection of others to thwart or reduce the impact of others' criticism or rejection of them.

Borderline

The intense, unstable interpersonal relationships characteristic of *Borderline Personality Disorder* often predispose men to depression. Borderline men have an extensive need for, coupled with a paradoxical fear of, closeness, commitment, and intimacy. They characteristically shift between dependent merging and independent distancing. When in the merger phase they feel somewhat high as they feel pleasantly submerged into the oneness of boundary dissolution. But they also feel somewhat depressed because they feel controlled and engulfed, as if they have lost their independence and identity, and because in overvaluing others they come to feel that they are by definition devaluing themselves. Also, when in the emerging, distancing phase they feel depressed, but now because they believe that they have completely lost their moorings, have nobody, and will never find anyone again—and they react in this fashion even though they were more likely the ones to do the abandoning than they were the ones who were themselves abandoned.

A borderline patient who had a history of unsettling women by merging and emerging with them finally got the following insightfully revealing comeuppance letter from a girlfriend breaking off their relationship:

> You came all the way to New York to tell me you were coming because you finally saw the light and wanted to make plans to live together. After several days went by without your mentioning these "plans" I asked you

what they were, and you said that as a result of my question you felt so attacked by me that you couldn't say a word more about it. And you didn't, except to say on the last day before you left that had you not felt attacked you would really have sat and planned something with me. Yes, that is when I lost it. I felt duped and began crying like an asshole desperado, and even threw a bag of store-bought biscotti at you for not even caring that I was crying over the fact that you had lied. I know it became a Neapolitan scene right in the Big Apple. But it's you who make me feel incredibly stupid and quite the caricature of the woman who clings to the man screaming/pleading. Okay, but then you get home and have an epiphany, write me poetry and say you are now feeling depressed without me and "looking into ways to make it happen?" I don't think I can take this anymore. My psychiatrist was right when he fell off his chair laughing at this dynamic, and told me I needed to think again about someone like you who spends all his time thinking twice about me.

In a bi-directional way, a man's depression can give rise to his borderline personality problems/disorder, that is, it can be as much the *reason for* as the *consequence of* borderline personality features/disorder. In a typical scenario, depressed men feel desperately lonely and isolated to the point that they seek relief in a full merger, only to feel that they must break free of what turns out to be unacceptable closeness, only to then rue what turns out to be an equally unacceptable, and poignantly depressing, distancing.

TYPE II: ANGRY AND GUILTY

Sadomasochistic

A close relationship exists between depression and *sadomasochism*. In part this is because both are alternative ways of expressing the same psychic turmoil; that is, both can be, and often are, created out of the basic emotions of *anger* and *guilt*. Both depressed and sadomasochistic men struggle with *angry* and even *violent* feelings.

I get the impression that on average depressed men tend to be angrier than men who are not depressed. Some take their angry/violent feelings and fantasies out on themselves by creating their own suffering in the form of lowered self-esteem, suicidal fantasies, or suicidal behavior. Others take their angry/violent feelings and fantasies out on the world, causing others to suffer, doing so either passive-aggressively or openly in the form of verbal temper tantrums or physical abuse of others. Many do both, such as the man who blew up his own house to get back at his wife for winning the home in a divorce settlement—injuring her emotionally, injuring passers-by emotionally and physically, and hurting himself in the process.

Angry depressed men desire to create misery in others. They want to spread the pain around, so they attempt to dominate, control, and castrate others. They might do this to have company in their misery, so that they punish others in a way that resembles how they themselves feel dominated, controlled, and castrated. Or they might wish to elevate a flagging self-esteem or to repair a damaged masculine self-image by being the tyrant instead of the tyrannized, and the castrator instead of the castrated. A man appealed to all his friends to tell him what to do to feel less depressed—precisely so that he could reject all their suggestions as unhelpful and inadequate. As he once admitted to me during a therapeutic hour, "My impossible depression is a way to be as angry with others, and make others as angry with me, as I feel angry with myself."

As a practical matter, all depressed men should be examined for violence to themselves and others, and all men who are violent to themselves and others should be examined for depression.

Both depressed and sadomasochistic men are also struggling with extreme *guilt*. Many depressed men are primarily *masochistic*, and both their depression and their masochism arise out of an excess of guilt. Guilty depressed/masochistic men constantly blame, disparage, and apologize for themselves, zealously self-flagellate and self-abnegate, and routinely seek out and accept self-punishment and punishment from others. They punish themselves and accept punishment from others for a number of *psychological reasons*, doing so in a number of manifest *psychological ways.*

The following are some of the *psychological reasons* depressed men punish themselves and accept punishment from others.

- They want to bring about suffering actively to hurt themselves at a time, in a place, and in a way that they feel they have under their complete control. That way they feel in charge and prepared, and can avoid being unpleasantly surprised by being unexpectedly hurt.

- They cannot tolerate experiencing pleasure. They willingly postpone pleasure in life now for some future reward, exchanging the dull present for the bright future, hoping that the bright future will never come, which is the main reason they agree to the exchange. The few indulgences they permit themselves are of the simplest and most modest kind, or those they can somehow link to suffering—their way to see to it that nothing comes easily in life, and that they instead have to struggle for everything they get.

- They believe all their legitimate needs to be excessive or inappropriate, and feel compelled to forgo them.

- They believe that getting something for themselves means hurting others, along the lines of each time the "bad I" is gratified, someone else, someone truly good, dies. They feel remorse, regret, pangs of morality, and guilt over surviving because they believe that in outlasting they have vanquished, and in vanquishing, they have murdered the competition.

- They fear success and relieve success-anxiety through renunciation of joy and achievement. Men who fear success willingly seek out and settle for second best, or make some other form of self-destructive compromise and stick with that. They lower or arrange to not reach their goals and then rationalize their self-limiting actions in a number of ways. They rationalize settling for any mate, not selecting the best they could find, as "just being practical." They rationalize a decision to stay in a bad marriage as a good thing because "the familiar is better than the unknown devil"; or, "I am actually trying to reduce my suffering by avoiding that difficult interim period between partners, which I know by experience to be very painful." They rationalize as appropriate their desire to stick too close to their family to the detriment of outside relationships by convincing themselves that they do so to assure an inheritance. As does the writer who tears up all his opening salvos because they are not completely original, or the project person who sets up a successful restaurant then loses interest in it and lets it fail, they convince themselves that they are not seeking failure but just avoiding stagnation. Those who gamble their life savings away often rationalize their actions by covering up their self-punitive with a self-protective motive, fooling themselves into thinking that they are just trying to get out of a hole, when in fact they are really just trying to dig themselves into one.

- They need the moral reassurance that their guilty desires have not gone, and will not go, unpunished. Truly believing that pain is conducive or even essential to physical and moral superiority, they develop a depressive asceticism consisting of a "to do is to die" Spartan ideology where discomfort is not merely an inescapable fact of life but a glorified and heroic builder of character, with beneficial punishment the equivalent of the ancient's "laudable pus"—the one and only indication that true emotional satisfaction is being obtained, and that actual emotional healing is taking place.

- They feel it is only right for them to buy into society's guilt-inducing, self-punitive-enhancing prohibitions calling for renunciations. In a bidirectional way they allow guilt that is already in place to lead them to selectively buy into the social prohibitions that they want and need to hear. They pay the most attention to those who criticize them for self-fulfilling and being good to themselves. Some become scrupulously religious individuals who go beyond simple honest faith to become fanatically and selectively preoccupied with their religion's harshest and severest tenets. Others listen hardest to those in their society who tell them to become a failure because it is wrong to be too successful, as if there is a zero-sum accounting in this world where others' success necessarily means their demise. Many listen to those in their society who tell them that winning competitively involves destroying or killing off the competition. Nonmasochists move away from, but masochists stick with the impossibly strict tenets of the punitive society into which they were born or otherwise find themselves. For masochists, doing so does not mean that they are throwing their lives away; it means that they are living to the fullest.

Here are some of the *psychological ways* that their self-punitive nature manifests itself.

- In low self-esteem that takes the form of a self-vote of no confidence lived out as minimal self-expectations and a feeling of lack of entitlement, as if one's reasonable needs are excessive, and available and appropriate gratification should therefore not be sought.

- In self-destructive behavior that takes such a form as failing to defend oneself personally, and even politically, for example by denying the existence of social danger such as the reality of an impending flu epidemic or the possibility of becoming a victim of terrorism.

- In self-deprivation taking the form of extreme self-sacrifice associated with empathy and altruism that is so excessive that it can but ultimately lead to a sense of personal depletion. Excessively altruistic men become too self-sacrificial, and hence too needy, not by preference, or by choice, or because they believe that true happiness can only be derived from inculcating the happiness of others, but because in spite of having legitimate needs which they recognize and acknowledge as such they refuse to ask for anything much for themselves, because "anything much" becomes "too much." Of course, they get depressed as they come to recognize that they have little or nothing at all in their lives. While the narcissistic man gets depressed because others don't give him what he wants and thinks he must have, the overly altruistic man gets depressed because after feeling that he has too much he gives it all away since he doesn't need and really shouldn't want anything—only to then feel unworthy because he has so little, and depressed because no one ever gives him anything back.

- In relational distancing as they drive others whom they need and love away, not, as with narcissists, by constantly going from one to the other seeking more and more attention and love and better and more worthy companions, but by brushing and pushing off, and driving away, potentially worthy companions based on the irrational belief that they do not deserve to have good friends and a close family—the familiar "I am leaving you not because I don't love you, but because I want to spare you what would otherwise be a lifetime of pain if I stayed."

- In self-sustaining viciously circular processes involving escalating guilt. Here guilt goads the man to actively accept and welcome his guilty feelings—then to act them out self-destructively, then to become even guiltier in retrospect about having acted stupidly, and so on.

- In accepting depression and its ravages as inevitable, then rationalizing the depressed state and so not doing anything about it. Such men remain passive in the face of their depression by convincing themselves that they are simply beset by misfortune and that fate has abandoned them permanently, and by rationalizing their failure as due not to their depression but to circumstances and bad luck that they cannot change. If such a man is depressed about having a bad job he convinces himself that that is a good thing, because the most painful jobs are the best jobs—for they are the ones that come with the most job security, or that benefit society the most.

- In enjoying their depression as if it is such sweet sorrow. Some men even have an addiction to depression, where depression becomes a singularly pleasurable way of adaptation—a friendly habitual thinking, feeling, and behaving mode not to be gotten rid of but to be clung to enjoyably, like one's best and last friend in a cruel, friendless world. For such men what seems to others to be inordinate self-deprivation and lack of self-indulgence becomes a preferred way of feeling and living, and indeed the source of some of life's greatest pleasures.

- In not getting or using treatment as their way to keep their illness and with it their depressive suffering. Men like this when in therapy often favor the masochistic triumph, where they say to themselves, and to others, including their therapists, "See, you can't help me, for try as you might I am destined to always be sick, and I am fated to always be depressed."

- In hurting themselves physically. They may slowly commit suicide by drinking to excess, taking harmful drugs, injuring themselves at sports or having purposeful auto accidents, or exposing themselves to severe illnesses—such as alcoholism or HIV. Or they may actually mutilate themselves physically. The depressed woman who slashes her wrists or cuts her body or develops a suicidal anorexia nervosa to self-punitively waste down to nothing has as her counterpart the depressed man who has a sex-change operation less to be true to his inner self (perhaps the more common motivation) and more to self-punitively mutilate his genitals precisely in order to devalue what he already has, is, and does.

- In relating mainly or only to others who treat them shabbily. They find and form the closest relationships with society's major guilt-inducers. They deliberately seek out and try to enlist the approval of people who are negative to them, trying hardest to get those who openly disparage them to change their minds, come around, and think otherwise—the typical masochistic mission to convince one's worst enemies to become one's best friends. Such men actively take on those challenges, such as romantic challenges, that are the most difficult to impossible to meet. Typically they deliberately look for love in all the wrong places, and are lonely because they refuse to compromise in their choice of whom they love, along the lines of, "For me *only* the *very best* will do." They also passively accept without protest what victimization comes (or they can bring) their way, because it offers them satisfaction to know that they are in fact being brutalized in exactly the way they feel they deserve to be.

- In developing "writer's cramp" where instead of getting openly depressed they deliberately work below par, or do some specific mechanical damage to themselves. They become like the pianist who manages to damage his anatomy, as according to legend did Robert Schumann—who was later to develop symptoms that might have signaled the presence of a deep psychotic depression. Schumann, according to this legend, invented a device to strengthen his fourth fingers that actually did the opposite and damaged them to the extent that he could never become a concert pianist. A pianist patient of mine accidentally on purpose lost some of the function of his left hand because he tensed when he should have been relaxing it, and a carpenter patient of mine accidentally on purpose cut off his thumb. A patient of mine sought and stuck with menial and otherwise unsuitable jobs and took every opportunity he could find to make self-destructive career moves. He would find decent work then self-destructively do his job badly by becoming unpleasantly competitive with his coworkers, to the point that they would ultimately retaliate by being the ones to put him down. When he, almost in spite of himself, was actually able to rise through the ranks to become the boss and CEO, he indulged in risky business ventures, taking unwise gambles in an attempt to artificially elevate a self-esteem that was in the first place needlessly and inappropriately lowered.

Many depressed men are less masochistic than *sadistic*, and both their depression and their sadism arise out of an excess of guilt. However, sadistic depressed men prefer punishing others over punishing themselves but they punish others in a way that involves ultimately punishing themselves considerably. For example, they might beat others over their heads with their own bloody bodies, as did the gambling man who after losing all his life savings at the tables spent years writing letters and giving speeches trying to make the individuals who operated the casinos feel guilty, hoping to show them how they ruined his life and shame them into looking at themselves, and realize the harm they were doing to him and to all of society. In like manner, a sadistic landlord seriously hurt himself in the wallet by selling a desirable property under disadvantageous circumstances. As he put it, "It hurt me more than it hurt my tenant, but it was worth it to punish her for being late with her rent three months running."

Passive-Aggressive

Passive aggression, like depression, is a possible clinical outcome of poorly modulated, badly integrated, inadequately handled, and indirectly discharged anger. Both have an underlying sadistic component to them. A depressed man discharged his angry impulses passive-aggressively by constantly lamenting his poor health, keeping his family in a perpetual state of alarm about the possibility that he might get sick or die and leave them personally and financially bereft. He also constantly lamented what he imagined to be his wife's delicate health, and made her go from doctor to doctor so that she did not die and leave him alone. This man was using his depression as a form of covert warfare—for him, depression was not merely anger turned inward but also anger turned outward—a way to say "I am angry with you" in the guise of saying, "I am so depressed about what might happen to you."

Paranoid

Both paranoia and depression arise out of the primeval turmoil of anger. *Paranoia*, like depression, often starts with an inappropriate, excessively negative response to a neutral or actually positive event in a suspicious, highly sensitive man who is attuned more to the hidden, personal, and negative than to the actual, impersonal, and positive meaning of events. Men like this tend to overreact to minor irritants, which they come to view as last straws. In addition to feeling slights that are not there they let actual but minor slights affect and offend them too deeply. Then they get depressed, or more depressed, because they become demoralized over feeling like mistreated innocent victims of assault at the hands of others who are remiss by being antagonistic players in the critical and unfair world in which they believe themselves stuck. They tend to distort well-meaning attempts to guide them into personal assaults on the part of their guides. They see an offer of help as infantilizing them, attempting to control them, or criticizing them for needing help in the first place. The last time I saw a friend who had been partially crippled by a leg injury he was recovering slowly and was using a cane. The next time I heard from him, in an e-mail, he told me that he was tired after walking three miles. I responded, I thought, quite helpfully, naturally, sensibly, and supportively, "Hey, three miles, that's great!" He replied, angrily, flaming me in caps that made his e-mail look like a prolonged shriek of anger at me and an expression of the pain he felt I caused him, "Hey you, back, you should have known that I wasn't bragging, I was complaining."

Both paranoid and depressed men tend to have very violent fantasies. They direct their violence both against themselves—in the form of low-ered self-esteem, suicidal fantasies, or suicidal behavior—and toward others. Some fantasies become complaints about others, such as, "You make me feel bad"; threats about what they are planning to do to others, such as "I intend to sue you for malpractice"; or actual violence toward people where verbal abusive outbursts in the form of temper tantrums go on to become physical abuse like slapping a partner around, shaking a crying baby, or killing someone—a stranger or family member.

However, some so-called *paranoid depressives* are not so much inher-ently paranoid as they are provoked by depressogenics who are mean and devious enough to make anyone feel angrily suspicious. This was likely happening to the boyfriend in the following vignette. A neighbor complained to me that her boyfriend frequently became angry with her for no reason and mistreated her both emotionally and physically. I felt pity for her for being stuck with a paranoid partner until one day she collared me to tell me that she was going dancing at a certain bar down the street, and if her boyfriend should ask me where she was to not tell him—because tonight at least she wanted to be free to go with all the men in the bar, and he was a jealous person who objected to her even looking at another man.

TYPE III: ANXIOUS
Paranoid

Both *paranoia* and depression arise not only from anger but also from the well of severe present and future anxiety. Depressives and paranoids alike share some of the same anxious fantasies: that the world is full of enemies; that all negative events refer to me and me alone and are planned, not accidental; that everyone picks on me and blames me for everything; that whenever I turn to someone for help or rescue no one seems to be there for me; and that disaster is predictable because any fool can see it coming, out there on the horizon.

Anxious Neurotic (Neuroticism)

Men who are depressed are often simultaneously highly *neurotic*: overtly anxious and phobic. It is but a short step from the worrisome anxious fear that something bad *might* happen to the painful depressive conviction that disguised catastrophes are in fact all around and about to land. As one patient put it, "when I feel depressed I also feel as if I am back in the nightmarish experience I felt when my dog was attacked by a pit bull—and though I yelled for help, and it was 2:00 o'clock in the afternoon and on a crowded street, absolutely no one came to assist her or me."

Depression often arises out of one or more of the following four specific anxieties:

1. *Separation or abandonment anxiety.* Anxiety is related to the potential or actual loss of someone loved and needed.
2. *Social anxiety.* This, involving shyness, is in some ways the direct opposite of separation anxiety, because social anxiety involves not a fear of distance but a fear of closeness and commitment.
3. *Control anxiety.* This involves a claustrophobic-like feeling that the person is no longer in charge of his life but is instead overwhelmed by outside forces that pin him down, such as people who boss him around, tell him exactly what to do (whether or not he wants to do it), subordinate him, regiment him, and trap him in a difficult or unpleasant situation from which he cannot escape.
4. *Success anxiety.* Success anxiety arises out of guilt over achievement, as the man panics over the possibility not of a loss but of a gain, that is, not over losing but over winning.

In a bi-directional way, depression can be viewed as a defense against neuroticism—a way to reduce anxiety by the conceit that there is no reason to fear anything at all because all is already lost anyway. Depression is also a way to handle shattering anxiety by becoming inured to it—a numbing learned helplessness or hopelessness installed to manage seemingly insoluble situational problems as well as forbidden impulses that are threatening to become conscious, take over, and catalyze the release of a flood of unbearable, intolerable emotion.

Obsessive

Both obsessionalism and depression arise from primal anxiety. *Obsessionalism* is anxious worry manifest in scrupulosity and ritualism. Depression is anxious worry controlled by abdicating to it.

Obsessives and depressives also share a number of symptoms. Both tend to be uncertain individuals unable to make up their minds and then problem solve by committing to a practical effective course of action. Both tend to become emotionally paralyzed due to an inability to get started, make decisions, move forward, act forcefully, and keep on keeping on, as they shift instead between alternative plans often of equal value without being able to synthesize, merge, and blend opposing tendencies into a meaningful whole. An obsessional depressed man is functionally paralyzed due to his inability to make up his mind between being and acting altruistic and being and acting selfish— between "should I be charitable to others" and "no, charity begins at home." He cannot decide whether to have fun now or later—to enjoy the present or save for the future, so that when spending money he thinks he should be saving it, and the other way around. He also has serious conflicts between the spiritual and mundane and the Spartan and the hedonistic, so that when renouncing pleasure he would think, "I should be having fun," and when having fun he would think, "I should be working." When it comes to his therapy he not surprisingly has a great deal of difficulty being compliant. Such a patient typically would make an appointment with me, then, worrying about what might come out of his mouth, not keep it; he would accept a prescription from me, worry about the side effects of the medication and then not fill it, or have it filled, and then not take it.

Also obsessionalism can *predispose* to depression. In typical fashion, depression is preceded and even precipitated by a surge of obsessive-compulsiveness characterized by constant worrying over matters of very little importance. In one case a man's depression started with the worry that bad things, however unlikely to happen, were in fact certain to occur—in particular an unexpected cancer diagnosis made after a visit to a doctor for a routine checkup. It also started with his brooding about things that were inherently of some significance but that most people could easily relegate to the background—that he was mortal and would die, that nothing he touched was certifiably hygienic, and that the rules of etiquette were often contradictory, making it impossible for him to know for certain how to behave in public, and especially how to avoid losing control and being impolite when he found himself in "polite company."

TYPE IV: WITHDRAWN
Avoidant

Avoidance often defends against depression as the man steps away from others in the belief that "If I don't get close and involved, then I won't get rejected." Many observers make the point that men with a wide circle of friends are protected from the depression that can develop out of loneliness. However, it is also true that wide connections can set the stage for troublesome interpersonal interactions that can lead to many painful depressing experiences, particularly rejections that can undo the benefits that having an extended family can at least theoretically confer.

Schizoid

Schizoid men install mechanisms defensively to render them insensitive to depressing negative interpersonal input, particularly rejection. Such men often also use depression itself as a defense as they harness their depression to avoid interpersonal interactions which they find distressing.

Passive-Dependent

Passive dependency is perhaps the one character trait that most readily predisposes to depression. Passive-dependent men easily become depressed when they do not feel completely and absolutely fulfilled and succored. Unfortunately, they rarely feel totally fulfilled, because for them fulfillment is predicated on others giving them *all* the supplies (gifts of love) they want and feel they need. Such men tend to be depression-free when in a stable long-term relationship where they feel they have fallen safely under the umbrella of perpetual care. However, the slightest indication of a partner's distancing makes them feel as if they have been deliberately and completely abandoned. They start to feel blue, think that they have lost everything, fear that they will be cast completely adrift, and anticipate that they will wind up alone. Next, instead of setting out to make any repairs that might be indicated, they feel that doing so will, given their precarious interpersonal state, only make matters worse; they become meek, submissive, and excessively self-abnegating—in a panic willingly accepting little so that they don't lose it all. Unfortunately, that doesn't help enough, for now they get depressed both because they recognize how little they have and how precarious their situation is, and because they condemn themselves for the complacency and compliance they themselves installed to sustain the little they believe they still have, and to protect all they fear they might lose.

Paradoxically, their underlying anxiety about being abandoned predisposes them to actually being abandoned when, as often happens, it leads them to become disloyal to established relationships. They are so desperate for any relationship and so easily feel slighted and rejected, that they constantly keep one eye open for a welcoming port in their anticipated storms—that is, a new and perhaps better relationship where they can be even more, and more safely, dependent. As such they ultimately come to treat vital relationships as interchangeable, for that very interchangeability reassures them that they can avert a depression, at least as long as their supply of substitutes—of which they keep many on hand just in case—does not run out. This is, of course, an ultimately self-defeating mechanism; it soon becomes apparent to those they depend on that they are being used. So these others leave, realizing the passive-dependent man's worst fears. Now he gets and stays depressed until he can hook up firmly with new relational substitutes. Unfortunately, his characteristic lack of enterprise and tendency to avoid engaging in anything taxing or potentially dangerous often make that difficult, thus predictably prolonging and making his depression even worse.

Passive dependency and depression are also alternative expressions of anxiety—especially anxiety about being active. Both depressed and passive-dependent men fear activity, as if that can but create intolerable stress. Both believe that nothing ventured, nothing lost. Though we often call such men lazy, in fact they are not so much lazy as they are fearfully inhibited. They remain in the shadows as the safest place they know, for they can hole up there, and avoid calling attention to themselves and how they are failures in life. Unfortunately, hiding from the world and becoming reluctant to engage in self-satisfying and self-fulfilling activities can intensify the typical depressive inability to experience pleasure in most, and sometimes in all, realms of life.

In a bi-directional way, passive dependency is also a symptom of depression, for depression gives rise to passive-dependent attitudes and behaviors. In a typical sequence a depressed husband goes to work but becomes a hermit at night and on weekends. When he gets home he feels too depleted to take his wife out for dinner or visit friends and family, and feels too depressed to do anything but sit at home watching TV or surfing the Internet. He mostly refuses to do anything around the house, but instead complains bitterly should his wife ask him to help her out. To quote one such patient exactly, "As I said to my son, 'With all those big football games going on it's depressing for me to have your mother constantly demanding that I get up from my comfortable lounge chair and help her put up her damnable shelves.'"

TYPE V: IMPULSIVE, UNPREDICTABLE, DANGEROUS
Psychopathic

Psychopathy can be a hypomanic-like defense against depression. The psychopathic man becomes the opposite of the depressed man as he comes to feel little or no guilt whatsoever. His oppressive sense of shame becomes shamelessness. Self-abnegation becomes pleasure-seeking behavior with little regard for consequences. Self-deprivation becomes exploitation of others. "I deserve nothing" becomes "I will get whatever I want, whatever I have to do to get it." The depressed man's passivity becomes the psychopath's full control—less subjugated than powerful, less on the bottom than on the top. Some teenage psycho-pathic wilding and violence is the adolescent's way to mug the world to avoid feeling mugged by it, and to feel less deprived by a world that seems to want to only take and to not give anything back. The material acquisitions arrived at through psychopathic behavior also serve as a symbolic prop to the depressed man's low self-esteem—as he acquires objects that compensate for and enable him to deny feeling impover-ished, allowing him to create a rosy out of a bleak present. Therefore, it is not so surprising after all that a depressed millionaire can heist a gewgaw from a Dollar Store to give himself a little gift, or a depressed poor man can gamble to excess just to get complimentary services from the casino—with both attempting to reverse the ravages of inner disap-proval by turning their negative self-view around with small and sym-bolic compensatory gifts and personal victories that, being snatched unlawfully, satisfy more than big and real gains, come by honestly.

Addicted

Observers generally recognize that *addiction* to alcohol and/or drugs (substance abuse) is a common *symptom,* that is, an outgrowth of, depression. Many men who "party hearty" are drinking and taking drugs in an attempt to adjust their mood, that is, to treat an underlying affective disorder. Men who overuse such painkillers as Oxycontin, and men who abuse such sedatives as benzodiazepines, are often doing something similar. Many of my veteran patients used painkillers to obscure the depression that was part of a severe and intractable Posttraumatic Stress Disorder characterized by wearisome, debilitating, constant flashbacks to battle scenes from World War II and Vietnam.

The depressed man longs to experience not only the satisfying phar-macotherapeutic effect of the addictive substance but also the direct (oral) satisfaction obtainable from the accoutrements of substance intake. He gets direct relief from the sucking, swallowing, and ingesting behaviors and restitutive relief from the almost personal relationship with the bottle or the dealer as "my friend in need." There are also real pleasures to be obtained from the social activities associated with drinking and taking drugs. Also he obtains enticing secondary gain by using his addiction to get others to care for him while relinquishing responsibility for himself, managing to gratify regressive tendencies without fully having to own up to so doing, and managing to satisfy his passive needs without feeling that he is weak, powerless, and sissified.

Depression-driven addiction is tenacious because self-treatment of depression with substances actually works to some extent as it effectively, if only temporarily and at great cost, substitutes rapture for pain. Depression-driven addiction is also tenacious because it is easily rationalized using such cultural arguments as, "I only drink to be with my buddies." Also other men and women accept and encourage the addiction as part of their own addictive morality and life-style such as for their own transcendental purposes—for example, because they like and want to keep their bar buddies. Of course, the therapeutic value of addiction pales beside its ultimately destructive properties. This is particularly true for alcoholism in depressed men, because alcohol releases both anger and love, that is, the alcoholic when high either hates completely or loves abjectly, only to become guilty about both responses so that his depression predictably gets worse, leading to even more self-destructive addictive behavior. Clearly in men who are both depressed and addicted, to become sober and avoid a relapse after a period of sobriety, it is necessary to identify and treat not only the addiction but also the underlying depression.

There are some men who may be pseudoaddicted—to sex, or junk food, or television, or exercise, or even to the use of cell phones. Pseudoaddictions like true addictions are often put into place to treat depression. This stereotypical male couch or mouse potato may be treating his interpersonal angst by becoming addicted to living a cushy hermetical life, or a gymnast addicted to constantly exercising may be training out there to avoid conflicts back home. In pseudoaddictions there at least at first appears to be an absence of primary physiological dependency. However, in a bi-directional way, the behavioral changes, and particularly those behavioral changes associated with depression, can ultimately bring about actual and meaningful secondary changes of a physiological nature, which can go on to create a kind of substance dependency of their own, such as the "endorphin high."

TREATMENT

Chapter 15

Psychotherapy

Part III, Treatment, is divided into several chapters. In this chapter I discuss ways to treat the depressed man psychotherapeutically. In Chapter 16, I discuss the treatment of atypical depression and hypomania. Chapter 17 focuses on errors therapists often make with depressed men—a discussion that is also applicable for a depressed man's family, friends, wives, and partners who hope to act in a therapeutic fashion with the depressed men in their lives. In Chapter 18, I discuss self-help methods for the depressed man to help manage and cope with his depression. Chapter 19 discusses a way for the targets of a man's depressive fallout to ease their pain, and cope. I then conclude in an appendix with a brief overview of some general principles of pharmacotherapy, one that does not, however, go into specific therapeutic protocols, for I consider those to be beyond the scope of this, a descriptive, basically psychodynamically oriented, text.

Depressed men can be very difficult to treat. Many respond most not to the helpful things that their therapists say and do but to the mistakes that their therapists unwittingly make. For example, a depressed patient of mine once said that now that he was approaching eighty years old he fatigued easily. He described how he could only do four hours of work a day without feeling tired. I, trying to be supportive and reassuring, said that in my opinion he was doing quite well for his age, only in response to hear, in essence, "You don't understand how much I am hurting. Like all my other therapists you are cruel, uncaring, and unsympathetic. And, anyway, what exactly do you mean by, 'For your age'? Is there anything wrong with my age?" Clearly treating such a depressed man requires that we exercise the utmost care in what we say and do to avoid being ensnared in his sometimes excessive and often almost paranoid sensitivity, thus offending his sensibilities and falling short of his expectations.

In this chapter I discuss some of the classical therapeutic modalities that can be helpful for treating men who are depressed. This discussion does not pretend to be inclusive. Instead it represents an overview of the most common methods therapists employ when treating men (and women) who are depressed.

SUPPORTIVE THERAPY/AFFIRMATION

Being Accepting

Just agreeing to see a man in therapy offers him a degree of acceptance that contrasts with the rejection to which he has likely by now become accustomed, if not inured. The therapist who accepts the depressed man into treatment is in effect giving him a sanctuary—a hideaway where he can at last get some respite from the turmoil of his inner life and the stresses of what are often some very difficult day-to-day problems and harsh everyday circumstances.

Calming

Real's belief that to treat a depressed man you must first "'get at' him [and] 'crack him open' ... bringing his depression up to the surface"[1] is the antithesis of the calming that is the goal of the supportive, affirmative approach. Real's approach can, in the hands of an inexperienced therapist, and used on a brittle patient, prove to be a dangerous psychic invasion if it abrades on the depressed man's considerable sensibilities and thereby runs the risk of re-creating rather than relieving his pain. As Bemporad says, it is often unwise to

> arouse ... strong affects and require ... a relative lessening of control over usual rational thought processes. Some individuals cannot tolerate these stresses and may respond with an exacerbation of illness. Bipolar patients, even when maintained on medication, may not be able to withstand the extremes of emotion engendered in the therapeutic process.... For such patients, modified therapy, in which defenses or resistances are left intact and transference is discouraged, may be beneficial.[2]

I have learned through sad experience that digging too hard and going too deep is only safe, if ever, in an inpatient setting where there is staff about in case the invasion enhances rather than reduces a depression or provokes rather than relieves suicidality.

Being Patient

Patience, always indicated with men who are depressed, is the cornerstone of effective supportive therapy. Though one episode of depression is often time-limited, many depressed men become demoralized bec they overlook how they can get better in a period of weeks or months a they spontaneously integrate and replace losses; learn to control controlling people; and ultimately and effectively defang those castrative people who are trying to cut them down to their size or make them even smaller. Therefore, a cornerstone of treatment consists of reassuring the man that the prognosis for a single episode of depression is good, so that excellent results can often be expected just from waiting it out.

It is especially important to be patient with men who have experienced a loss and are grieving. Supportive therapists treating grief understand that they must allow the griever time to recover. They do not demand that a grieving man get over his grief right now and replace his loss immediately. Instead they allow him all the time he needs to grieve at his own rate. He may want to wallow in someone old without replacing him or her immediately with someone new, as when he is prolonging his grief to avoid feeling disloyal to the person lost. This said, it is also unsupportive to take the harsh position that all depressed grievers must wait a year or two to replace a loss, and that if they seek to replace a loss immediately they are necessarily acting out by acting on the rebound.

Giving Advice

Supportive therapists can sometimes profitably offer the man a specific doable plan to help him relieve his ennui and jumpstart himself and his life. An example of such a plan might be: "Get out of the house and stop hibernating, because hiding out at home will not help you recover, but will instead more than likely make you worse. I say that not to tell you what you should do, but to help you release a bit of energy through activity, then harness that bit of initially released energy so that you can become even more active, so that you can release a little more energy, and so on."

Depressed men sometimes respond to commonsense advice which they were unable to give to themselves because they were too preoccupied with being depressed to think of it. Many depressed men need to be reminded of the benefits of developing a physically and emotionally healthy life-style, of the need to get a new and better job when the old one is lacking, or of the wisdom of starting a new relationship to relieve their loneliness. They may need reassurance that they are not too old at thirty to go to school to make a career change, if this is what they desire. Medical advice is often indicated and welcome, for example, "If you continue to take that sleep medication every night you may find it stops working well and that you are becoming addicted to it."

Advice always turns out to be ill-considered when the man asking for the advice is offering a one-sided presentation of a complex situation.

fficiently different, what works in the therapist's
to the patient's advantage. Often the best course of
...an to make his own decisions about what he wants
...ife, then offer to help him implement the decisions
...as made.

...ould recognize that many depressed men view giving
...fering. Advice angers many depressed men who bridle,
...ven quit therapy because they hate being told what to do.
This ... ...cially true for the independent man who prefers to make his own decisions and doesn't like someone interfering in what he considers to be his private world.

The following is a request for advice that I received from a gay man asking me what to do about relational problems he felt trapped in. I finessed this request because the information was incomplete, because I didn't actually see the individual asking for the advice in face-to-face therapy, and because there was no one right way to respond in this situation—as is true of many of the difficult situations depressed men find themselves in, and passively lay at, the therapist's door. If I were seeing this man in therapy I would ask him to determine where he wants to go with his relationship, then offer to help him realize those goals that are entirely his own.

> Hi, my name is Ronald. I was hoping that if you had a couple moments to look over this e-mail and then answer back, you could be a life saver, and would be my new hero! I am twenty years old; I came out the closet when I was eighteen. I'm not "flaming" as some put it, and still am not "out" to most I don't know well. I have been with my boyfriend for a little more than two and one-half years, and there have always been little troubles with us. He is thirty-eight now and I'm into older men, so that works out in that area.... But he is in the closet, none of his friends or family know, which most of the time is ok. We get along really great; I'm a little more emotional than he is, but other than that we are very much mannered the same and equal in temperament. We also mostly like the same activities, and enjoy doing them together. So here comes the problem.... I'm not one for a crazy amount of petting or any for that manner, but I am a very affectionate person, and find him very attractive. He takes good care of himself, I do too, but I have sort of let myself go a little the past year or so ... anyway I end up looking for a lot of hugs, kisses, and fondling when we are by ourselves. He doesn't like this too much and really just puts up with it for me, but with a dirty look, or a moan here and there ... Also, being twenty, I do like sex, and with him being very attractive doesn't help very much. He would be happy with once or twice a week, if that, and I even have to push for that most the time; when we do it, he has a tendency to get it over fairly quickly, and basically just wants to hit and run. I love Randy with all my heart. People I know always say dump him because of things like this, or "can you see yourself with him in ten years?" and to be honest, I think I can. He is truly the greatest man I have

ever met ... it's just that these little things that really shouldn't be that big of a deal, drive me nuts some times, and I will say that I get little spurts of depression here and there ... we talk about everything, so he knows where I stand, and I know where he stands. The thought of him dying or something similar and me not even being able to be part of the funeral, etc., I don't like that.... I really don't want to change Randy, I just want to either make it easier for him to deal with my affection, and/or for me to be able to deal with him being like that, and somehow be ok with it. I have looked to family and friends, Web sites, etc., but it always turns out with Randy being the bad guy, which it really isn't that way ... so I don't know what to do. To be honest I would rather be slightly depressed than not be with him and he won't do counseling. I haven't brought it up more than once or twice, but I'm lost on what to do or think! Any thoughts or suggestions would be of great help, I'm sure you are a busy man, and that you probably get a ton of e-mails like this, but if you have the time to answer this I would like it most definitely! Thanks a bunch!!! :)

If Ronald were my patient I would ask him to come up with his own design for living. Instead of giving him advice on how to live his life, and run his relationship, I would help him see the necessity of intervening on his own behalf. Then I would offer to support him in his quest to put his own personally chosen interventions into effect.

Reducing Guilt

The supportive therapist can encourage the depressed man to creatively pursue healthy relationships, professional activities, and interesting and rewarding hobbies not directly but indirectly through reducing his guilt and shame. Guilt and shame reduction have as their goal, as Real puts it, "bringing [the man] up from shame states."[3] There are at least five methods for doing so.

1. *Offering absolution.* The therapist offers absolution to, as Real puts it, help the man give up "penance ... and sentence[ing] himself...."[4] The specific absolution given should be based on a thorough understanding of the man's depressive psychodynamics as these reveal the source of his guilt. It should be directed to helping him become more forgiving of some of the things he actually did and feels he shouldn't have done, and to altering specific ongoing destructive personal and interpersonal behavioral patterns that cannot help but leave him feeling guilty after the fact.

2. *Countering specific unhelpful self-punitive cognitions.* The therapist challenges the specific self-critical punitive messages that come from the conscience. The therapist offers a professional assessment that stands in contrast to the depressed man's personal belief that he is a bad person who does not deserve to give himself a vote of confidence, or to get better.

3. *Modeling.* This involves using the therapist's thoughts about how he or she avoids and reduces guilt as examples.

4. *Reparenting.* As Real suggests, the therapist helps the depressed man "give to himself the functional parenting he never received."[5]

5. *Setting limits.* This is based on accepting the man as a person while at the same time discouraging specific thoughts and prohibiting specific behaviors that might actually be unacceptable and therefore rationally "worthy" of feeling some guilt.

Conversely, tactless, overly resolute probing; excessive correcting cognitively; or overly focused desensitizing behaviorally can increase rather than decrease guilt. It is very easy for depressed men to misread analytic interpretations as criticisms, cognitive corrections as knuckle-rapping, and behavioral interventions as controlling. The therapist who says, "You react this way because you perceive your wife to be your mother" may fail to recognize that in his or her attempt to impart insight he or she is also saying, "You are wrong-headed"—not necessarily something that the man who is already flagellating himself wants or needs to hear. That is why I believe that whenever possible interpretations should be softened with a qualification such as, "That doesn't mean that I think you are bad," or with reassurances such as, "That is just a part of you, but you are struggling against, not endorsing it."

Therapists can inadvertently enhance guilt even when merely giving advice. To avoid this, it helps to give advice from the positive side, not, "Here's what you did wrong," but instead, "Here's what to do to make things right." Giving advice is discussed further below.

Too often therapists enhance guilt by setting overly harsh and overly punitive behavioral limits via the issuing of warnings, strictures, and caveats. They might instead consider identifying what troublesome behaviors exist and gently asking the patient to first understand why these are there in preparation for seeking alternate ways of expressing discerned feelings and resolving uncovered conflicts.

Paradoxical Limit Setting

Some therapists attempt to set limits paradoxically via exaggerated equanimity, as when they respond to suicidal thoughts not by saying, "Please don't kill yourself," but by saying, "It's your life, so take it if you like, just leave me out of it." This can work in selected cases, and in hindsight appear to have been very effective, but it is a dangerous maneuver because the patient can make a suicide attempt to prove how serious he is about his threats, and how he is literally a man of his word.

In conclusion, men who are depressed tend to take anything that the therapist says that falls short of complete affirmation as severe and shattering deaffirmation. That is why true affirmation is, at least in the initial stages of therapy, one of the most helpful things that a therapist can do to tide the man over what can be, even in some of the severest cases of depression, a self-limited disorder. Actually being unaffirmative can lead the depressed man to rightly think not that he is getting help, but that he is being once again the victim of all the old accustomed put-downs, criticisms, and devaluations that have been his lot throughout his lifetime.

That does not mean that all supportive therapists ever do is hand-hold. The supportive therapist remains a technician meeting depression head on in a clear-eyed, understanding, knowledgeable way—sugar-coated, however, as much as possible, to avoid rubbing salt in the depressed man's already open, and very sore, wounds.

INSIGHT-ORIENTED PSYCHOTHERAPY

An Overview

Insight therapy can help the depressed man diminish the hold his past has over him in a way that leads to his feeling presently helpless, frustrated, demoralized, and bitter. Insight therapists often start by asking the depressed man to take a large share of the responsibility for his depression and to not blame it entirely either on the world and others in it, or on a chemical imbalance. They then work to help him understand his depression through and through in terms of its origins in the past and how the past affects the here and now, creating maladaptive, rigid, automatic, defensive attitudes and behaviors that lead to unhealthy thoughts and self-destructive actions.

Depressed men often get a measure of relief from learning that it is their inappropriately harsh *conscience* or *superego* that leads them to become divided against themselves and to become their own worst friends. They also get a measure of relief from identifying messages from their *ego-ideal* that need to be modified in the up direction—to become more inspiring; and/or in the down direction—to become less demanding. Depressed men often benefit from recognizing and understanding all about their troublesome anger and how to integrate and manage it with the goal of replacing id with ego so that they can civilize their psyche by reducing inner rage and dealing better with any of its leftovers. (Anger management is discussed further below.) Depressed men also can discover how to accept and integrate their own sexuality and permit themselves a reasonable amount of sexual gratification without hewing to unreasonable, hypermoral standards that ultimately lead to painful renunciations. In short, as the depressed man learns about himself, he learns to synthesize the disparate forces within into a consummately healthy whole, thus creating an inner harmony between his needs and his regrets, so that he can now fulfill his needs without allowing his regrets to poison his life, and completely destroy his happiness.

Psychodynamic understanding blends well with other approaches, especially ventilation and cognitive therapy. For example, the man who is depressed about being alone might profit from understanding the origins of the distortions of his loneliness that lead a little loneliness to become a lot because being alone for a minute brings him back to his boyhood when his mother left him alone in the crib with only a few toys and the radio on for company. He can simultaneously benefit from talking about how lonely he feels and getting that off his chest, *and* from understanding the cognitive errors that make his loneliness seem worse than it actually is, as when he comes to believe that his feeling lonely now necessarily means he will be lonely forever, and fails to recognize that while his loneliness is punishing, it is not his punishment.

Reducing Anxiety

Almost all of my depressed male patients suffered from what the literature calls a *Comorbid Anxiety Disorder*. But their anxiety was specific, not generalized—the product of losses whose meaning they distorted to make the losses into personal recriminations and rejections; of commitment fears; of a fear of being controlled by others to the point of being unable to control their own destiny; of a fear not only of failure but also of success; and of a fear of castration.

Overcoming a fear of commitment. Depressed men who are simultaneously avoidant feel anxious about relating closely to others. Theirs is a paralyzing fear of being submissive, engulfed, and abandoned. So often the dependent woman who has to be helped to become more independent has as her counterpart this independent man who has to be helped to become more dependent—to not fear and deny his dependency but to instead accept and adapt to it without thinking that it necessarily means that he is a wimp or acts like a wuss.

Overcoming a fear of success. Some men become depressed for realistic reasons, often because they cannot meet their goals. These men may have to learn to resign themselves to the disappointments in life that come to all men, no matter how manly, gifted, well-situated, and powerful they happen to be. They may need to tolerate being second tier as they understand and accept their limitations without viewing themselves as limited. But other men become depressed because they fear failure even though their worst nightmares about failure have yet to be realized and may never actually come true. A third group of depressed men are neither failures now nor fear failure in the future. They are potentially or actually successful men who fear not failure but success, and it is that fear that keeps them from meeting their goals in life. They cannot accept winning—because winning leaves them feeling vulnerable. Yet they have little choice but to at least try meeting their life's goals anxiety free and begin the journey on the road to achieving real world successes. To do this they need to work through their guilt about achieving to the point that they can actually accomplish something. Accomplishments help them win back their self-respect and earn the respect of others who can now come to hold them in higher regard. Respect from others inculcates further self-respect, and increasing self-respect almost always leads to decreasing depression.

Overcoming castration anxiety. I use the term *castration anxiety*, in a way that is more figurative than literal, to refer to how men get depressed when they feel that they have been deprived of, or have otherwise lost, a manhood consisting of power, glory, status, position, and supremacy. They may feel castrated by fate. But more likely they feel castrated by a wife who is henpecking them, by children who are taking them for granted or humiliating them, or by a boss who does not appreciate them or actually lacerates them. They believe that all concerned are diminishing their self-pride by invalidating their significant accomplishments—demoralizing them and leading them to lose their self-confidence by treating them like a "big nobody" and thus taking their "somebody-ness" away.

Here is an example of depression originating in castration anxiety arising in the setting of father-daughter conflicts. A man asked his daughter to hold off getting married until she finished college, only to have her become defiant, elope, and then refuse to speak to him at all. Then, to ice the cake, when he sought help from a radio talk show psychologist, the host castrated what was left of him for "driving his daughter away." As he said to me:

> Well, I am not exactly a national statistic, but I had a bad situation with the radio psychologist Happy Greenville, whose books I have and whose show I like listening to—until the other day when I called her to ask her opinion on whether to try and keep contacting my daughter or not. She tarred and feathered me for public consumption as she let me get only the first few words out and said this was all my fault because I probably bad-mouthed my daughter's love choice and now I got what I deserved. When I tried to explain the situation further, she hung up on me, telling me not to waste her time on national radio if I didn't want to fess up to what I had done to cause this situation. I went into such a depression I couldn't stop crying all day (you know how I am consumed with guilt anyway). I ought to sue her. But I guess that's entertainment.

The following is an example of castration anxiety induced by a ball-busting boss, as one of my patients called him.

> I was desperately trying to please my boss but to no avail. You'd think he would be happy that my work got a mention in one major magazine and had an article about it in another. But he just didn't even seem to care.

Instead he turned away when I tried to show him my work and continued to treat me in the same shabby manner he always does. I'm just too fearful of the future and too depressed to go on with this job, and I think I will quit on him before he hurts me even more.

Some men can best deal with their castration anxiety by looking within to see if they are feeling more vulnerable than they actually are, or are even doing something to create much of their own anxiety-inducing circumstances. Other men can best deal with their castration anxiety by avoiding those who castrate them—by getting a divorce or finding a new job with a better boss. Still others can benefit the most from taking steps to gain ascendancy over their current castrators rather than the other way around. One good way to do this involves using knowledge as power: understanding their castrator's motivation to see if it is irrationally neurotic and mainly transferential and therefore by definition basically impersonal.

I worked with a man for months to help him stand up for himself and express his legitimate concerns and needs instead of hiding in the shadows and yielding, resentfully and depressively, to others' dictates. We worked hard to get him to speak up at a town meeting—to say what was on his mind about his concerns over a used car lot being opened up right next to his house. When he spoke up to express his alarm about his quality of life and property values, a local councilman told him that he was just a complainer and thinking only of himself, not of the entrepreneur who wanted to start a legitimate business, or of the town's tax base and ratables. First, I made it clear that he had a right to express himself and to go after satisfying his needs, which I believed to be as legitimate as anyone else's. Next we looked into why the councilman rapped my patient's knuckles when he was merely expressing legitimate concerns and trying to satisfy legitimate needs. After studying the councilman's history, he felt better when he determined that the councilman had a long track-record of criticizing others for standing up for their rights, and in doing so was talking less about them than about himself. For as my patient subsequently discovered through personal contacts, the councilman, a depressed man himself, was putting others down to uplift himself, devaluing and even vilifying them personally so that he could value himself more highly. "Now we see," as I told my patient, "you are not the bad guy after all. He is, for trying to become a saint by virtue of calling you a sinner."

Adjusting One's Ego-Ideal

Most depressed men need help identifying, understanding, and relinquishing any self-expectations, however highly cherished, that enhance the likelihood of their becoming depressed. Many depressed men need to relinquish *excessively high* aspirations. Perfectionists, as Real puts it, need to learn "to hold [themselves] in warm regard even when colliding with [their] human shortcomings."[6] Most men cannot live comfortably with an unbridled need for success that drives them to approach unreachable heights. Instead such men can benefit from not continually striving to do better and have more. They can stop stretching themselves to the point that they can never be pleased with who they are and what they have, and instead of always being dissatisfied just make the best of things or make things better. Many depressed men need to relinquish purely achievement-based self-esteem that is counterproductive because it entirely overlooks the centrality of their humanity. They need most to rethink a masculine ego-ideal that depends exclusively on being rich and famous; strong in every way as distinct from weak in any respect; cruel rather than kind; dominantly controlling, aggressive, and assaultive as distinct from appropriately cooperative and rationally submissive; completely independent as distinct from healthfully interdependent; and entirely selfish as distinct from reasonably empathic and altruistic so that they create a harmony between what they need and what they feel others must have.

One of my seriously depressed gay male patients sorely needed to readjust the following ego-ideal and align it both with reality and possibility: "I would like to be thirty-five forever, dancing on a box, and able to take all the drugs I want without ever becoming addicted to any of them."

Other men need to relinquish *excessively low* aspirations that result in their expecting too little of themselves. In my experience many depressed men expect too little for themselves because they are overly empathic toward others. It is an admirable trait to want to give to the world—but so often depressed men take it to the point that, gone mad, it exists at the expense of being giving to themselves.

Identifying, and Understanding the Effect of, Specific Precipitants

Insight psychotherapists should determine if a man's depression starts with a precipitating event that becomes significant for him because it interlocks with his psychology to create his psychopathology. As Bemporad suggests, therapists should work toward developing insight consisting of a

> search [that] involves the patient relating the precipitating factor for the clinical episode to his particular personality organization [determining how] the environmental loss, frustration, or rejection that provokes a severe depression has a deeper meaning for the individual, which threatens his needed sense of self and his sources of narcissism. Therefore, what appears to the casual observer as a trivial event may reverberate with a deep-seated fear and shame in the vulnerable individual.[7]

For example, some men get depressed after a loss. But I have treated a number of men (in short-term therapy) who got even more depressed after a gain—that is, not after they lost their jobs, but after they were promoted. These men got depressed because they felt that they were getting something good for themselves, and that was forbidden.

Dealing with Resistances

Insight therapists treating depressed men routinely find themselves in the position of having to deal with the man's resistances to therapy. Some of these resistances are listed in the following discussion.

"I don't need help." Women often assert themselves by finding and using a therapist. Men often assert themselves by refusing to see one, either when someone close to them wants them to, or when on their own they recognize that they need help. Men typically refuse to start therapy by convincing themselves that they have no time or inclination for treatment and would prefer to heal spontaneously, with the help of a trusted friend, or through reading self-help books. Once in treatment they often have a flight into health where they say, "I'm fine now," and quit therapy prematurely to continue with their depressive "business as usual."

"I like myself just the way I am." As Bemporad writes, men often like their personality as it is even though it is that "personality that forms the basis of [their] very dreaded symptoms."[8]

"I don't let anyone tell me what to do." Men act stubborn and oppositional in therapy because they confound being helped with being controlled and being advised with being criticized. They then act out, for example, by overlooking an appointment with the therapist, or by forgetting to take their medicine as prescribed. I once treated a depressed man who later confessed to me that to stay free of my influence he mentally kept his fingers crossed throughout the entire course of his treatment. His was the magical belief that that way it wouldn't affect him, hurt him, or make him so dependent on me for a lifetime that he would be, speaking of the fee, turned into an annuity strictly for my benefit.

"I know more than you do." Some men turn their therapy into a fresh opportunity to compete with authority—this time in the person of the therapist. Men who have built their self-esteem on being the smart one—smarter even than those from whom they seek help—often competed with me by ignoring, resenting, or refusing therapy because they felt that listening to what I said and taking me seriously made me look good—and they didn't want me to look any better to them than they looked to themselves.

"I need someone to blame." Those men who are paranoid in addition to depressed tend to hear but not follow my therapeutic suggestions just

so that they can then blame me for the unfortunate outcome that they planned all along for their therapy—and for their lives—so that they can hold on to the belief that they would have done better with a better therapist—one who doesn't ruin their lives by giving them ruinous advice.

In especially unfavorable cases the man yields to the allure of the emotional advantages that comes from feeling miserable. He enjoys having a masochistic triumph—staying the same or getting worse, simply to spite and to get back at a therapist trying so hard to be of help.

"No matter what you do you can't make me better." This form of noncompliance is often due to a fear of success. It may also be due to the feared loss of a favored identity through positive change. For such men getting better also means getting worse because it means suffering a significant loss—that of the therapist. The man thinks about his therapist, "If I get better that will mean the end of our relationship."

"Nothing helps anyway." Depressed men are often pessimists who reason, "Since I am having so many problems and feel so bad it must mean that my life is a study in futility, so why bother trying to fix things?"

"I can't afford it." Too many depressed men refuse to come to treatment because they don't want to pay for therapy even when they can easily afford to do so. They say it would impoverish them and that they need to conserve their money, which is all they believe that they have left in life. There is often guilt about getting something for oneself. One man quit therapy after the first session because he "even felt guilty about buying himself a cup of coffee in a coffee house when he could have made it at home for a lot less."

"It's too much trouble to change (inertia has taken hold of me)." Some depressed men stay the same not because they do not want to get better but because they feel that it takes too much effort for them to do what they have to do to improve.

In conclusion, the goal of psychoanalytically oriented psychotherapy involves obtaining insight into those factors that cause a man to get depressed. This insight is productively sought in the context of a therapeutic relationship that is supportive to the extent that negativity toward the therapist is muted by positive transference feelings. Insight helps the man on many levels, both intellectual and practical. It helps him recognize that in addition to the inevitable real miseries that are part of every life he is self-creating even more, unnecessary misery for himself. It helps him understand the damage he is doing to his life and to his relationships with others who love him. Therefore, he ought to change his behavior now before it's too late so that he can undo past damage that can still be undone, work around past damage that cannot be undone, and do less damage to himself in the present and future. It keeps him from getting into and staying in toxic relationships. He is able to resolve ongoing personal problems through discussion instead of by acting them out—such as by walking out and prematurely abandoning a valid personal or professional relationship or job as he yields to his problematic rage instead of calmly looking for solutions. It helps him distinguish the here and now from the past so that he can stop viewing current events as primarily symbolic of earlier, truly bitter occurrences. He is able to identify the "small stuff" and distinguish it from the "large stuff" so that he can learn not to "sweat the small stuff" and so not to react catastrophically to minor rejections and losses. He can accept his inadequacies without feeling personally inadequate. It helps him get comfortable with himself through reassessing scrupulously moralistic attitudes that lead to excessive self-blame and self-faulting. He can understand and repair leanings that make him vulnerable to set-backs or tempt him to actually provoke them. When he accomplishes these things he is in a better position to triumph both over himself and over the real adversity that comes to every man at some time in his life.

COGNITIVE THERAPY

Cognitive therapists help depressed men recognize and correct the cognitive errors that form the basis of their automatic, pervasive, distortive, negative thinking (as described in Chapter 11). Many men become less depressed when they exchange inner reality (things as they perceive them) for truth (things as they are). Now they can begin to think less catastrophically about nothing and respond to extant catastrophes in a healthier, more effective way so that they can cope with adversity instead of dissipating their energy in ill-conceived panic over the possibility that all is lost.

However, it is important for men receiving this form of therapy to be aware of exactly what they are getting into before they start, and to agree to do the work based on knowing what it involves. Cognitive therapy can be jarring, and depressing in and of itself, especially to the man who discovers that he came for insight, or support, only to learn that he is instead having his faulty thinking corrected by a therapist who is doing only that, which is helpful, but little or nothing else, which is inadequate.

ENVIRONMENTAL MANIPULATION

Depressed men who are somewhat isolated not by inclination but as a result of their depression should at the very least consider looking for ways to improve the quality of their isolation. Better still, they should try to become less isolated. A good way for them to do that is to make connections with other depressed men, say on the Internet to form what amounts to a leaderless group discussing mutual concerns and shared problems. (There are Web sites for depression in men.) Scattered throughout Rosenthal's book are a number of suggested tactics—such as volunteering and helping the less fortunate—that depressed men (and women) can use to occupy their time, help with their loneliness, and come to feel better about themselves.[9] One should, however, not forget that there are downsides to such obvious-appearing solutions. A serious one is that depressed men whose chief complaint is that nobody is being charitable to them resent, often deeply, being told that the only way to their own salvation is to be the salvation of others.

GROUP THERAPY

Group therapy offers the isolated depressed man an opportunity to meet new people who can fill a void in his life. It can provide a scheduled, structured activity for the man who is floundering because he has nothing to do. The group leader and the group members can tell the depressed man the things he needs to know to survive and prosper, such as how he might handle the difficult people in his life. The group members can offer him advice—either directly or indirectly by modeling a healthier outlook and approach to living that embodies the changes depressed men need to make in how they respond and behave. One group member helpfully told of how he avoided getting anxious over nothing by thinking about alternatives to catastrophes he anticipated but never actually occurred. Another helpfully suggested specific ways he went about feeding himself a little pleasure and, refusing to accept defeat, achieving at least a modicum of success. The group can also sift through a man's ideals, and help him determine whether they make sense given his circumstances, are too high given his innate capabilities, or are too low given his real-life possibilities.

The group can also offer a depressed man a corrective emotional experience in the form of a life-changing interaction with new, different, and perhaps healthier, or at least more forbearing, people—the group members. The group might act the part of someone who acquiesces appropriately where others have stood their ground inappropriately or the part of someone who hears the man out for the first time in his life and then responds to his revelations of secret embarrassing sexual fantasies without shock or dismay and thus reassuringly without inducing guilt or more guilt. The group can react to a depressed man's anger not by making him feel as if he is a bad person for feeling and getting angry, but by reassuring him that anger, under many circumstances, is a normal, appropriate, and even unavoidable emotion.

FAMILY THERAPY

The family therapist treats the family along with the patient, with three goals in mind. The first is attempting to resolve the man's problems more efficiently by resolving them in the setting in which they occur. The second is attempting to involve the family in doing something about the man's emotional and physical problems. So often the family, less resistant to the therapist and therapy than the patient himself, can pressure the man into listening to his therapist. The third is helping the family take direct healing action. In one case a wife helped her husband get over his depression by agreeing to become less dependent on him after recognizing that he was getting depressed because she was making too many demands on him, as she finally saw, totally depleting him "with all my orality."

ANGER MANAGEMENT

Anger management is a process consisting of one or more steps. When one's anger is inappropriate, such as when the other person is not out of line, it may involve finding a way to feeling less angry. That often involves understanding the irrational aspects of one's own anger thus becoming more objective about it so that one can become less retaliative to others so that they do not then themselves angrily retaliate, starting a vicious cycle of angry point and angrier counterpoint.

When the other person is truly out of line it can involve becoming more charitable and forgiving—by becoming more empathic, after seeing where the other person is coming from so that one can pity rather than condemn him or her. Or it can involve coolly having it out with the other person in a problem-solving way. It is always wise to express in a relationship-sparing way anger that cannot be eliminated or held in, avoiding temper tantrums marked by cursing and yelling that can only generate guilt within oneself and foment ill will on the part of others. In this respect, a good device involves simply referring to one's anger calmly and in a controlled, dispassionate fashion. Many people are reasonable and will listen to anger expressed unaggressively to make a needed point and bring about called-for changes. This method avoids alienating a true sympathetic friend, family member, or loved one—someone a man might need on his way up to promote him, and on his way down to console him.

SHORT-TERM THERAPY

Peter Sifneos in a personal communication in 1966 recommended short-term therapy for those depressed men whose depression contained a significant oedipal component. He offered such men twelve sessions focused on resolving two central oedipal aspects of depression:

- Conflicts about being competitive, with guilt originating in fantasies about overthrowing the father, with the guilt appearing whenever success of any kind threatened.

- Loneliness due to interpersonal difficulties arising out of an (oedipal) mother fixation. As an example, a man avoided unattached women who wanted him to commit to a relationship and instead formed triangular relationships with married unavailable women because for him these represented mother figures. Only he then got depressed because the women he loved were either too much like his mother for comfort, or not enough like her for satisfaction. This man profitably saw how his oedipal fixation put him in a no-win situation characterized by his alternating between loneliness that was unacceptable, and closeness that was forbidden.

BEHAVIOR THERAPY

Behavior therapists view depression as a learned response that can be unlearned, or as a conditioned response that can be deconditioned. Many depressed men bring themselves down by remaining in contact with depressogenic individuals who deliberately set out to hurt their feelings. Then they go back for more in the hope that such hurtful people will treat them better the next time around. For example, to keep from getting depressed I have to avoid the depressed neighbor who always stops me on my pleasant morning walks to tell me about the book that is currently the most meaningful in his life and to quote many long, depressing passages from this self-help book entitled, *What to Do When Your Whole Life Falls Apart*. Depressogenesis is discussed further in Chapter 12.

As Hoberman and Lewinsohn suggest, behavior therapists often attempt to get a slowed depressed man moving again by "'activation' of [his] motivation via an increase in [his] behavioral output."[10] In my version of this approach, which I call "fake it until you make it," I ask a depressed man to virtually force himself to get moving—partly to push himself into a state of activity through defensive denial, and partly to encourage him to shake himself free of his lethargy so that he can release a little positive energy, making that available for catalyzing the release of a little more.

Some behavior therapists try to undercut the secondary gain of depression by asking the depressed man to identify and renounce some of the illusory benefits of being depressed. These often include unhealthy relational gratifications such as those extracted from excessive clinging dependency; using depression manipulatively as a form of control ("If you don't ... then I will kill myself"); and getting sadistic pleasure from hurting others assumed, often incorrectly, to have acted in a provocative disappointing way. The depressed man who relinquishes these unhealthy gratificational methods can focus on developing better relationships with others characterized less by selfishness and more by cooperative mutuality, interactive caring, and altruistic consideration and concern.

EDUCATIONAL THERAPY (COACHING)

Educational therapists teach, or coach, the depressed man by telling him what he needs to know to survive, prosper, and become and remain less depressed, or even depression free. They may teach him how to avoid problematic interpersonal interactions in the first place and how to handle those difficult interpersonal situations he cannot avoid. They may teach him how to wrest free of double binds in order to be released from the state of learned helpless that is a "what's the use" response to situations that appear to have no real solutions, such as, "If I spend too much time at work my wife complains, but if I spend too much time with my wife my boss complains, so I think I will just give up, for, after all, life sucks." (A compromise approach is often the best way to keep everyone happy.) They may teach him how to communicate better with others, and how to ascertain his legitimate needs and get others to gratify those that are appropriate. They may teach him how to go about making and keeping healthy personal relationships and integrate them into his job and career. For me the most important teaching task involves helping the depressed man learn how to get past his complaints and to instead shift onto focusing on correcting his problems.

INTERPERSONAL THERAPY/COUPLE THERAPY

Interpersonal therapy focuses on the interactive personal events that contribute to a man's depression. The therapist focuses less on how symptoms arise out of interactions with others that constitute a repetition of past traumatic relationships and more on how symptoms arise out of here-and-now contacts that create, maintain, and worsen depression.

Interpersonal therapists should, but too infrequently do, focus on the depressed man's negative effect on others via his maladaptive behavioral patterns. Depressed men can profitably stop threatening suicide to control and manipulate significant others to give in to their inappropriate expectations, gratify their unhealthy needs, and yield to their excessive demands. They can profitably stop their depression-inducing vicious interpersonal cycles involving pessimism, remoteness, anger, and neediness that lead others to respond negatively in a way that creates more of the same. For example, the depressed man who confides to others that his self-evaluation is low, hoping that they will disagree and tell him he is okay just the way he is, too often discovers that that approach backfires because others perceive his protestations of being lowly not as the neurotic self-effacements that they actually are but as a realistic self-evaluation by one who ought to know. Now others go on to treat the man badly the way he seems to be asking to be treated, shattering more of what is left of his self-esteem. In short, the core vicious cycling of depression comes down to this: almost all depressed men are unable to function optimally socially because they are depressed, and almost all depressed men are depressed because they are unable to function optimally socially.

The interpersonal therapist might model healthy interpersonal behavioral responses for the patient by showing him what the therapist in parallel situations might him- or herself think and feel. Also as Real suggests, the interpersonal therapist might offer the patient a "'corrective emotional experience'"[11] that "consists of reparent[ing] the patient [to help him] gradually internalize ... new, benevolent 'interjects' [sic] that modify his structural damage."[12]

I believe that a solid relationship/marriage, straight or gay, helps protect men from a depression. So I endeavor to help many of my male patients find, achieve, and maintain a stable relationship with a significant other. When I do couple therapy, I always keep in mind how many depressed men need the relationship that their very disorder threatens to disrupt. So I often don't solely attempt to rescue the man from the ravages of his relationship but also attempt to rescue his relationship from the ravages of the man. To do this I view his situation bi-directionally, that is, while a man's marital problems create his depression, his depression also creates his marital problems. Therefore, I have twin goals: removing the marital problems from the depression and removing the depression from the marriage.

Not surprisingly, then, a major focus of my interpersonal therapy will be the depressed man's personality/personality disorder. For as Glick, Clarkin, and Hass say, "Those individuals who experience episodes of depression are also likely to have personality disorders that affect their interpersonal relationships prior to, during, and after the depressive episodes."[13] Especially with couples I emphasize resolving personality difficulties affecting intimacy. These include an excess of dependency paradoxically coupled with a fear of closeness and commitment, and an excess of off-putting interpersonal hostility meant to protectively handle a fear of annihilation or a fear of castration. My goal is to resolve these problems through developing interpersonal insight in a setting where blame is avoided in favor of problem solving, and acting-out is avoided in favor of working through rather than living problems out. Personality problems related to depression are discussed further in Chapter 14.

When doing couple therapy I am especially careful not to assume that the woman is always and purely the victim and in no way the victimizer. There are situations where the provocations are mutual; these need to be identified so that they can be properly resolved. First, any violence must stop. Second, the violence must be understood in an interpersonal context. I do not agree with those observers who suggest that the very act of attempting to understand the interpersonal nature of violence necessarily condones, and therefore detracts from containing, it.

In a general way, interpersonal therapists must take special care to avoid affixing blame and taking sides in intrafamily struggles. They owe it to couples to avoid falling into the "spousal trap" where a couple lures the therapist into taking sides with one or the other—man or wife—then closes ranks, joins forces against the therapist, and expels him or her completely from their lives.

MISCELLANEOUS FORMS OF THERAPY

Light therapy is generally considered to be an effective remedy for *Seasonal Affective Disorder* (SAD). As Rosenthal suggests, this syndrome consists of the classic symptoms of depression in the form of "recurrent fall-winter depressions, at least two of which occurred during successive years, separated by nondepressed periods in spring and summer"[14] with "atypical vegetative symptoms [like] carbohydrate craving, and weight gain; fatigue, and social withdrawal."[15] The details of how to do light therapy as well as of other newer therapeutic approaches such as vagal stimulation are beyond the scope of this text.

INTERGRATION OF THE DIFFERENT SCHOOLS OF THOUGHT

I believe that each depression has developmental, interpersonal, cognitive, behavioral, and reactive aspects, although of course the blend is different from one depression to another.

Along lines explainable in psychodynamic terms, I myself tend to get depressed when someone reminds me of my past experiences with a remote, cruel, critical parent—my own mother. Afterward I have abandonment dreams such as trying to call up my last friend in the world only to be unable to locate him or her because I forgot to put the number in my cell phone, or because my fingers are too small to press my cell phone's keys.

Along interpersonal lines, when I feel as if I am in a double bind it leaves me not knowing what to do because, if I try to set limits on someone who is aggravating my depression, I will be rejected and lose the relationship, but if I don't say something to set limits then I will lose my comfort, my defined sense of self, and my intactness and sense of firm boundaries. The following incident reflects this and a related problem: my going back for more in the belief that I can change the other person's mind and rescue a relationship even though it is not one, as it should be clear to me by now, that is at all worth saving.

The following message from my neighbor appeared on my answering machine after I came home from a special event dinner.

> I know you are at a special celebration dinner. I remembered you are at an award dinner but I tried to call your cell phone but you didn't answer and I didn't mean to bother you. I was just trying to get a coalition of neighbors to call the cops for a barrage of noise complaints that are ruining my life. It's 8:00 P.M. and two women are out there in front of my apartment banging on some bongo drums and singing with a guitar and I have just had it, I have just had it—so we should all call the cops and make a noise complaint—that might shut them up. I dunno. This is a joke. We went though the whole weekend with all the noise and now it's Monday and they are continuing so if you get this message and they are still playing out there can you call the cops? Thank you. Bye.

It struck me as a highly narcissistic in-character attempt to figuratively speaking vomit all over me, and had a chilling effect on me because this was a special night—and he knew it. The effect was akin to my response on hearing someone run fingernails along a blackboard. Yet I still go back for more from him, partly because he seems to be so desperately needy, partly because I feel guilty about not helping him, and partly because (hope against hope) I anticipate that, however unlikely, some day he will be there for me when I need him.

Also in interpersonal terms I get somewhat paranoid along the lines of "with me others can't win." If I don't hear from someone for a while it means they don't like me. If I do hear from them too often it means that they are trying to extract something from me. Along cognitive lines, I distort the import of trivial issues that mean little in my or in most other people's personal infinite scheme of things.

Should I feel I need treatment I believe that for me the best form of therapy would involve an eclectic approach attuned to all the levels of my depression—one that used a holistic blend of those techniques that have proven affinity for resolving the particular underlying issues that are of special concern to me as an individual.

THERAPEUTIC GOALS

The two overriding goals of the psychotherapy I do with men involve: helping the man improve his relationships with others, as Real puts it, "opposing the force of disconnection, and reentering the world of relationship,"[16] and helping the man improve his relationship with himself, so that men who are guilty, self-punitive, self-critical, and self-abusive to the point of becoming their own worst enemies can learn, perhaps for the first time in their lives, to give up their self-denigrating attitudes and start giving themselves a vote of confidence, and a beginning, tentative offer of self-love.

* * * *

SOME DIFFERENCES IN THE THERAPY OF MEN AND WOMEN
Course and Prognosis

I cannot find any literature that reliably differentiates the course and prognosis of depression in men from that in women, and have not in my own practice noted any special distinction in this regard. In fact there is some scientific and anecdotal evidence that no significant differences exist and that after the first episode of depression, not only its incidence but also its course and prognosis are remarkably similar in both men and women.

Treatment-Seeking and Treatment-Utilizing Behaviors

Women tend to seek help more than men, who tend to prefer to at least try to resolve their problems on their own. More men than women seem to resent having to get into psychotherapy, and if they do go for treatment, have issues with the treatment process itself, because they feel embarrassed about revealing personal secrets and telling their therapists that they suffer from a problem they view not as an illness but as a weakness. Men, being less introspective and less in touch with their emotional side than women, are on the whole less likely to make satisfactory psychotherapy candidates than women.

Goals of Therapy

The goals of therapy necessarily differ in women and in men. Many women need to find their true identity from within. In contrast, many men need to suppress parts of their true identity within and to accept a new identity imposed (therapeutically) from without. Many women do not have to get in touch with their more masculine side. Many men can profit from permitting themselves to allow their feminine side through—without becoming depressed over being weak or alarmed by the possibility that they are gay.

Content of Therapy

I tend to talk about and try to resolve different things with men and women, for to get over their depression women and men often need to solve just the opposite sorts of problems.

- The woman who needs to deal with being too dependent has as her counterpart the man who needs to deal with being too independent. The woman who needs to break away from an overly dependent relationship has as her counterpart the man who needs to get into one but cannot because he is too self-reliant for his own good due to seeing all dependency as a troubling threat to his status, to his masculinity, and to both his professional and personal goals in life. So he stays out of what could be a succoring relationship—doing so less to retain a true desired advantage than to cling to an abstraction such as "my masculine freedom." In short, the woman who needs to focus on resolving problems resulting from an excessive longing for intimacy has as her counterpart the man who needs to resolve problems related to being unable to become intimate in the first place. The woman who must always be in a committed relationship and gets depressed because she has no one to commit to and depend on, has as her counterpart the man who is afraid of commitment and gets depressed when he feels he needs to or is being forced to commit and become dependent in a situation where all he wants to do is to hang loose or break free.

- The woman who needs to deal with being unassertive has as her counterpart the man who needs to deal with being too assertive or too aggressive. The woman who needs to become more in tune with her power side has as her counterpart the man who needs to become more in tune with his passive or feminine side.

- The woman who is too passive and submissive and might reasonably protest about being overly dominated has as her counterpart the man who is compulsively overly footloose and ought to allow others to have at least a measure of dominance and/or control over him.

- The woman who may need to get her anger out more has as her counterpart the man who may need to keep more of his anger in.

- The woman who cares too much about others and too little about herself (and is always disappointed in what others give her in return) has as her counterpart the man who cares too much about himself and too little about others (and often finds himself unloved for being too selfish).

- The woman who is excessively masochistic and gets depressed as part of her need to suffer has as her counterpart the man who is excessively sadistic and gets depressed because he has made others suffer, feels guilty about it, and is now all alone.

One must not, however, opine that all therapeutic goals are necessarily or ought to be gender specific. Some women need to learn to become less, some more, dependent, while the same is true of men. Both men and women may need to pull out from under a relationship that in reality involves losing too much of their freedom; both may need to accept being devalued less—treated unequally for the woman, castrated for the man. The goals I just presented represent general guidelines and are not meant to advance or advocate a fixed, generally applicable agenda more stereotypically conceived than actually present.

The following patient needed to become not more but less dependent. A woman offered to marry one of my male patients, an undocumented alien, just so that he could gain United States citizenship. She held all the power in the relationship through her money and personal connections. He was just a poor immigrant trying to survive and send money back to his family at home. She knew right from the beginning that he had a girlfriend and that she was the one he truly loved. The man took the woman up on her kind offer of marriage, not realizing what he was getting himself into. He thought that the marriage would be pro forma. She, having an entirely different agenda, thought otherwise, for all along she planned to ensnare him, subjugate him, and use him for her own ends. As soon as they got married she showed her hand. She didn't want a full husband—but she did want some company and someone around the house to do the hard work involved in keeping up the place. As a result, fearing that attaining citizenship would make him independent of her, she dragged her feet about helping him gain legal status as promised. Instead she put her own plan into action: to keep her new husband subservient and beholden. When he asked her to start the citizenship paperwork going she refused to fill out the required forms. He was trapped. There was nothing in this marriage for him, only for her. She completely controlled and thoroughly emasculated him by threatening to cut off his money supply and to report him to the immigration authorities if he didn't do her bidding. As he saw it, his only way out was to distance himself from his life. So he developed severe headaches, stopped eating, started crying all the time, and soon afterward had to be hospitalized for a severe depression.

In therapy we first had to come to appreciate and understand the full emotional impact his failed marriage was having on him. Next we had to find a way out for him and develop a clear-eyed plan of action. The centerpiece of this action involved his taking on two jobs to become financially independent of her. Once he had attained a measure of independence we were able at leisure to go back to discussing the emotional hold she had on him and how it was this that led him to tilt toward giving her what she wanted even when it wasn't what he needed—a bent he had to relinquish if he were to ultimately put his life together again.

Chapter 16

Treating Two Common Presentations of Depression in Men: Atypical Depression and Hypomania

In Chapter 15, I outlined some general principles of psychotherapy for men who are depressed, recommending an eclectic approach that incorporates relevant features of supportive-affirmative therapy, insight-oriented psychodynamic psychotherapy, cognitive-behavioral therapy, interpersonal therapy, and environmental manipulation. In this chapter I briefly describe some interventions that I have found particularly helpful for aspects of two common presentations of depression in men: atypical depression and hypomania.

ATYPICAL DEPRESSION

This section offers miscellaneous ideas for treating such symptoms of atypical depression in men as irritability, constipation, insomnia, and passive dependency.

Irritability (Anger Management)

Irascible, irritable, depressed men often respond positively to improving the way they deal with their anger using the anger-management techniques outlined throughout.

Constipation

Whenever possible, treatment of the constipation often associated with depression in men should go beyond the use of strong laxatives, enemas, or disimpactions to focus on the underlying mood disorder. However, mild laxatives such as supplemental dietary fiber derived from air-fluffed popcorn may, depending on the patient's overall medical status, occupy a place in the therapeutic regimen.

Insomnia

Medication to treat insomnia is best reserved for short-term usage, for example for acute insomnia whose symptoms are associated with discrete troublesome external events and so are sudden in onset and hopefully short-lived in duration.

Some depressed men find that they can lull themselves to sleep by the night-eating of comfort foods. However, to avoid weight gain they should take in no more than the calories they save from their daytime meals. Sometimes either the steady whir of a sound machine used to mask room noises or soothing music (while avoiding radio announcers with a rise-and-shine mentality) can help. It is important to adjust the temperature of the room to one's liking—factoring in what might make one's partner comfortable. Some men find it helpful to hire an acoustician to reduce the noise that comes into or originates in the bedroom. Some of the depressed men I treated were bothered by outside noise because they relished sleeping with the windows open—and refused to close them and turn on a fan or the air-conditioning because they gave priority to defeating their noisy environment over just accepting and working around it. I saw a patient who regularly called the police about a nearby coffee house's guitar player, saying that the music was keeping him awake. Sheepishly he subsequently admitted that he could have closed out the noise if he had only shut the windows, but he didn't do that because he liked having fresh air—and more importantly, the freedom to live as he pleased. My patient did not need sleeping pills, but less of a self-destructive, depression-inducing mindset. He needed to give up feeling that he had to be in control of all situations at all times and to instead start making the personal compromises and adjustments necessary to adapt to a somewhat unfavorable but essentially unalterable environment.

Handling the psychological components of insomnia can help many men get to sleep and stay asleep. Three important ones are narcissism, anger, and cognitive distortions of reality. In the realm of narcissism, men who allow a wife or a partner's snoring to be off-putting might benefit from not thinking primarily of themselves and their annoyance and instead becoming more altruistic as they start rejoicing that at least their wife or partner is able to sleep. The narcissistic man is often also an angry man. For such a man it isn't the wife's snoring that keeps him awake as much as it is his rage at her for making noise, and it is his brooding, stewing, and fuming that is making it so difficult for him to fall asleep. In the realm of cognitively distorting reality, many men cannot sleep because they view insomnia as an emergency, after maximizing its import so much that they feel desperate to sleep. That only perpetuates the tossing and turning as they anxiously think that "I will not be able to function effectively the next day without sleep—and that will be a big catastrophe." Such men may benefit from recognizing that insomnia is rarely the matter of life and death that they fear it to be. Most men can get through tomorrow with little sleep the night before, and even if there is a bad performance it is unlikely to break their career. Also to my way of thinking, not taking too many sleeping pills can be as important as being professionally on top. Correcting cognitive errors of this nature can often help men avoid seeking radical interpersonal remedies ranging from sleeping in a separate room to forcing their wives or partners to have a medical procedure that is not fully indicated.

Too many accepted psychological remedies for insomnia are based on myths. One is that if you cannot sleep you should get out of bed, leave the bedroom, and stay awake and read or perform some other activity until fatigue sets in. While this works for some, many men find that the best plan is to simply stay in bed and lie there quietly until sleep comes, without agitating themselves, while trying to work out in self-analysis what might be keeping them awake. Many psychologists also suggest that men avoid wide-awake activities, such as reading, in the room they sleep in. Psychologists believe that that can only lead to autoconditioning—that is, the man conditions himself to stay awake because he connects wakeful activity with the sleeping room. While some men might benefit from following such advice, introspective depressed men, who are often more attuned to internal than to external matters, are often in a position to safely disregard it. Insomnia was also discussed in Chapter 6.

Pseudofatigue, that is, feeling tired no matter how much sleep one gets, is often best treated not with increased rest but with increased activity, such as medically approved strenuous exercise (not, however, done just before bedtime). A better mattress may also help. But often what helps the most is definitive treatment for the underlying affective disorder.

Characterological Problems

Men's characterological problems were discussed in Chapter 14, and treatment methods were implied. Here I revisit passive dependency as perhaps the commonest characterological trait that leads men to develop and succumb to depression. In particular, many depressed men need to be helped to become more assertive about taking charge not only of their lives but also of their depression. While some men report that they do best by not fighting their depression and instead letting it work itself through, other men report that what works best for them is attempting to push their way through their depression and live as if it doesn't exist. Men who have tried that often praise the health-giving effects of not decrying their plight and instead just forcing themselves to extricate themselves from it. Instead of bemoaning how the worst has happened they arrange for the best to come about. Instead of complaining about their fate they do something to change it. In other words, they replace a preoccupation with their problems with a total concern for, and a taking action toward, developing their solutions.

A man was depressed because instead of setting new goals and meeting them directly and forcefully he could do no better than brood about how bleak things looked for him. He constantly complained that he hated where he lived, wasn't making money in the office he operated, had no one to love and no one who loved him, and was the local therapist everyone unloaded on when they had a problem. Yet he was reluctant to either sell his apartment (which he could have done at a great profit) or keep it and save money by closing his office and moving it to his spare room. He also went through life looking for love in all the wrong places—seeking relationships in singles bars and settling for substitute relationships in therapeutic groups he entered not for treatment but to make friends—using the group setting as a place where he could find, if not the real thing, then at least a substitute for it. He also refused to stay away from those people who were mistreating him by unloading on him. Instead he convinced himself that complying with their demands was the best idea because standing up for his legitimate rights would necessarily give others offense, and they would drop him. So he became a toady who did what he was told, whoever told him to do it, and whatever they wanted him to do. He felt much better when at my suggestion he took charge of his life. He made three resolutions involving three new goals:

1. I will make enough money by taking odd jobs and a part-time teaching position to support an acceptable life-style and keep my office open without having to clutter my apartment with things that are work-related.

2. I will stop substituting therapeutic for real-life encounters and instead start meeting women outside of group therapy through personal introductions.

3. I will start cutting off people who unload their problems on me, but have no patience for my problems when I just want to "spill my guts," by politely but firmly saying, "Sorry, but I am busy now," rescuing myself from people I see as predators who bring me down with their self-indulgent tirades meant to make me their company in their misery.

TREATING HYPOMANIA

The approach to treating hypomania is in some ways the obverse of the approach to treating depression. Whereas treatment of depression involves a degree of affirmation, treatment of hypomania involves a degree of deaffirmation. The therapist needs to ask for not more but for less self-expression. Because lifting too many controls is absolutely contraindicated for men who are cyclothymic or hypomanic, the therapist treating a hypomanic man should assiduously avoid using Real's approach of "crack[ing the depressive man] open."[1] Hypomanic men need not to be opened but to be closed up. They need to be deflated by being told, as gently as possible, that they feel too good under the circumstances. They also may need to be asked to moderate their excessive outlandish behavior. For example, I suggested one of my patients save some time from his constant pursuit of sex so he would have some time left over to do some productive work. I also believed he needed to become more thoughtful, that is, to talk and act less, and to think more about what he was saying and about to do. He needed to accept, not frantically deny, the narcissistic injuries of his life. He was becoming hypomanic as his way to handle a male midlife crisis/male menopause, so he needed to start accepting his ageing gracefully and with equanimity—and to stop striving for what was impossible given how old he actually was, and to instead start looking and acting in an age-appropriate manner so that he could savor pleasures suitable for and available to someone at his stage of life.

Unfortunately, hypomanic men are often resistant to many forms of treatment. They have more than their share of the male's usual "I can do it myself" mentality, which is in these cases one manifestation of their serious denial tendencies. Their tendency is to be flippant about the importance of therapy, to not take what the therapist says seriously, and to even condemn their therapists, as well as all advisors, as squares, spoilers, and medical establishment lackeys. Resistances like these need to be identified and handled properly in a timely fashion. The hypomanic man's therapist should consider telling the patient up front, and without mincing too many words, that the cure he must accept will likely involve being at odds with the elevated status in life that he appears so reluctant to forgo.

Chapter 17

Therapeutic Errors

This chapter is written primarily for therapists, but it is also for the loved ones of depressed men who hope to act in a therapeutic fashion with the depressed men in their lives. The goal of all concerned should be to avoid making the errors discussed here to keep from inducing a depression in a man they love and to avoid making one he already suffers from worse and instead help him feel better about himself and more positive about the world he lives in.

Some therapists have fixed (and inaccurate) ideas about what constitutes normal affect. Some go to one extreme and call any sadness depression (or, diagnosing hypomania, any resolute preoccupation with a topic of interest or concern a "flight of ideas"). Others, in a state of denial, go to the opposite extreme. Starting with the premise that we all get depressed from time to time, just as they do, they deny that a clinical depression exists unless the man suffers from a severe form of melancholia. *Conclusion*: helping the depressed man starts with correctly identifying his depression after casting aside personal prejudices about what is normal and what constitutes deviation from the norm.

Some therapists simply push the depressed men they treat too hard, virtually demanding that they get better. They truly believe that the best way to help a depressed man is, as Real suggests, to "peel ... back the layers of [his] disorder."[1] However, uncovering and exposing the deep layers of a man's psyche in what amounts to a form of Real's "jack-hammer therapy"[2] can leave a depressed man wide open and defenseless, and so even more anxious and depressed than before. For depression is a defense, and as such it serves a need, meaning that it should not be undermined too precipitously. Many of the men I treated needed a degree of defensive depression to protectively tide them over the rough spots in their lives. Removing their depression prematurely (when such a thing was even possible) was detrimental to their health and impeded rather than enhanced their progress. Some of these men complained that their antidepressants made their depression worse. In many of these cases I found that the drugs made their depression not worse but better, and what made *them* worse was no longer having the depression that to some extent they relied on to reduce their anxiety and structure their life, albeit in an unhealthy, counterproductive manner. *Conclusion*: getting over a depression takes time. Rushing the cure can interfere with the natural healing process. Some men want and need to remain in the comforting shadows of their depression for just a little while longer. All concerned should not push them to emerge from their depression too precipitously, but let them bear their burden until they are ready to have it lift.

Some therapists, becoming angry or impatient, threaten to throw a resistant patient out of therapy or to put him in a hospital if he doesn't comply, get better fast, or stop making suicidal threats. Setting limits on depressed men is often necessary, however harsh that may be. But some therapists set limits arbitrarily, punitively, and often strictly for moral reasons. *Conclusion*: depressed men should not be coddled because they are depressed. But neither should they be punished for feeling the way they do.

Some therapists develop strongly negative (countertransferential) feelings about their depressed patients—particularly those who appear to inspire feelings of rage, helplessness, and disdain in other people, and therefore in the therapist. Some therapists feel uncomfortable with men who unload nonstop on them, for they feel flooded by them, and dislike the implied narcissism. Many therapists dislike men who cling too hard to them. They also feel impotent in the face of a depression's chronicity. Some cognitive therapists feel challenged unless they can immediately and radically correct persistent, negative cognitive distortions. Many therapists feel put down by patients who criticize their best endeavors, and some develop an almost homophobic dislike for the feminine passivity and whining that characterizes occasional depressed men—in private even referring to them in such pejorative terms as drama queens or wimps. *Conclusion*: it is not necessary to like a man's depression, but to help a depressed man feel better one has to basically like the man who is depressed.

Too many therapists make the mistake of debating philosophically with the depressed man. They have arguments with him about what should and should not depress him, such as what he should find moral and acceptable or immoral and forbidden. In effect they are foisting their philosophy on someone who prefers his own, and does not need others' dictates to follow but help in rethinking any self-destructive, rigid presumptions he has by himself unthinkingly accepted and firmly integrated. *Conclusion*: hear what the depressed man is telling you about himself, without foisting yourself and your theories about life, truth, justice, and good versus bad on the depressed man.

Therapists who indulge in biological reductionism overlook the emotional causation of depression and scour the world for the right drug or drug combination even when pharmacotherapeutic regimes haven't worked previously—and won't work this time—not because the right prescription drug has not been found, but because the right interpretations haven't been given. *Conclusion*: in some cases it is not that the depression is unresponsive to drugs—it is that the man needs something besides drugs, like the right prescription for living. (An overview of my philosophy of pharmacotherapy is offered in the appendix.)

Equally problematic is deemphasizing the biological to fixate on the psychological causes of depression. Some therapists do that even in those cases where mood and mood swings are clearly primarily endogenous and so likely to be in great measure the product of organic (biological) factors. Sometimes psychological factors precipitate a depression with organic features. Sometimes organic factors precipitate a depression with psychological features. *Conclusion*: many depressed men need to take both stock of themselves and their pills.

Some therapists forget that each man's depression is unique. Some overemphasize the here and now when the main problem is in the past, and vice versa. Some suggest that men are depressed because they are suffering the effects of early trauma when in fact it is their depressing attitude that has just driven their last friend to traumatize them right now. Too commonly, therapists focus on loss and abandonment in a man who is actually focused on issues of control and castration. *Conclusion*: the topics of discussion with a depressed man, in and out of therapy, should reflect not preset theory but individual cause; that is, they should come from the individual man's unique dynamics. Depression is a destination arrived at by many roads. One should not oversimplify the route taken by the individual man in his journey into darkness.

Therapists who overidentify with their patients run the risk of applying theories to them that are more applicable to themselves. They project what makes them depressed onto their patients. I get the impression that throughout his book Real focuses mainly on the traumatic causes of depression because Real himself had a father who traumatized him. Trauma lies in the shadow of many depressions; but not all depressions are shadowed by events that are traumatic. *Conclusion*: it's a good idea to put yourself in the depressed man's shoes, but only when those shoes fit.

Many therapists have subtle ways of inducing guilt in their depressed patients. Some do this by criticizing their patients directly, others by belittling their fears, still others by demeaning or overinfantilizing them by treating them as if they cannot take care of, or take responsibility for, themselves. Many wreak havoc with their patients' self-image by giving interpretations that are insightful but given in a critical, confrontational manner with punitive content and intent. Conversely, some therapists wreak havoc with their depressed patient's self-image by being too permissive. They overlook that depressed men (like everybody else) to an extent ought to feel guilty over some things, for guilt is controlling, and helps depressed men feel valid and moral for having acted in a restrained way. Giving a man permission to continue doing things he should never do again can, if he continues to do them, ultimately enhance his shame and increase his guilt. *Conclusion*: some depressed men got depressed not because they were too guilty from the start but because they, having behaved badly, and still behaving that way, are not guilty enough in the end. In dealing with a depressed man's guilt it is necessary to impart not only absolution but also a sense of responsibility.

Some therapists believe that you can only change yourself, not others, so throughout therapy they work from the premise that all depressed men are entirely responsible for making themselves undepressed— overlooking the simple fact that while some depressed men are masochists who bring on their own victimization, others are caught up through little or no fault of their own with sadists eager to cause them intolerable and unnecessary pain and suffering. *Conclusion*: don't blame the depressed man for his depression when it is not only he but also his family, partner, or child who needs the treatment. Some depressed men need to change themselves. Others need to get a whole new set of acquaintances and good friends.

Some therapists feel that they need to remain neutral without ever showing their human side. But in truly sad situations, an honest expression of empathy may be indicated. A patient complained to me in tears that he had lost all his tropical fish, which were "all I had left in life." He was receiving chemotherapy and the poisons came through his skin, contaminated the fish food when he handled it, and killed off the whole tank. He was truly heartbroken, and so was I for him, and I felt I should say how sorry I was and how I could actually feel his pain.

Some therapists unwisely feeling that they are out of the woods relax just at the moment when their patients start improving. But this is the time to become increasingly alert and especially cautious. For in my experience depressed men often attempt suicide not when they are getting worse, which does happen, or when they are staying the same, which unfortunately happens often enough, but when they are getting better and so are becoming more energized and, less anergic, are both more willing and able to take harmful action against themselves.

Conclusion: never let down your guard just when the depressed man has finally let down his and has started to improve.

Therapists and laypersons alike sometimes make men worse by offering them bad advice that ranges from the merely trite to the actively harmful. Here are some possibly countermanded offerings. These can at times be helpful, but they should be dispensed with care and sensitivity. Advisors should always remember that many depressed men fear getting better because they fear success, and that that fear can turn what is actually helpful advice for some into useless or counterproductive instruction for others. Even such apparently bland and harmless advice as "devote yourself to your work," or "improve yourself by losing weight and dressing better," can be discordant with the depressed man who is still depressed enough that for now he needs to do some serious tithing to his punitive conscience.

Here are some examples of advice that for any number of reasons isn't right for all depressed men.

Keep mentally and physically active, stay and keep busy. Many depressed men are too anergic to follow such advice. Even if they could follow it they would soon discover that substitute gratifications amount to "basket weaving." They temporarily divert them from their anguished self, but they ultimately focus their minds on trivial and peripheral diversions that can give them an illusory sense of accomplishment and pull them away from satisfying their true important desires and working toward actually getting their lives together. "Basket weaving" advice is especially counterproductive for a man who is depressed because he feels he has fallen short in the first place by living and working beneath his capacity, and for the man who is depressed because he has antagonized or lost someone he loved by putting the relationship last, and putting less important life considerations, like his hobbies, first.

Take a long vacation. Advice like this, or such related advice as advice to quit your job, retire, and "go enjoy yourself; the fish are biting," will mostly resonate positively only with those depressed men who got depressed because they were working too hard and now need relief by pulling back. Workaholic men hate being idle and feel guilty about being lazy, while men whose self-esteem depends on toughing it out will view taking time off as a failure of bravery and view themselves as cowards who instead of going on vacation should be facing, working on, and mastering their problems. Obsessive depressed men will find it especially depressing not to be working. They hate being unoccupied, they brood constantly about going broke, and in any event when these men go on vacation they predictably take their troubles with them and can't wait to get home to finally do something about what bothers them.

Devote yourself to your work. This advice implies that work should come first, before people. In unfavorable situations that advice can induce or worsen workaholism, and that can have serious negative consequences on the man's interpersonal relationships.

Help the less fortunate. Some depressed men find that helping the less fortunate gives their self-esteem a boost. Others find that helping the less fortunate leads them to feel personally slighted, ignored, depleted, and deprived, as if they are doing everything for others and little to nothing worthwhile for themselves. My depressed male patients did best when they struck a compromise between giving to others and getting for themselves, and only gave what they felt they had left over after they got enough to satisfy their own needs. Giving makes some men feel full. Giving too much makes many men feel empty.

Analyze yourself thoroughly. Depressed men should self-analyze—but only if they can do so without simultaneously being narcissistically focused and excessively self-critical. Too many depressed men have a habit of going too deep and depressing themselves, contemplating their navel when they should be working on their professional and personal relationships, and going deep without a therapist around to guide them through the depths.

Just get over it. Some therapists have a "cut-it-out" mentality. They give the depressed man advice to cheer up, smile, look on the bright side of things, and think positively, and tell him that he is better off than he thinks because things aren't as bad as he sees them, because there are worse things in the world than what is happening in his life. Advice to not worry about the things that bother him and instead smell the roses belittles the man's concerns, demeans him for seeking help, and slaps his wrist and shames him for being a big crybaby. Therapists who give such advice are in effect exhorting the man to drop his symptoms and get better by the very act of will that his illness keeps him from exercising. A depressed man would stop being depressed if only he could. Ordering him to cut it out belittles the significance both of how he feels and how difficult it is for him to feel otherwise. It also says to him, "You are bothering me, so stop being an annoying crybaby over nothing, and stop it right now" and tells him, "You are once again a failure." Though it is true that serious physical illness, disability, or death is actually worse than having one's creative ideas rejected by a publisher of little books of poetry, for the moment an unaccepted poem is the worst thing in the world for the poetically inclined depressed man who already feels personally unacceptable. Suggesting otherwise is dismissive and rejecting, and can lead to his believing that you, like everyone else, do not care enough about him to take him seriously and pay attention to him personally. In short, advice to not let little things bother you is destructive because it asks too much of a depressed man, because a depressed man's illness so often consists mainly of letting little things bother him.

Instead of telling the depressed man to cut it out, I tell him to occupy and divert himself as best he can while his depressed mood improves—that is, to put his mood on the back burner, so to speak, trying to ignore it, yet checking back with it every once in a while to see if it has lifted. Or I might sum up his prior successes in preparation for helping him make further course corrections along similar lines. Finally, I often suggest that he convert the energy that goes into creating his depression into energy that goes into relieving it—moving on from a need to erect a wall of worry into constructive action meant to tear that barrier down.

Don't take things so personally. Hostility, cruelty, and rejection are often meant personally. Even when there is a transferential component to them, the transference has a personal element to it because it is, after all, directed to you, not to somebody else. A better suggestion is to agree with the man that he is right to think that attack(s) on him were meant personally, then wonder with him why a personal attack should matter so much.

Don't care what others think. Most depressed men, concerned as they are with being loved and accepted, find it difficult not to care what other people think. A good piece of advice for the man who gets depressed is to remove himself from people whose thinking is seriously at odds with his own and find other people who think the way he does, and validate him for thinking it. Sometimes a depression lifts when a liberal man can leave his conservative society, and vice versa.

Be a nicer person. You catch more flies . . . Depressed men have to walk a fine line between being nice to others who deserve it and being nasty to those who don't. It is often a tradeoff between being untrue to yourself then feeling regretful, and expressing yourself honestly in an assertive or even angry and aggressive fashion then being alone. Deciding how to make that tradeoff is an individual matter—one that requires taking both one's personality and one's individual circumstances into account.

Get the anger out. Too many therapists encourage a man to get his anger out without considering the downside of his being an unduly angry person constantly acting in an unduly angry fashion. Some depressed men do feel temporarily better after they get their anger out. But many others discover that the benefits of getting the anger out can be far outweighed by two downsides: antagonizing people one cherishes and needs, by insulting, humiliating, and hurting them; and (when there has been a temper tantrum) feeling guilty about not having behaved in a way that makes you sufficiently proud of yourself to give yourself a vote of confidence, and to in turn reasonably expect one back from others.

Also, too many therapists treat all anger as born equal, and fail to distinguish anger that is inappropriate (and needs to be resolved internally) from anger that is appropriate (and if anything needs to be resolved with the person who is fomenting the anger). Depressed men often need to somehow come to terms with their anger in a way that involves not getting it out but getting over it, while perhaps expressing what anger cannot be resolved, but limiting that expression to one that takes place in a relationship-saving way.

Moreover, depressed men may need to be distracted from what is making them depressed, and being and getting constantly angry means being excessively and continuously steamed up over depressing matters. Angry depressed men need to ask themselves why they let difficult but unimportant things get to them and upset them, so that they can stop getting angry in the first place and start thinking about other, healthier, more calming things.

Be true to yourself. Self-fulfillment is a difficult goal for the multilayered depressed man who rarely knows which layer of his personal self to fulfill. It can also be dissonant with the altruistic personality's important goal of becoming fulfilled via fulfilling others.

Start all over again. Many advisors routinely tell depressed men that they are young enough to get a divorce or start a new career, when in fact that is not entirely true. They are trying to reassure the man that he can still be as future-oriented now as he was when he was young, and that he is not too old to continue developing along new and fresh pathways. While it is true such advice can keep hope alive, on the downside it can involve belittling what the man already has accomplished and is presently doing. Also, advisors must always consider that with age comes restrictions, for every day that goes by can make it too late for something. Some demoralized depressed men need to acknowledge that their ideals are never reachable—especially when these ideals are so age-specific that they are inappropriate for the man who has gotten somewhat older. Certainly any life changes to be made should not be constructed out of depressed mood. Men who think that it is their bad marriage that puts them in a bad mood should consider the possibility that it is their bad mood that puts them in what they believe to be a bad marriage. Such men should be finding a therapist, not getting a divorce.

Try to keep the family together (no matter what). Marriage *can* be a source of greater stress than divorce. The decision to make or not make significant changes in one's marital status should be left entirely up to the depressed man. It is usually unwise to push a man to reconciliation or divorce, for though he complies today he may resent it tomorrow if the decision he makes at a therapist's suggestion turns out to be the wrong one for him.

Be a more moral person. All men, but especially men who are depressed, need to distinguish between morality on the one hand and guilt and remorse on the other. Being moral is one thing, but being excessively self-punitive in reply to understandable and unavoidable human imperfection is quite another. The depressed man should either stop what he did that led him to feel guiltily amoral or continue in his old ways without feeling quite so sheepish about doing so.

Get a pet. Some therapists underestimate the liabilities of pets. Pets are often loving companions who help with anxiety and depression. But for some depressed men even the best of pets can become antitherapeutic. A dog that barks constantly may be a great annoyance, or even a personal catastrophe if it requires so much care that it keeps the depressed man from doing the things that will enhance his mood by reducing his loneliness.

Conclusion: the role of the therapist, or any other advisor, can and should generally be confined to asking the man to make his own decisions about his own life then offering to help him implement those decisions once he has made them.

In summary:

- Depressive affect is a model of specificity; misidentifying it leads to under- and overdiagnosis.

- Depressed men may react badly to excessive probing by getting worse.

- Disliking a depressed man because he is depressed overlooks that depression is a symptom or a disorder, not a conscious, off-putting, willfully hostile form of communication—with oneself, with you, and with the world.

- Criticizing and punishing a depressed man for being depressed is seriously antitherapeutic.

- Depressed men's sense of righteousness, morality, and sensibility is often determined not by his conflict-free cogitation but by his pathological affect. Therefore, arguing with him about what is right, moral, and sensible is not only counterproductive—it also diverts from treating the pathological affect behind the distortive cognitions.

- A holistic view of depression considers its organic and psychological underpinnings and where indicated treats both.

- Depressed men need to be understood as they are, not as others project their own selves onto them.

- In the treatment of the depressed man guilt reduction is not always indicated, for sometimes guilt enhancement is more appropriate and effective.

- Letting down one's guard just when a depressed man's depression begins to improve can be dangerous; this is often precisely the time the depressed man makes a suicidal attempt.

- Using caution in getting the anger out importantly involves distinguishing between rational anger and irrational rage.
- Getting the anger out may be the wrong approach. It may be better to keep it in and come to terms with it—by thinking things through with the goal of "just simmering down."

Chapter 18

Self-Help for the Depressed Man

Most men get depressed from time to time. Some fall into a depressed mood that merely lasts a few hours or days. But others develop a lingering clinical depression. Men whose depressions are mild and transient are able to shake off the blues rapidly and effectively before they develop into a full-blown clinical disorder. Here are some trouble spots that depressed men should be on the alert for and try to work through internally or with significant others so that they can either avoid a clinical depression or keep one from firmly taking hold.

ARE YOU BEING BULLIED?

Depressed men tend to allow themselves to be bullied and then allow their bullying to continue. Many are unassertive individuals who believe that if they refuse to be bullied they will lose their partners, all their friends, and family. To some extent they are right—for friends and lovers of depressed men tend to be people who prefer men they can bully, only to drop them should they try to wriggle out from under their assaults. It is true that in many cases the depressed man has to make a choice between (1) being bullied and staying depressed, and (2) leaving the people who bully him behind and finding a way to get through that difficult, harsh, lonely period in-between giving up his old best friends and making a whole set of new ones.

One of my patients got depressed in part because he shied away from setting limits on friends and family who were bullying him. He would never say, "Please stop that, it annoys me," or "I warn you that this cannot continue." As he put it, "I feel it is better to accept being abused and have friends, than to become abusive to my friends and have nobody." So he made excuses for his friends' bullying, such as, "He can't help it; he is under so much pressure," or "She can't help it; she is sick." Once he managed—after a long inner struggle—to ask a neighbor to bring in his barking dog at least at night so that the barking did not keep him awake. The neighbor cursed him out, in the process saying many hateful things and even added a homicidal threat or two. All his friends advised him, "Call the cops" and "Get a lawyer." He replied, "I don't want to make trouble. I'm afraid that if I hire a lawyer that guy will burn down my house." Follow-up revealed that though the problem continued he still thought that he was right to have avoided confrontation. As he put it, "On their own, things have gotten a bit better for me. Now the dog only barks for 12 hours—during the day, but thankfully, not at night."

However, here is a vignette that illustrates how cautious one must be when attempting to set limits on bulliers, and how it is sometimes better to be a bit bullied and feel temporarily depressed than to stand up for oneself and be emotionally intact but run the risk of being physically hurt. I was in a restaurant where I am friends with one of the waitresses, a woman who was severely depressed because she just had many losses in her life, including the loss of three members of her family from heart disease. This waitress had finally almost literally dragged herself to work after a few weeks' absence, and I was overjoyed to see her back and looking better. In the midst of her telling me that things were going well for her now and that she was slowly improving, a patron at the next table interrupted us both with a warning for her: "Stop talking and start doing your job." The intrusive man's entire mien indicated to me that it was a good idea for us to just give him what he wanted. I surmised that it was better for me to temporarily feel down about being put on than to have provoked someone who could have easily acted in a dangerous way.

In some extreme cases the best idea is to send straightforward messages to bulliers simply stating one's position—not to cow or to hurt them but to get their attention to open up peace negotiations. I have found that many difficult people actually appreciate an honest, straightforward approach that makes their position clear and leaves them knowing exactly where they stand. Many people prefer doable recommendations that constitute a blueprint for change over having to constantly hear a litany of passive-aggressive complaining that is no substitute for handling specific problems that are potentially resolvable.

ARE YOU LETTING YOUR LOW SELF-ESTEEM STAY LOW AND GROW EVEN LOWER?

Men with inappropriately low self-esteem feel worthless and guilty though they are in fact no worse than, and are often better than, the people they compare themselves to. If this is you, you might benefit from fully understanding why your self-esteem is so inappropriately low. Here are some possible reasons, each implying a specific antidote. You might be:

- Contaminating today with yesterday, treating yourself as that completely bad child you might have been then even though you in fact have grown up to be a pretty good man now.

- Evaluating yourself strictly and negatively according to how others view you, abdicating to sadists and beginning to believe yourself to be unworthy just because others find you to be so, according to the formula, "I don't love myself because you don't love me."

- Being overly perfectionistic using self-standards that are too high because you overlook that "no one is perfect" and that "everyone wins some and loses some."

- Being excessively angry with yourself because you are keeping your rage at others in and taking it out on yourself.

- Being appropriately angry at yourself for mistakes that you should have avoided making, are still making, and may still be able to correct—but are doing nothing about correcting.

- Condemning your anger that is reasonable and within bounds though anger is a normal, acceptable emotion and sometimes even an appropriate response to provocation.

- Identifying with someone you perceive to be or who is actually unworthy, for example, "I am just like that bad father of mine."

- Punishing yourself by getting there first with a self-criticism to forestall criticism from others.

- Blaming yourself for things that others are really responsible for, as if you are entirely responsible for creating your difficult situations and for not properly dealing with situations that are in actuality impossible to handle. I long blamed myself for what I consider to have been my underperformance as a medical intern. Just recently I recognized that maybe it had something to do with the fact that for a whole year I was on duty every other night, and up all night each night I was on duty. With such an impossible work schedule how could I expect myself to deal adequately with everything that came my way?

- Being too altruistic toward others while not caring enough about yourself and ultimately even condemning yourself for your excessive altruism. Excessively altruistic men are often actually masochists suffering from a deficiency of self-interest. They are like my patient who tolerated and even coddled his abusive, critical mother because he believed that her need for him was greater than the suffering he experienced at her hands. So he spent his entire life catering to her, using as his excuse that it was the best way to insure his inheritance. In a similar position was the child who was literally rescued from the streets by a couple that took him in and virtually adopted him. He was unable to move forward and find a significant other for himself out of gratitude to what they had done for him—a self-sacrificial attitude that at this writing still threatens to compromise his personal and sexual life completely and forever.

- Globally condemning your humanity by experiencing severe sexual guilt after forgetting that sex is a biological function.
- Living in a society that doesn't approve of you and often of your best characteristics, for example, a gay man living in a homophobic society or a Jewish man living in an anti-Semitic society.

If your self-esteem is low at least take care to not live out your excessively low self-image via self-defeating behavior. For example, do not self-punitively give up a successful business to become an unsuccessful artist or give up being a successful artist to become an unsuccessful businessman. Do not deliberately work beneath your capacity, work up to capacity until you are about to finish a project and slack off at the end, or tear up your good work and in a transport of self-criticism throw it away.

ARE YOU GRIEVING SELF-DESTRUCTIVELY?

Some men grieve following a loss while others go beyond normal grieving to become depressed. They feel that they will never recover or heal, and so will be unable to survive. They unrealistically believe that "I simply cannot live without him or her," though such thoughts are more a symptom of their grief than an adequate assessment of their reality.

Some grieving men should try to make new friends or find a new partner immediately or as soon as possible. But others should try to take their time replacing losses, even if that means being alone for a while. Individual preference, not conventional wisdom, should determine the chosen path. Men who are uncertain which path to choose should consider seeking temporary substitutes for, rather than exact duplicates of, what they have lost. That is, they should search for "transitional objects," such as a therapist in place of a long-term lover, or peers in group therapy in place of new best friends. Some grieving men have done well literally going home again to their family, using them as a substitute/temporary crutch to tide them over this difficult period in their lives.

Here are some things grieving men should avoid:

- Making irrevocable financial or personal decisions, such as impulsively selling a house, getting a dog, or marrying someone they hardly know.
- Abdicating to difficult people just to have some company—and the opposite problem.

- Treating everyone as not good enough for them and instead searching for the perfect replacement while simultaneously bypassing people that could potentially satisfy them somewhat if only they would accept them for what they are.

- Burning interpersonal bridges they may later need to cross, for example, by becoming remote from, or angry and paranoid with, friends and colleagues they need now and/or might need later.

It is often important for a grieving man to continue to work instead of taking a lot of time off. He might feel better sticking with the regular and productive activities that organize, structure, and improve his life and keep him in touch with important familiar significant others. He should avoid going on a long vacation if that will leave him feeling isolated in the midst of strangers and simultaneously detract from his staying home and restructuring his life along more satisfying and productive lines. He should also avoid getting mired down in impractical and dangerously diverting symbolic substitute strivings that will not make him feel as whole as he might hope. For example, many of my male patients dealt with a divorce by becoming house proud—seeking and finding the perfect apartment or house for themselves then feathering their empty nest, only to find themselves both financially strapped and emotionally bereft.

Here are two helpful psychological defenses men can employ to deal with their grief. First, they can identify with the lost object to dilute, diminish, and postpone the impact of the loss by temporarily resurrecting the object within. (Identification with the lost object as a psychological defense is described further in Chapter 5, Grief.) Second, they can resurrect the lost object by returning to old familiar shared haunts or leafing nostalgically through picture albums. To be avoided are counterproductive and dangerous defensive regression into alluring infantilism, especially the kind that is associated with overdrinking and overeating.

An especially important psychological task for the griever is to reduce the guilty feelings associated with his grief. Guilt during grief originates in

- The belief that one's anger killed off the relationship or the person.

- Selective amnesia, where the man views the lost person as all good and himself as all bad.

- Survivor guilt over having been spared someone else's suffering.

- Self-condemnation for being an inadequate griever because you want to move on, not to continue to be mired down in grief.

- Emotional assaults from sadistic people, including: those who go on an attack they have been saving up because it is safe for them to do so now that you are down, and those who induce guilt in you as a way to handle their own guilt for not helping you out during your difficult times by offering complaints of the "it's you not me" variety such as "Why didn't you tell me that your wife was so sick? How was I to know? I would have done so much more for her." In another example, "Now I find out you lost your mother? As her niece I should have been warned in a timely fashion that her condition had suddenly taken a turn for the worse so that I could have made one last visit before she died." Yet another example: those who tell you to snap out of it just so that, as one insensitive wife put it, "I don't have to listen to your whining anymore."

Finally, grieving men should always keep in mind that the tincture of time is one of the best remedies. With time many if not most men somehow work through their grief. When grief is a response to traumatic life circumstances, grief lessens when the difficult circumstances change for the better. Grief is more thoroughly discussed in Chapter 5.

ARE YOU BEING CUCKOLDED AND NOT DEALING WITH THAT ADEQUATELY?

Men often get depressed because their partners are cheating on them. My female depressed patients mostly seemed to forgive their husbands for cheating, but my male depressed patients rarely truly forgave their wives for the same thing. Instead they constantly brooded about how they had been betrayed, and some even blamed themselves for the betrayal, along the lines of, "What did I do wrong?" and "How could I have avoided this?" These men needed to be open with themselves and with their wives about how they felt in preparation for deciding once and for all whether or not they could forgive and forget. Then they needed to firmly implement whatever decision they made about the future of their relationship. If they decided to stick with the marriage they needed to once and for all relegate the cheating to an unpleasant past, hopefully with minimal implications for the present and future.

ARE YOU DEALING INADEQUATELY WITH PEOPLE WHO CRITICIZE YOU?

We often hear about the relationship between artistic talent and depression. We often hear both that depressed men are creative and that creative men are depressed. Some observers note that depressed men (and women) make good artists because depression opens up an abyss from which they draw inspiration out of pain. The reverse process also occurs: some artistic men who at first become successful creatively without being at all depressed subsequently get depressed and become less successful after becoming the butt of infantile, paranoid, self-serving, self-aggrandizing, and sadistically satanic critics who mete out punishment out of a personal agenda. They envy the artist his ability, become jealous of his accomplishments, feel slighted by an author's having failed to direct his work toward their personal needs, or get mad because an author failed to spare the critic's personal sensitivities— raging at the author even though he could not have possibly known (or cared) what these personal sensitivities might have been.

The harsh critic is the potentially depressed man's nemesis and the already depressed man's worst nightmare. Yet too many depressed men (and their therapists) fail to make the connection between getting depressed and being criticized by their boss, wife, or child. Too many men accept all the criticism that comes their way as if it were benign background noise when instead they should be identifying their critics and their criticism, recognizing how seriously abusive they are being toward them, and making it their priority to take remedial action.

In fact, I have seen many cases of so-called chronic depression where the therapeutic focus has been on finding the right antidepressant drug cocktail to cure a chemical imbalance when the problem really consisted of an emotional imbalance caused by ongoing criticism. Many men thus treated got even more depressed because they basically sensed or knew that their therapists were overlooking their real problem and by ignoring it were in effect criticizing them further for having such a problem in the first place.

When treating depressed men I start with the hypothesis that even criticism that at first appears to be modest can be nevertheless so pervasive, clear in direction, and unalterably motivated to go forward that it makes up in devotion to purpose what it lacks in strength and focus. I then employ a multistep approach to help depressed men deal effectively with criticism so that they can avoid getting unduly depressed over it.

Step 1 involves distinguishing between types of criticism. Men should distinguish unjustified (unwarranted) from justified, and destructive from constructive, criticism. Constructive criticism involves an assessment rather than an attack. It is meant not to wound but to be helpful via suggesting healthy, self-fulfilling, therapeutic ways to reduce vulnerability and enhance self-approval. It is directed to problems that can be solved in a way that falls within the individual's capacity to solve them. Where the target behavior is a mixture of tempting fate and bad luck it affixes blame where appropriate, but gives absolution where indicated. Men should accept constructive criticism and use it to make needed improvements. Of course, they may strive for perfection, but they should also consider the possibility that the best they can do is to perfect the imperfect at least somewhat and learn from their failures—then put them behind them once and for all and finally give themselves enough absolution so that they can rise onward and upward in life, after starting off in a new direction, and with a clean slate.

Destructive criticism is the reverse of constructive criticism. It is consciously or unconsciously meant to be harmful. It is a selfish response to the needs of the critic, not to the needs of the object of the criticism. It is unsolicited, forced on an unwilling victim. It is full of hubris, like the following statement made in a blog written for Amazon.com by the author of a book competing with my earlier-published book on passive aggression: "We wrote about [Passive Aggression] since there was very little literature or consumer writing featuring this [topic]."[1] This was not a case of simple oversight. The author of the blog knew of my book because she quoted it extensively in hers, and we had much correspondence via e-mail about my writing a blurb for her forthcoming work.

Step 2 involves understanding how one's critics operate, which they often do in a characterologically disordered fashion. Some critics suffer from serious personal pathology. A psychoanalyst, perhaps going too far, and perhaps not, once told me that he believed that all male critics were a "bunch of latent paranoids." By that he meant that the way they came to terms with their own perceived flaws was by castrating others to make their own equipment seem bigger and better by comparison. Many of the critics I dealt with both personally and therapeutically were, as he suggested, overly *paranoid* men hiding a faulty self-image by externalizing it, externalizing the low self-esteem that came from self-humiliation to become a humiliation of others as a diversion, release, and self-esteem enhancer. They are like those homophobes who deal with their dislike of their own homosexuality by queer baiting and bashing.

While the more paranoid critics project their own inadequacies onto others, the more *narcissistic* critics criticize others as an extension of their belief that they alone have what it takes and know what it is all about. Theirs is the narcissistic premise that "I am better than you" and the self-serving need to shine by displaying how much brighter they are. We also see an implied cry for admiration and love based on the implied or stated belief that "I know better than the rest." Many such narcissistic critics embrace in an infantile way the egoistic viewpoint that something is per se defective if it doesn't speak to *me* personally and address *my* needs specifically—like my mother either did or ought to have done. Thus I have had one of my scientific books narcissistically reviewed essentially as follows: "No good at all. I was looking for a manual on *this*, but *your* book was all about *that*," and "It contained doctor talk, not at all suitable for someone like me with no scientific knowledge."

Histrionic male critics criticize others as part of an ongoing oedipal compulsion to best their rival father (and female critics to best their rival mother). These are envious, jealous individuals, often rivals without a cause, who luxuriate most in knocking the competition, typically over something exquisitely trivial. Thus I once quoted John Simon, reviewing the musical comedy *My Fair Lady* in *New York Magazine,* as seeming to have been narcissistically fanning his personal feathers when he should instead have been scientifically and dispassionately bird-watching: "Yet splendid as this Lerner and Loewe musical is, it has one blemish that has always bothered me, even though Kenneth Tynan beat me to it at getting it into print (for which I've never forgiven him): the solecisms that Lerner put into the learned Higgins' mouth—*hung* for *hanged*, 'equally as ... than,' for 'equally ... as,' both of which are pretty gross."[2]

Seriously histrionic critics are at times best characterized as "ball-busters." They tend to accept only men who fit the stereotype of being masculine and dislike men they stereotype as passive and feminine, whom they criticize for being "wusses" and, confounding personality style with sexual orientation, "faggots."

Obsessive critics criticize others for not being as perfectionistic as they are, or at least as they feel they should be. *Sadistic* critics criticize others as part of a primary hurtful need to make everyone feel bad. *Psychopathic* critics criticize others as part of their personal search for palpable, and often ill-gotten, gain, as when they knock a rival book to obtain increased sales for a competing book they wrote.

Clues that negative criticism is a symptom of the critic's emotional disorder can be discerned without knowing the critic personally when they appear in the body of the criticism itself. For example, the written criticism contains too many exclamation points—put there to drill through logical and emotional protective barriers to its acceptance. The criticism is not measured but rather consists of an outburst driven not by its subject but by sadistic joy over having found something to object to. It often smacks of irrational exuberance installed to cover paucity of idea and can call to mind the kind of irrational prejudice implied in the oft-heard statement that "I don't have to read that book; I already know what is in it," as it makes its unsustainable point entirely out of the need to affirm preconceived notions, personal leanings, or group loyalties. The overly liberal critic who cares little for victims' rights will not approve of a book that speaks of the fallout of mental illness onto those in the mentally ill person's orbit, while the overly conservative critic who thinks mainly or only of the suffering of the victim at the hands of someone mentally ill will not like a book that condones in any way the legitimacy of the concept of not guilty by reason of insanity.

With such criticism the dyslogic employed fits the criticism to the emotions while making it seem as if it is the other way around. This dyslogic often consists of cognitive errors, such as

- Some=all, as when I wrote that *some* men don't marry due to emotional problems only to find myself quoted as having said that men who don't marry are emotionally disturbed.

- Part-to-whole, along the lines of, "If it's not all good then it's no good at all," using the selective process of identifying weak points and flaws while downplaying or entirely overlooking strong points and virtues.

- Selective abstraction, along the lines of paying attention to what serves one's critical purposes, and only to that.

- Arbitrary inference, typically supported by playing the following cards: the professional superiority card (for example, my degrees); the status card (for example, "I am entitled to criticize you because I am your mother"); the free country card (for example, "I am entitled to crush you based on my right of free speech"); and the altruistic card (for example, "I am just protecting society's right to know").

In too many cases in a final conceit to thwart effective self-defense the critic resorts to flight as he or she retreats to a safe anonymous perch by becoming unavailable so as to not have to respond to protests—the spiritual equivalent of screaming sexist/heterosexist/homophobic epithets not to the victim's face but from a racing motorcycle or moving car.

The men I know who best survive such assaults without significant defect are those who are one or more of the following: divinely inspired, masochistic, megalomaniac, insensitive, whose personality is such that they can comfort themselves by intensifying their creative efforts to prove themselves to themselves and others, or those who just get good and mad and don't put up with it anymore. The men who hardly survive tend to spend too much time and effort trying to prove their critics wrong; react emotionally to the onslaught based on feeling instead of purposively based on insight; fail to live well to get the best revenge; or endlessly attempt to satisfy a retaliative urge to have a heads-on battle and to win it decisively without considering that real and moral justification does not by itself necessarily constitute the basis of actual triumph.

In conclusion, the man who understands what the critic (and his or her critical society) is doing and why it is being done is the man most likely to detach himself personally from criticism and thereby become less of its victim. The man who understands that criticism is an inexact science is often in a better position to evaluate those critics who are (supposedly dispassionately) evaluating him. For mostly even the best criticism is only one person's opinion, and this is the case no matter how expert the critic, how official his status, how impressive her credentials, and how high his manifest self-esteem—with much criticism a form of self-acclaimed, self-important, self-appointed authoritarianism with an emotional, arbitrary, one-sided, prejudicial aspect to it. The man who understands all this is in the best possible position to avoid submitting to a critic's bullying authoritarian presumptuousness, for he is at least partially immunized from the all-too-common child-like need to grant expert status to anyone with a forceful personality and an official position, whose main or only qualification is, however, the self-proclaimed, "I am superior to you in status, knowledge, and experience." He can now reassuringly say to himself, "The problem is not in me but in you," enabling him to respond to negative critical judgments as if they mostly speak more about the one doing the judging than about the one being judged—that is, as if they are little more than self-statements carried over from the critic's childhood then projected and externalized to become statements about others. He can be assured of how many critical judgments are less passionate than pathological, and how there is no reason for him to get depressed over symptomatic displays of inner bitterness spilled transferentially onto him as object when the critic's main criterion for selecting him, as object, is that he makes a suitable blank screen for the critic's clear and present need, as subject, to find someone and something to defile.

Step 3 involves responding appropriately, effectively, and in a healthy fashion to criticism. A man instead of becoming overly involved on an ongoing personal level with his critics and their criticism can benefit from recognizing that almost any attempt to get his critics, many of whom are uninsightful and well-defended, to back down is counterproductive, inspiring not apology with retreat, but attack with intensification. He can avoid spending a great deal of time trying to appease his critics, especially when that involves compromising his ideals to the point that he completely loses his self-respect. As much as possible he should avoid getting involved in a prolonged struggle with a critic where he continues to fire off volleys at someone who has by now probably completely lost interest in him. In short, men who consider starting a fight should instead consider flight—far short, however, of abandoning talents and abilities or abdicating by giving up in masochistic compliance to the machinations of sadists. That way the man will avoid exposing himself to the increased criticism and the worsening depression that is likely to come to those who compulsively hunt their critics down to start up a self-defense or to pursue a nonproductive vendetta.

This said, there are times when it is a good idea to mount some form of self-defense, and there are certain self-defenses that might be worth trying. For example, it might help to write a rebuttal to a critical review to get a wrongful critic to back off. In the case of the implied criticism of my book on passive aggression, I first thought, "Maybe I will just ignore this." Then I thought, "I can't let her invalidate me and my work." So I countered with a public statement: that I didn't feel that my book deserved to be relegated to the category of "very little." I decided that there was no practical benefit to my being Mr. Nice Guy, and even if there were, it would not be worth the psychological cost to me of abdicating to her, then getting depressed because "no one ever appreciates me or gives me credit." In some cases it's a good idea to just get mad and get it over with—to identify the critic as the villain and go on the attack. When that anonymous reviewer stated that a medical book I wrote was deficient because it was full of doctor talk my first response was, "Oh boy, here I go again being too complicated"—and I got depressed. My second response was, "Maybe the problem is that my book isn't too complicated, but that you are too simple." Now I felt much better.

But my advice is: pick your battles very carefully and realistically, so that you don't win the skirmish but lose the war. Also pick your weapons carefully. There are times when it is a good idea to try to outwit rather than confront your critics. At other times it is a good idea to confront them passive-aggressively by attempting to induce guilt in them. To do this you might respond positively to their negativity, for example, acknowledging what is right about what they say and thanking them for their perceptive analysis, while gently pointing out its flaws. It is often a personal choice: between being nice to your critics to keep the peace with them, and being nice to yourself to be at peace within yourself.

It is never a good idea to respond to criticism with self-destructive, self-punitive ideation and action that lives out how demoralized you are from having been put down. It is never a good idea to respond with self-destructive, compulsive cruising for sex; acting childish and impulsively at work; having rages at your wife or partner; or verbally abusing or even physically beating a significant other just to get your anger and disappointment out of your system.

Step 4 involves trying to understand and master any special sensitivity to criticism you bring to a situation. Decouple what your first critics—your parents—thought about and said to you when you were a child from what you think of yourself now. That way you can avoid incorporating your parents' negative view of you into your own view of yourself, which puts you at great risk for buying into the negative view others have of you as you let any positive view others might have of you drop completely out of sight.

While you should master your tendency to accept others' negative opinions unquestioningly, you should also not be too hard on yourself if the criticism that comes your way does have a demoralizing effect on you. Many passive depressed men tell themselves and allow themselves to be told, "Why do you let your critics bother you?"; "Why do you care what people who buy ink by the barrel think?"; "We all have to take a little criticism, so why should you be any different?"; or "Don't be such a crybaby about this"—all self-excoriating comments that imply that as a man you are behaving badly by being oversensitive when the likelihood is that you are just behaving normally out of an average amount of sensitivity, so that you are reacting understandably and acceptably as a result of having been put down so savagely that the modest psychological equipment you, like most of us, have for defanging critics is inadequate to handle something that is spiritually the equivalent of a murderous onslaught of a vicious mountain lion when all you did was go out for a hike.

Step 5 involves avoiding unnecessarily bringing criticism, or further criticism, on yourself. Men with a potential for getting depressed often behave in a way that encourages potential critics to criticize them. Some men bring criticism down on their own heads because they are excessively guilty masochistic individuals—so guilty that they allow unhelpful guilt and a need to suffer drive them into the arms of malignant others as they figuratively put their heads into the lion's mouth hoping that this time they will not be bitten. Others enhance a critic's sadism by groveling—begging their critics to let up on them—only to give their critics the scream of pain that is exactly the opening they look for. Such men forget that to avert criticism and its sequelae they should develop the silent strength that deprives their critics of the pleasure of the kill. Here is my rule: if you have been weeping, never let them see the red of your eyes.

Step 6 involves seeking sympathy and consensual validation from simpatico friends. Support from a close friend or family member, from therapeutic support groups, or from a self-help book judiciously selected for being rational and having a proven track record can help a man recover from being criticized. Particularly helpful are good listeners who also model how to be depression-free by remaining detached from adverse criticism and continuing to be self-accepting without succumbing to excessive guilt, shame, and remorse in situations that parallel those that are troubling you.

Here is how a friend got me out of a depression after a critic said, in very broken English, some extremely negative (among the positive) things about a book I wrote:

> This review does not surprise me. First of all, you can tell by her grammatical errors that she does not have full command of the language, and probably not full command of the concepts she read about in your book. Foreign academics like her are known as "barroni"; they need superiority status; when they get a chance to intellectually attack their American counterparts, they do so with an enthusiasm that takes your breath away. I have first-hand experience with this underlying quest to look scholarly—a kind of a bella figura in academia. The review was about Elisabetta, not about the merits of your book.

Step 7 involves finding a therapist if steps 1 through 6 prove inadequate. Find one who does not say to you every chance he or she gets, "Here is what is wrong with you," as do some overly dedicated psychodynamically oriented therapists who become excessively critical in the guise of seeking understanding and deep truth. Also try to avoid overly dedicated cognitive therapists who, without first getting your acquiescence and permission to correct your thinking, assiduously carp on your wrong-headed beliefs, and effectively put you down by challenging your most treasured and creative ideas. Consider instead seeking a supportive affirmative therapist who uses these techniques but also dilutes them by saying, "Here's what you do that is right but let me show you where there is room for self-betterment," and then guides you by telling you what you need to do to better yourself.

ARE YOU STRUGGLING WITH A SUCCESS NEUROSIS?

Many depressed men fit into Freud's category of "Those Wrecked by Success."[3] These men ought to recognize that in their fear of success they are living out a surfeit of low self-esteem; self-blaming tendencies due to guilt; and overly altruistic/masochistic wishes to please everyone but themselves. They need to become not less but more self-centered—to start looking out for number one instead of giving everyone else's well-being priority over their own, then resenting it later.

A problem for depressed men with a success neurosis is that they get even more depressed should they achieve too much too quickly. One of my depressed men thought that he would feel better if he found a better job, only to discover that when he changed positions his success neurosis fomented even more depression because he became anxious and guilty about having achieved his goal. He was unprepared to go so far so fast. He would have done better if he had stayed put and worked out his problems with moving forward before taking action and venturing out.

SPECIAL TECHNIQUES
Acceptance versus Denial of Depression

Two diametrically opposed approaches can help men recover from depression. The first approach involves accepting depression and letting it work its way through you as you go into retreat and pull back from life until you feel well enough to reenter stronger and healthier. Men who wake up depressed, feeling as if they had a crushing weight on their chest and are unable to shake their depressed mood, might consider not panicking and trying to force themselves to feel better. Instead they might consider backing off and just waiting it out while their depression dissipates, remembering that many times bad moods vary not only intraday but also interday, and therefore, sooner or later lift as if spontaneously. The man who treats his bad mood cavalierly, as a passing event without extreme significance, can sometimes master it by ignoring it and leaving it be until it becomes quiescent as if on its own—or when the circumstances causing it just happen to improve significantly by themselves. Conversely, the man who meets his depressed mood head on and struggles with it may discover that it is an enemy that resists and even enjoys direct confrontation. Here is something I almost always tell my depressed male patients: no man should expect to always feel normothymic. All men need to accept a certain level of depression as part of life. Those who don't often get doubly depressed—that is, they get depressed about having gotten depressed.

The second approach, which I call "faking it until you are making it," involves actively forcing yourself to continue to function as well as possible even when you feel deeply depressed, in effect denying your depression at the very time that it is at its height. Here the goal is to disrupt the vicious downward cycle of depression breeding depression. The method involves feigning health—to yourself and others—to avoid allowing your sickness to make you feel sicker. This approach allows you to become active enough (without becoming hypomanic) to release a bit of energy from its depressive moorings, making that energy available for working your way further out of your depression. It also involves holding back tears so that other people feel more relaxed and comfortable with you, to the point that they can respond to you in a more positive way—thus giving you a real reason to stop crying.

Bibliotherapy

Bibliotherapy involves reading both self-help books dedicated to the topic of how to overcome depression and the classic scientific works on depression, such as Freud's paper on *Mourning and Melancholia*.[4] Men who are depressed should take care to avoid self-help books with a one-size-fits-all approach inapplicable to them personally, such as those that are organized and written with the intent more to sell books than to help people, or those that promulgate ideals the depressed man cannot and should never even try to live up to, such as books that suggest emulating people the depressed man, and most of us, can, or should, think twice about aspiring to become. Some depressed men should avoid reading material that stirs up unmanageable violent or sexual fantasies, especially fiction and nonfiction books that revive the very trauma that they are having the most difficulty mastering and integrating.

Trying General Toners

Exercise. Exercise relieves depression both directly/physiologically by releasing endorphins, and indirectly by increasing your attractiveness to others so that new self-esteem-enhancing relationships can develop.

Diet. Improved diet generally helps depressed men look and feel better. Dietary supplements can benefit depressed men who do not eat right, for example because they live alone and don't know how, or don't care, to cook.

Appearance/behavioral makeovers. A compromised appearance can make men unappealing to others, who in turn go on to reinforce the man's defective self-image. Men who are not natively good-looking can compensate with diversionary maneuvers such as a smile or an optimistic, welcoming body posture. Many depressed men can benefit from taking in brutally honest feedback from good friends who have their well-being at heart and are able and willing to tell them the things they need to hear about themselves to promote the changes in their manifest image that they ought to be making. Hopefully the shock of brutal honesty will wear off, but the good effects of the sage advice will last.

Here are some looks my depressed male patients benefited from altering:

- The "schlemiel" look that says, "It's not important to be neat and clean and it's okay to let yourself go."
- The shabby or "I didn't buy it, I had it" look and the "I got it on sale" look that says, "I have an eye for a bargain, but not for a style."
- The sensible look that says "function not fashion."
- The dirty look that proclaims "I don't care what others might think for it's obvious to me that cleanliness is next to nothing."
- The parsimonious look that says, "I am an uptight, regimented person unlikely to become excited or to be exciting."
- The sheepish look that says, "I have poured my sense of guilt into a fatal flaw." Particularly destructive to the overall appearance of some of my male patients was carrying a wretched shopping bag instead of a briefcase, wearing frayed collars or cuffs, or wearing badly scuffed shoes—particularly when these are installed to lend a contrastingly negative effect to an otherwise well-done outfit.

However, some depressed men only get more depressed when they follow the suggestions made to improve their appearance. These include:

- Depressed men who long to be accepted for themselves and not for how they look.
- Men with a phobia of success who need the plain, homely look as a defensive "stay away" shield.
- Masochistic men who need to deliberately compromise their looks for self-punitive reasons.
- Paranoid men who take advice to improve their appearance as an unwelcome attack on how they already look.

- Rebellious men who wanting to be free view even advice meant to be helpful as controlling.

Financial makeovers. Many depressed men can benefit from differentiating preferential thriftiness meant to ensure a happy future from compulsive, masochistic, self-punitive parsimoniousness meant to ensure a painful present. Many of my depressed male patients hoarded money for a number of neurotic reasons. Some envied rich people and wanted to emulate or outdo them. Others were getting rich as a substitute for getting involved—especially with other people. Some were saving too much money as a response to delusions of poverty associated with the belief that others were out to steal their assets and completely impoverish them. For example, I once treated a depressed man who wouldn't sign my Medicare forms because he felt that I would use his signature to raid his bank account. It is particularly unhealthful for depressed men to refuse to spend any money at all on entertainment because they believe that they will need all their money to compensate for being alone later in life, after their friends and family abandon them, or die off.

Using the Geographical Solution

The geographical solution is a form of environmental manipulation involving changing one's surroundings to resolve one's problems. In spite of the folklore that says, "The geographical solution is no solution at all," it can work for some depressed men at some times. It is a particularly good approach for men who cannot effectively defang their torturers and so are best advised to wisely and properly leave them behind. These torturers include such people as:

- Those who buy their dependency on you by eliciting your guilt about being independent.
- Those who do not defend you when you need them to be there for you.
- Those who spill their problems onto you because loving company in their misery they make a life out of announcing and re-announcing how they are victims, too readily sharing traumatic experiences at the hands of lovers who have abandoned them, doctors who made the wrong diagnosis and gave them the wrong treatment, and ungrateful children who ruined their lives.

Sometimes the best way to go about solving problems geographically is to make only small changes in a stepwise fashion. I often advise men to try changing their position within the company instead of changing their job or retiring completely, or to have a trial separation in lieu of getting a divorce. Some men instead of moving might profitably dispassionately revisit their decision to go. They may decide they are better off staying and doing what they can to make a bad situation better. Instead of trying to get away from enemies they might try turning them into friends. Or they might decide to accept things as they are as "the known devil." A patient saw the light and realized that his geographical solution would ultimately make very little sense for him. He was selling his beautiful loft in an area where he had made many friends and moving to a house in the suburbs so that his dog could have a yard to play in. He was planning to give up his life for his dog's life. He decided to stay put after he listened to what his friends had to tell him: "Dogs put out in a yard just wait at the door until you let them back into the house."

Since no man can move away from himself, the geographical solution does not work well for a man whose problems are mainly self-inflicted or who mainly suffers from an endogenous depression.

Zen

Some depressed men correctly identify how real situations are creating their problems only to find that they actually have no way of getting out from under them. Here the Zen approach, which involves finding comfort and reassurance from within, that is, not through geographical but through inner removal, can help. Depressed men can effectively stop thinking negatively of themselves just because others think badly of them. They can start holding themselves in high regard whether they do or don't match up to the irrationally lofty standards others impose on them—and which are the only ones they ultimately come to impose on themselves.

Enhancing Your Relationships

Depression is loneliness, and loneliness can sometimes be avoided by developing and maintaining relationships, as you avoid:

- Treating your parents badly only to regret it later. Don't abuse them secure in the knowledge that they love you too much to complain about or put a stop to the abuse. Yes, it is a good idea to avoid regressive symbiotic relationships marked by excessive attachment to your parents when that attachment works to the detriment of mature outside relationships. But it is also true that a good solid relationship with your parents is an excellent platform for a good solid relationship with everyone else—and ultimately, or especially, with yourself.

- Allowing your masochism to take over and turn you into a depressed man who self-punitively arranges to avoid having sustaining relationships with significant others or makes certain that those he develops fail.

Such men often complain that they cannot meet anyone suitable where they live. Yet they are reluctant, or outright refuse, to travel to a nearby place where they *can* meet people. They also favor hurting others by hurting themselves, in effect cutting off their noses to spite someone else's face. For example, they leave someone out of spite, rejecting a good prospect at their own expense just to make the other person feel bad, as when they walk off the job to get back at the boss, or out on a partner just to air their grievances.

- Unloading on your friends, employing them as targets for your existential despair, driving away people you need after forgetting that most people do not want to be around someone who is constantly taking their misery out on their company. Most people don't want to be around others who attack with their own suffering, drawing them into their black moods because they envy them for not having lost anyone or for being healthy when they are ill—as they deliberately traumatize others to get back at a world they feel has traumatized them.

- Allowing your excessive dependency to goad you into acting jealous and possessive to the point that you stifle your relationships by smothering them.

- Not giving others the benefit of a doubt and instead making "who has done what to whom" the most important aspect of a relationship—while expecting the worst from everybody, thus ensuring that that is exactly what you will get.

- Playing puerile adolescent games with people, like "You can't be friends with me if you are friends with someone I had a fight with and don't speak to anymore."

If you have not been able to avoid acting badly at least apologize for your ill-conceived actions. If you have been difficult to get along with, confess it, and start becoming easier to live with. Apologize if you have threatened to leave a healthy relationship that disappointed you not because it was inherently disappointing but because you were too easily disappointed. A patient invited a friend to join him for dinner. She accepted and confirmed. My patient suggested that the place he was taking her to was somewhat chilly so that she should bring a sweater along. She replied, "I'll take a rain check for cold and I don't mix," leaving my patient's plans for the evening uncertain. She never apologized. He never saw her again.

Correct cognitive distortions that lead to unfortunate avoidances. It is important to see relationships as mixed blessings and to recognize how most people have virtues as well as flaws. Men who make a negative whole out of a relationship's one or two negative parts give up prematurely on relationships that they might have otherwise enjoyed and might have sustained them for the whole of their lives.

Chapter 19

Coping with Depressed Men

Depressed men can be a burden to those around them. For as Real suggests, "those who do not turn to face their pain are prone to impose it."[1] As a result, friends, family, and loved ones of depressed men are often in the path of depression fallout—and they are usually ill-equipped to recognize and handle it. This chapter suggests one good way to go about coping with the seemingly endless agony imposed on others by depressed men, while helping the depressed man turn things around so as to lift his spirit, and the heavy burden from his life.

The depressed man who lives next door to me is depressed for a number of reasons. He is depressed because he is losing his mother to Alzheimer's disease and is struggling over what is the best way to care for her. He is depressed because his girlfriend is an alcoholic who makes plans with him only to break them at the last moment to go out and get drunk and then disappear for a day or two. Once in a drunken stupor she locked him on the roof and then left his apartment door wide open so that his dogs and birds got out into the building's halls and lobby. He is depressed because he is an artist and gallery owner who cannot keep up with his bills because his paintings aren't selling well; he is trying to sell his loft in a down market but has no takers; and to make things worse, he wants to stay there anyway because it is the only home he knows and loves. He is also depressed because a bar opened downstairs from his loft, and the noise and music are keeping him from concentrating on his work during the day and from sleeping at night. He often complains to the police, who come after he calls, but do nothing to help. But perhaps he is mainly depressed because he suspects that his neighbors don't like him very much. They have a number of

complaints about him: he has a tendency to be very pleasant and charm-
ing up to a point, yet without warning, and when least expected,
become cutting and jump down their throats over nothing because they
said the wrong thing, or did some little thing that made him mad. They
also don't like his involvement in fostering homeless dogs and rescuing
birds with broken wings—creatures who are as unsanitary as they are
noisy. They also don't like his constant complaining about the bar
downstairs and how it is ruining his life or his calling the police and
trying to ruin its business, because they like the bar. Since it opened it
has enlivened the area, rescuing what was a slum from oblivion by
bringing people and businesses to the street while discouraging some
criminal types who used to hang out there. They also don't like his
unloading on them all the time, nonverbally, with his sad, gloom-filled
facial expression and monosyllabic hellos full of pain and angst, and
verbally, as he tells them about his problems and virtually demands that
they come up with instant solutions. Those who have tried to help him
have usually fallen into the classic trap some depressed men set: tell me
what to do, but I'll find reasons not to do it. I'll take your advice, but
see to it that in implementing it it goes nowhere, or wrong, so that I can
throw it up in your face and prove once again that few people love me,
and fewer still can be counted on to help me out at times of need.

The neighbors are now almost all as depressed as he is. He brings
them down on pleasant days. They exit their apartments dreading to
run across him because nobody knows what to say to him. If they say
hello he unloads on them; if they don't say hello he feels cut dead and
complains to the next neighbor that the last neighbor was uncaring
toward, and so, knowing how much he needs love, being abusive to
him.

The neighbors are now fighting with each other over just how to handle him. One is upset with the other for rejecting a man who needs help;
but the other is upset with the one for being too permissive—for trying
to help him when they should instead be referring him to a professional
for problems that are too big to be solved by amateurs out on the sidewalk. Two schools of thought have emerged. The first is to be kind and
helpful because he is a poor lonely wretch who needs a friend, a little
hand-holding, and a mother figure to care for him in his time of deprivation and need. The second is to set limits on him not only for one's
own self-protection and self-preservation but also to help him get back
in control of himself so that he can stop feeling so guilty after the fact
about his whiny off-putting behavior. Those who oppose being soft and
suggest setting limits on him say that coddling him only makes things
worse, for he deliberately maintains special sensitivities so that he can
continue to wallow masochistically in feeling that everyone is wounding
him; deliberately overstates his difficulties so that everybody will hold

his hand and come to his rescue; deliberately avoids responding positively to offers of help so that he can maintain his illness with all its distinct emotional and practical advantages of being the victim; and deliberately if unconsciously asks to be humiliated and devalued so that he can increase his guilt to the level he feels is appropriate for someone who is the bad person he believes himself to be.

The neighbors consulted with a counselor who lives in the neighborhood. She recommended that he see someone professionally, and perhaps ask to be medicated. Only when they passed that on he took that as her rejecting his pleas for help, and anyway came up with one excuse after another for not going for treatment, saying he couldn't afford it, claiming that he was not sick, and adding that if he were ill he could get better by himself because he knows how to find his own way out of his unhappy state.

How can the neighbors cope with this difficult man? How can you cope with a man like this if he is your boyfriend, son, or husband? Are your complaints that this depressed man is difficult to live with justified, at least to some extent? Do they reflect how he *intends* to be difficult to live with, that is, is he deliberately, if unconsciously, beating you up with his bloody body, so that you need to stop him before he kills his relationship with you, and even kills himself? Or by complaining and setting limits are you just being cruel and unkind yourself, and selfishly unwilling to give up your comfort to help a guy in desperate need of comforting from you?

Some of the neighbors did treat this man with firmness: by telling him to cut it out. Some lapsed into resentful silence followed by a big blowup that helped neither them nor him. Some treated this man permissively by humoring him, handling him with kid gloves because they believed that that was humane, only to find themselves wallowing with him in his depressive despair, their hopes of consensually validating him dashed by his lack of positive response. Still others continued to give him advice even though he continuously rejected it as ill-considered, uncomprehending, inadequate, wrong-headed, and even sadistic.

All these approaches failed because:

- He took their telling him to cut it out as a criticism, causing him to get angry and become more depressed.
- He took others' resentful silence as harsh and passive-aggressively punitive.
- He took others' permissiveness as condescending and even as encouraging that which he himself knew should have been discouraged.
- He took validating him as egging him on to do more of the same.
- He used all attempts at counseling as an opportunity to play with his advisors, as they fired advice at him only to have him throw it back into

their faces with a lot of reasons why it wouldn't work, until they were
out of sorts. He continued to demand more and better advice until his
advisors ran out of things to suggest.

I concur with Real's insightful formulation that failure to "put [your] foot
down [can] provide ... a rich medium in which ... dysfunctionality ...
flourish[es] and grow[s],"[2] for as Real continues, speaking of wives of
depressed men, "women who [are] afraid to make reasonable demands on
their depressed husbands ... [wind] up being left anyway."[3] It is true: permissiveness risks causing the man to escalate to the point that he becomes
intolerable to his wife, only to get so guilty afterward that he becomes
intolerable to himself, often to the point that he might have to leave to
spare her, as his victim, further victimization—from him.

I therefore recommend that amateurs respond to men like my
neighbor who are depressed, and to their entreaties and complaints, by
avoiding the traps I just mentioned. Instead I suggest that you as an
amateur counselor consider asking the man if he is comfortable following this game plan: lift the weight off yourself by moving on from your
acknowledged problems to focus on their solutions. Extricate the energy
from your depression and instead put it into developing a clear-eyed,
unemotional, problem-solving approach that leads you away from your
own depression, and spares you its pain and all others from your
depression fallout. Do this by dealing with your emotions unemotion-
ally, getting beyond the problem of your foul moods and your realistic
difficulties and going directly to solutions. In effect you are saying,
"Instead of wallowing in despair, separate yourself from it long and
hard enough to do something about all your despairing."

I even suggest that whenever possible amateur "therapists" think twice
about giving depressed men advice. Instead they might point out that
most depressed men already have all the advice they need right there
within themselves to conquer their self-defeating behavior. Many a
depressed man already has all the equipment he needs to look at his situation overall and ask, "What exactly is it necessary for me to do to stop
feeling so depressed?"—in preparation for coming up with a *real answer*
to his own question. Often depressed men blossom when they understand that they have their fate in their hands and under their control.
They can lift the weight of their depression when they recognize that they
are not the victim of unchangeable circumstances but the victim of their
own irrationally pessimistic belief that it will be impossible for them to
change the negative circumstances that are victimizing them.

This approach will not work wonders in the sense of curing a depression. Most depressed men need more than a layperson's sympathetic
ear or heart-felt intervention. They mostly need treatment from a trained
therapist. However, this approach, which represents a compromise

between being completely supportive of and distancing yourself from the man and his problems entirely, can work wonders in one limited sense: it can help the depressed man translate his complaints into remedial action, transferring the energy wasted in his depression to become energy harnessed for its relief. It can have the added advantage of keeping you and other victims of depression fallout from being sucked into the vortex of the depressive maelstrom. It is not the ideal solution and it is no placebo, but it is a workable and effective approach for the layperson to at least consider trying in an attempt to be helpful, and to all involved.

Once when I was very depressed I spilled my guts to a bartender who refused to listen to how depressed I was and made me more depressed by dismissing me as a crybaby. So many wives, friends, and lovers do the same thing by being dismissive or getting annoyed. They unwittingly make their men feel alone, lonely, and misunderstood. Of course, a little sympathy goes a long way for depressed men. But a little reality goes even further. For many depressed men are in a prison of their own making and so can, and should be, helped to see that the keys to the locks on their cells are right there outside of their bars. The victims of depression fallout who do not dwell on the prison conditions, but instead focus on the key ring right out there for the taking, help the man who is depressed grab it, open the door, and emerge at last free of the bars that confine, out of the fire of his personal hell, and back into the world of those who are living the ordinary lives of the encumbered, but not the sad, depressive, extraordinary lives of the damned.

Appendix: An Introduction to Biochemistry and Pharmacotherapy

A review of the literature suggests that we have not yet discovered a single definitive biological cause for depression that implies or suggests a specific pharmacotherapeutic cure using one or several targeting medications. It also suggests that we have not yet discovered precisely how the different classes of antidepressant medications actually work. What is clear is that depression can to some extent be understood as a chemical imbalance and that antidepressant drugs do affect one or more of the components of this imbalanced chemistry.

The symptoms of depression (and the mechanism by which antidepressants provide relief) can be related to biochemical function/dysfunction on that neurochemical level where neurons communicate with each other across a space between them called the inter-neuronal synapse, or synaptic cleft. They do this via substances that Cell I releases into the synapse to be picked up by the receptors in Cell II. Cell I produces and secretes a number of different neurotransmitters called biogenic amines: norepinephrine (which mediates mood), dopamine (which mediates pleasure and activity), and serotonin (which mediates aggression). (There are also cholinergic neurons which are generally antagonistic.)

The neurons and their communicative chemistry do not, however, constitute the whole picture of the biochemical basis of depression. An important substance is brain-derived-neurotrophic-factor (BDNF), which is, according to Constantino, Lembke, Fischer, and Arnow a "chemical in the brain that regulates growth and differentiation of neurons"[1] and is decreased with stress and increased with long-term administration of antidepressants.[2] Another important part of the picture is the hypothalamic-pituitary-adrenal axis. This ultimately affects the production of adrenaline, which also has significant effects on brain function. Too, the cells around the neurons (the neuroglia) have a place in the overall picture, as does the exact location of the neurons in the brain for a biochemical malfunction in the limbic system will tend to have different implications from a biochemical malfunction in the cerebral cortex.

Such attempts as the attempt to correlate location with function, like all attempts to create an overarching theory that correlates known biochemical/organic parameters, have, however, not yet come to full fruition. To the best of my knowledge, no one has been able to create a theory that adequately takes into account all the possible structural and biochemical variables, and documents with a degree of exactitude their causal and consequential relationship to each other and to depression. To my way of thinking, all present-day theories whose goals are to explain the biological basis of depression simply present limited slices of reality where the fit with other slices of reality, such as other theories, is not always determinable. As a result, a truly integrated view of the pharmacology (and pharmacotherapy) of depression still remains somewhat elusive.

Antidepressants certainly work—but why they work in a given patient and which antidepressants are best for which man's depression remain the subject of much speculation and ongoing research. What we generally accept is that antidepressant medications, as Akiskal notes, "raise the functional capacity of the biogenic amines in the brain,"[3] for example by increasing brain serotonin by inhibiting its reuptake or breakdown.

As Akiskal says, "Antidepressant agents, irrespective of specificity to one or another biogenic amine, are approximately equally effective in two-thirds of those with depressive disorders."[4] Therefore, it generally behooves the clinician to consider choosing drugs on the basis of their side effect profile, such as sexual side effects; previous response; and safety should the patient overdose with them. Mostly the side effects of antidepressant medication are tolerable. But sometimes their side effects can create more problems than the medication itself solves. Some of the more disabling side effects of medications are specific to men, such as decreased libido associated with problems in attaining an erection and difficulty ejaculating. This said, some clinicians suggest different antidepressants for different clinical depressive states. For example, they believe that those antidepressants that are more activating can best help the man who is withdrawn; those antidepressants that are more sedating can best help the man who is agitated.

Ultimately the final choice of antidepressant for a given man is often determined by a process of trial and error: seeing which antidepressant(s) work best for him and determining if other medications, such as benzodiazepines and antimanic drugs, can be profitably added to the antidepressant regimen.

Many therapists start treating men who are only mildly depressed with psychotherapy alone and initiate pharmacotherapy only if psychotherapy by itself appears to be inadequate. Conversely they start treating men who are more severely depressed with pharmacological agents, while often recommending simultaneous counseling or psychotherapy to supplement pharmacotherapy.

My practice guidelines are as follows: the depressions that are severe, primary, nonreactive/endogenous, mood displaying, non-characterological (especially those without psychopathic features or other severe acting-out manifestations), and recurrent strongly call for the use of pharmacotherapy. Depressions that are mild, secondary (the spin-off of another disorder such as a phobia or Posttraumatic Stress Disorder; a comorbid feature of another disorder, such as anxiety disorder; or even a relatively minor feature of a mixed disorder such as Schizoaffective Disorder), reactive (such as depressions precipitated or intensified by specific life experiences), cognitive-displaying, chronic, accompanied by acting out (especially psychopathic acting-out), and to a great extent reflective of the operation of premorbid and comorbid personality problems—that is, depressions that are as characterological as they are affective—may be good candidates for treatment primarily with psychotherapy, with antidepressants assuming a secondary role.

In my experience, pharmacotherapy alone for *significant* men's depression is not nearly as effective as pharmacotherapy combined with psychotherapy. Pharmacotherapy is quick and relatively inexpensive, but it is not always by itself fully effective. This may be because while a degree of symptom relief is a likely outcome, the initial causative factors often remain—and can ultimately lead to persistence and recurrence, although the therapeutic relationship with the pharmacotherapist can and often does resolve some emotional problems and even lead to subsequent real underlying personality change.

Even some men with a mild depression find that pharmacotherapy facilitates and improves on their psychotherapeutic experience. Medication can help a man with a mild depression feel better fast, making him more amenable to ongoing psychotherapy geared to help resolve the underlying reasons for his depression. Medication can also help avoid a recurrence so that the man can go on to live a happier, depression-free, more fulfilling life with, and sometimes without, further therapy. However, though pharmacotherapy can help the patient become more amenable to and use psychotherapy more effectively, it can also be counterproductive for those patients who, feeling too good too soon, lose their motivation to continue in psychotherapy and so fail to look into the root causes of their disorder.

To an extent the decision to use or not use antidepressants involves determining what form of treatment the man himself prefers, and that can in turn depend on his personality style/disorder. Perhaps he is a denier—an uninsightful man likely to prefer a nontalking form of treatment. Or, conversely, perhaps he is a brooder—an introspective man who enjoys and profits from naval gazing then talking about what he finds down there. While the man should have a vote in what his treatment will be, his voting power should be limited by consideration of the nature and state of his judgment and the extent to which it is conflict-free. Does he, for example, merely *think* he has a chemical imbalance that can only respond to pharmacotherapy when in fact his emotional problems are clear and present? Conversely, does he pick and yield himself up to expensive expressive long-term treatment because he is a masochist who likes to do everything the hard way, and to ultimately be unsuccessful at everything he does?

The decision to initiate pharmacotherapy should certainly not be made simply because the therapist believes that all depressions are the result of a chemical imbalance that is presumably correctable if only one could find the right drug or drug combination. That may be, but it is unlikely. Besides to the best of my knowledge, no pathognomonic chemical imbalance, and no cause-specific cure, has to date been identified for all depressions and with any degree of specificity. Another truth is that as with many disorders a good cure may not be directly related to the root cause. Thus, just because antidepressants change amine metabolism doesn't mean that amine metabolism gone awry has caused depression. Pharmacotherapy can work independent of cause much as a drink of alcohol can relieve anxiety even though anxiety is certainly not caused by alcohol insufficiency. Also, sometimes a chemical imbalance is there but as the *result*, not the *cause*, of a depression. By implication psychotherapy can have a pharmacotherapeutic effect, changing one's chemical imbalance by influencing the emotional pathways that are responsible for influencing one's biochemistry.

Antidepressants should not be given strictly to reflect a therapist's personal agenda. They should not be given to deny psychic causations when that denial reflects the therapist's own prejudices, particularly those arising out of unresolved negative feelings about his or her own personal therapist.

Antidepressants alone (without a covering agent such as a phenothiazine) should be used with care for men who are as paranoid as they are depressed. That usage may increase paranoia by intensifying angry feelings, leading to suicidality and possibly violence to others. Because antidepressants may activate schizophrenic delusions, it is crucial to distinguish between depression-based withdrawal and schizophrenic anhedonia. Antidepressants sometimes cause a swing into hypomania perhaps as a result of their amphetamine-like effect. Therefore, consideration should be given to covering men who are vulnerable to Bipolar II Disorder with an antimanic medication.

Antidepressants are relatively ineffective unless given in the proper dosage. Most clinicians recommend giving a full dose over an adequate time period, such as one year. Increasing the dose gradually from a low starting dose is often indicated. However, as Stark notes, because of the "hormetic effect, higher doses—beyond a certain point—may actually be less effective (and not because the drug becomes less well tolerated)"[5] so that effectiveness may follow a bell-shaped curve where a medication actually loses its effectiveness at higher doses. Should the doctor wish to stop antidepressants he or she should do so slowly, especially when nearing the lower dose ranges, always being careful to differentiate the anxiety and agitation of recurrent depression from the anxiety and agitation of antidepressant withdrawal.

According to Stark, "it has been suggested that some of the atypical antipsychotics may be more aptly termed 'broad-spectrum psychotropics,' because they are able to address affective states, such as mania and depression, along with psychotic symptoms."[6]

Antidepressants are generally preferred over symptom-specific palliatives such as pain killers for headaches or laxatives for constipation. Codeine plus aspirin for depression-induced headaches can be ineffective, addictive, and further depressing. Laxatives and enemas for depression-induced constipation are to be avoided whenever possible. Enemas are especially toxic psychologically to young boys, most of whom detest mother's manipulating the genital area. I have treated boys who after having been traumatized this way go on as men to develop an emotional connection between evacuation and sexuality, leading to a lifetime of shame about their body associated with severe sexual performance difficulties and sometimes even asexuality.

Amphetamine-like substances may do little more than add a level of stimulation to a continuing depression. Benzodiazepines have fewer severe side effects than antidepressants but are considerably less effective than antidepressants when used alone. They can also enhance the potential for anger outbursts/temper tantrums—especially when combined with alcohol. A discussion of the use of testosterone, thyroid hormone, and other newer forms of "organic" interventions such as vagal stimulation is beyond the scope of this text.

Vitamins can be useful for the malnutrition that is part of a depression, such as the malnutrition that is a consequence of depressive anorexia or a failed attempt to cure depression by strenuous bizarre diets. Many depressed men stint on their nutrition. Some eliminate vegetables and fruits from their diet entirely because they find them constipating. Too many have a bagel and coffee for breakfast, a sandwich and a soda for lunch, and a decorative but nonnourishing dinner using as their excuse that they are too busy to cook and sit down to eat, when in fact they secretly want to injure themselves to pay themselves back for something they feel guilty about—their anger believed unacceptably inhumane, their sexual fantasies believed abnormally perverse and amoral, or just for their having become more successful in life than they find tolerable and so can permit themselves to be.

Shock treatment can be especially useful for refractory melancholic depressions. It should not be withheld in the belief that it is excessively sadistic or dangerous. But it should also not be misused, particularly as part of a ritual exorcism, or, as it was in the past, for trivial indications such as weeping. What used to be said of a certain Boston psychiatric service—that electroconvulsive therapy (ECT) was both the medical handkerchief for a patient's tear in the eye and the financial restorative for the doctor's empty wallet—was then, and remains now, a completely unacceptable practice guideline for giving shock treatment.

✳✳✳✳

PHYSIOLOGICAL/BIOCHEMICAL DIFFERENCES BETWEEN MEN AND WOMEN

A number of observers have postulated that the increased frequency of depression in women over men can be attributed to hormonal differences, such as differences in levels of testosterone, estrogen, progesterone, and thyroid hormones. Also there are differences in (protective) serotonin levels, with women having lower serotonin levels than men. Women are also said to have higher concentrations of Monoamine Oxidase (MAO), an enzyme that breaks down protective catecholamines. Of course the hormonal ups and downs related to a woman's childbearing functions are not factors in men.

Notes

PREFACE

1. T. Real, *I don't want to talk about it: Overcoming the secret legacy of male depression* (New York: Scribner, 1997), p. 31.

CHAPTER 1: AN OVERVIEW

1. A. Solomon, *The noonday demon: An atlas of depression* (New York: Scribner, 2001), p. 176.

2. S. V. Cochran and F. E. Rabinowitz, *Men and depression: Clinical and empirical perspectives* (San Diego: Academic Press, 2000), p. 19.

3. Cochran and Rabinowitz, p. 56.

4. Solomon, p. 175.

5. Cochran and Rabinowitz, p. x.

6. Solomon, p. 176.

7. P. Kraemer, *Against depression* (New York: Viking, 2005).

8. Solomon

9. Cochran and Rabinowitz, p. 94.

10. T. Real, *I don't want to talk about it: Overcoming the secret legacy of male depression* (New York: Scribner, 1997), p. 83.

11. American Psychiatric Association, *Diagnostic and statistical manual of mental disorders* (4th ed.) (Washington, DC: American Psychiatric Association, 1994), p. 327.

12. Queen Victoria, http://www.female-ancestors.com/daughters/louise.htm. Accessed April 2007.

CHAPTER 2: MAKING THE DIAGNOSIS

1. "Challenges in the family practice setting: Recognition and treatment of depression, anxiety disorders, and medical comorbidities," *CME CNS News* (New York: McMahon Publishing Group, 2006), (Vol. 9, No. 5, 2006), pp. 28-35.

2. S. V. Cochran and F. E. Rabinowitz, *Men and depression: Clinical and empirical perspectives* (San Diego: Academic Press, 2000), p. xvi.

3. Cochran and Rabinowitz, p. 34.

CHAPTER 3: SYMPTOMS

1. T. Real, *I don't want to talk about it: Overcoming the secret legacy of male depression* (New York: Scribner, 1997), p. 194.

2. S. V. Cochran and F. E. Rabinowitz, *Men and depression: Clinical and empirical perspectives* (San Diego: Academic Press, 2000), p. 96.

3. Cochran and Rabinowitz, p. 95.

4. Cochran and Rabinowitz, p. 96.

5. Cochran and Rabinowitz, p. 95.

6. Cochran and Rabinowitz, p. 91.

7. Cochran and Rabinowitz, p. 95.

8. American Psychiatric Association, *Diagnostic and statistical manual of mental disorders* (4th ed.) (Washington, DC: American Psychiatric Association, 1994), p. 327.

9. American Psychiatric Association, p. 327.

10. Cochran and Rabinowitz, p. 73.

11. Cochran and Rabinowitz, p. 74.

12. Cochran and Rabinowitz, p. 74.

13. Cochran and Rabinowitz, p. xii.

14. Cochran and Rabinowitz, p. 83.

15. Cochran and Rabinowitz, p. 24.

CHAPTER 6: ATYPICAL DEPRESSION

1. T. Real, *I don't want to talk about it: Overcoming the secret legacy of male depression* (New York: Scribner, 1997), p. 22.

2. Real, p. 22.

3. M. Erman, "Overview of insomnia," *CNS News* (Special Ed.) (New York: McMahon Publishing Group, 2005), pp. 17–19.

4. Erman, p. 18.

5. Erman, p. 19.

6. M. Kantor, *Understanding writer's block: A therapist's guide to diagnosis and treatment* (Westport, CT: Praeger, 1995), p. 39.

7. M. Kantor, p. 12.

CHAPTER 8: THE PSYCHODYNAMICS OF DEPRESSION

1. T. Real, *I don't want to talk about it: Overcoming the secret legacy of male depression* (New York: Scribner, 1997), p. 199.

2. Real, p. 198.

3. S. V. Cochran and F. E. Rabinowitz, *Men and depression: Clinical and empirical perspectives* (San Diego: Academic Press, 2000), p. 46.

CHAPTER 9: DEVELOPMENTAL ORIGINS

1. T. Real, *I don't want to talk about it: Overcoming the secret legacy of male depression* (New York: Scribner, 1997), p. 205.

2. Real, p. 205.

CHAPTER 13: STRESS

1. T. Real, *I don't want to talk about it: Overcoming the secret legacy of male depression* (New York: Scribner, 1997), p. 105.

2. Real, p. 106.

3. O. Fenichel, *The psychoanalytic theory of neurosis* (New York: W. W. Norton, 1945), p. 394.

4. Fenichel, p. 394–95.

CHAPTER 14: PERSONALITY AND MEN'S DEPRESSION

1. S. V. Cochran and F. E. Rabinowitz, *Men and depression: Clinical and empirical perspectives* (San Diego: Academic Press, 2000), p. 96.

CHAPTER 15: PSYCHOTHERAPY

1. T. Real, *I don't want to talk about it: Overcoming the secret legacy of male depression* (New York: Scribner, 1997), p. 31.

2. J. Bemporad, "Intensive psychotherapy and psychoanalysis." In *Treatment of psychiatric disorders: A task force report of the American Psychiatric Association* (Vol. 3, pp. 1824–33) (Washington, DC: American Psychiatric Association, 1989), p. 1826.

3. Real, p. 279.

4. Real p. 295.

5. Real, p. 277.

6. Real, pp. 181–82.

7. Bemporad, pp. 1829–30.

8. Bemporad, p. 1830.

9. M. S. Rosenthal, *50 ways to fight depression without drugs* (Chicago: Contemporary Books).

10. H. Hoberman and P. M. Lewinsohn, "Behavioral approaches to the treatment of unipolar depression." In *Treatment of psychiatric disorders: A task force report of the American Psychiatric Association* (Vol. 3, pp. 1846-62) (Washington, DC: American Psychiatric Association, 1989), p. 1852.

11. Real, p. 278.

12. Real, p. 278.

13. I. D. Glick, J. F. Clarkin, G. L. Hass, "Couples and family therapy." In *Treatment of psychiatric disorders: A task force report of the American Psychiatric Association* (Vol. 3, pp.1885-90) (Washington, DC: American Psychiatric Association, 1989), p. 1886.

14. N. E. Rosenthal, "Light therapy." In *Treatment of psychiatric disorders: A task force report of the American Psychiatric* (Vol. 3, pp. 1890–97) (Washington, DC: American Psychiatric Association, 1989), p. 1891.

15. Rosenthal, p. 1891.

16. Real, pp. 158–59.

CHAPTER 16: TREATING TWO COMMON PRESENTATIONS OF DEPRESSION IN MEN: ATYPICAL DEPRESSION AND HYPOMANIA

1. T. Real, *I don't want to talk about it: Overcoming the secret legacy of male depression* (New York: Scribner, 1997), p. 31.

CHAPTER 17: THERAPEUTIC ERRORS

1. T. Real, *I don't want to talk about it: Overcoming the secret legacy of male depression* (New York: Scribner, 1997), p. 97.
2. Real, p. 150.

CHAPTER 18: SELF-HELP FOR THE DEPRESSED MAN

1. Blog on Amazon.com. http://www.amazon.com/Overcoming-Passive-Aggression-Spoiling-Relationships-Happiness. Accessed April 2007.
2. M. Kantor, *Understanding writer's block: A therapist's guide to diagnosis and treatment* (Westport, Conn.: Praeger, 1995), p. 34.
3. S. Freud, "Some character-types met with in psycho-analytic work: Those wrecked by success." In *Collected papers* (Vol. IV) (London: The Hogarth Press, 1915/1957), pp. 323–41.
4. S. Freud, "Mourning and melancholia." In *Collected papers* (Vol. IV) (London: The Hogarth Press, 1917/1957), pp. 152–70.

CHAPTER 19: COPING WITH THE DEPRESSED MAN

1. T. Real, *I don't want to talk about it: Overcoming the secret legacy of male depression* (New York: Scribner, 1997), p. 274.
2. Real, p. 303.
3. Real, p. 318.

APPENDIX

1. M. J. Constantino, A. Lembke, C. Fischer, and B. A. Arnow, "Adult depression: Features, burdens, models, and interventions." In *Mental disorders of the new millennium*, edited by T. G. Plante (Vol. 1, *Behavioral issues*, pp. 139–66) (Westport, Conn.: Praeger, 2006), p. 151.
2. Constantino, Lembke, Fischer, and Arnow, p. 151.
3. H. S. Akiskal, "Mood disorders: Historical introduction and conceptual overview." In *Kaplan & Sadock's comprehensive textbook of psychiatry*, edited by J. S. Sadock and V. A. Sadock (8th ed., pp. 1559–77) (Philadelphia: Lippincott Williams and Wilkins, 2002), p. 1568.
4. Akiskal, p. 1573.
5. M. Stark, *Psychiatric Times* (Vol. XXIII, No. 12, 2006), p. 6.
6. Stark, p. 3.

Index

ABOUT THE AUTHOR

MARTIN KANTOR, M.D., is a psychiatrist who has been in private practice in Boston and New York City, and active in residency training programs at hospitals including Massachusetts General and New York's Beth Israel. He also served as Assistant Clinical Professor of Psychiatry at Mount Sinai Medical School, and as Clinical Assistant Professor of Psychiatry at the University of Medicine and Dentistry, New Jersey Medical School. He has authored 15 other books, including *The Psychopathy of Everyday Life: How Antisocial Personality Disorder Affects All of Us* (Praeger, 2006), *Understanding Paranoia: A Guide for Professionals, Families and Sufferers* (Praeger, 2004), *Distancing: Avoidant Personality Disorder, Revised and Expanded* (Praeger, 2003), and *Passive-Aggression: A Guide for the Therapist, the Patient and the Victim* (Praeger, 2002).